Heidelberg Series in South Asian and Con[illegible]Studies - Volume III

The Many Faces of India
Law and Politics of The Subcontinent

Foreword by

Soli J. Sorabjee

Edited by

Malcolm MacLaren

SAMSKRITI

SAṀSKṚITI
C - 9020, Vasant Kunj, New Delhi - 110070
Visit www.samskritibookshelf.com

Price: ₹ 595.00

ISBN: 978-81-87374-69-5

Heidelberg Series, Vol III

Typeset by SNGT Publishing Services Pvt. Ltd.
Published by M. Sengupta for Saṁskṛiti, New Delhi.
Printed by Shivam Offset Press, Noida.

Contents

Foreword

This excellent volume comprises articles examining Indian law and politics from a comparative perspective. The contributors, who are scholars worldwide, analyse with clarity and deep understanding 'many faces of India'.

The range of the subjects covered in the articles is truly impressive: the Indian policy and legislative response to global climate change, mediation in India, sacred texts in Indian law, the codes of Manu, Indian federalism in international context, the Uniform Civil Code debate in India, the meaning of Indian citizenship, and Gandhi's concept of the political.

The articles' insights and perceptions provide invaluable material for the different political and legal systems. No nation is an island unto itself, and no legal or political system can claim to be a repository of all the wisdom regarding governance. Indeed, the importance of comparative scholarship cannot be overemphasized today. *The Many Faces of India* demonstrates how developments in Indian law and politics have significance and can be the basis for insights far beyond the country's borders. More importantly, this volume will foster comparative scholarship in India, for which there is great potential. I know from my experience as a senior advocate practising before the Supreme Court of India that the court frequently refers to comparative law and human rights jurisprudence when dealing with constitutional issues.

As rightly observed by the editor in the introduction, the beneficiaries of this volume will be its readers, who will range from policymakers and politicians, administrators, judges and lawyers, to academics and researchers - indeed, readers should include anyone interested in and concerned with the important subjects encompassed in *The Many Faces of India.*

SOLI J. SORABJEE

December 2010

Preface & Acknowledgements

PREFACE

Much about this volume, including its conceptualization and content, is explained by its origins. These are to be found in a special issue of the *German Law Journal* (GLJ), an online-only legal publication.[1] As its name suggests, the GLJ publishes primarily in the field of German law. It was founded a decade ago to cover decisions of the Federal Constitutional Court of Germany, but it now covers comparative, European and international law as well. The GLJ's editors realized that the journal cannot limit itself geographically or thematically if the journal is to be true to developments in theory and practice. The growth in the kinds and degree of international, transnational, supranational and global legal activity has elevated the importance of comparative law, especially for the journal's worldwide readership.[2] The journal itself must seek to contribute to the exchange of knowledge across jurisdictions and to the ongoing shift in perceptions of the nation state, legal systems and even the 'law' itself.

---

[1] The GLJ registers over 2,000,000 site visits annually and has, for several years now, been ranked as the world's leading online legal periodical.

[2] "Learning Comparative Law can prepare students for effective participation in an increasingly global and diverse legal profession". Nehaluddin Ahmad, *Adapting Indian Legal Education to the Demands of a Globalising World,* 10(7) GERMAN LAW JOURNAL 856 (July 2009).

The idea of putting out a special issue on India (as opposed to China, Japan etc.) was an acknowledgement that "India is everywhere" ("Indien ist überall"), as a Swiss newspaper recently put it.[3] The country – for reasons additional to its exotic culture a.k.a. "spice and curry" – has captured international interest. This interest is mirrored in the many submissions about developments in Indian law and politics that the GLJ receives.

The special issue on India was, in other words, intended to complement the GLJ's traditional coverage and to satisfy the burgeoning interest in comparative law, especially as regards the Subcontinent. The journal approached scholars in keeping with the broad concerns of its editors and subscribers and sought a selection of comparative legal scholarship on India that was representative of and relevant to contemporary interests.

The publication of the special issue in March 2008 was warmly received by our European readers. They were taken with the many faces of India that it presented. Specifically, they felt that its subject matter and perspectives overcame the parochialism that plagues such scholarship; that its mix of articles gave a panoramic view of the field; and that its contents offered new learning for those familiar with comparative law in the Indian context as well basic information for those unfamiliar with it.

Professor Subrata K. Mitra (South Asia Institute, University of Heidelberg, Germany), himself a contributor to the special issue, felt that there was "enough suitable material here for a solid book". He suggested to the co-editors of the special issue that it be converted from a virtual to a real publication as a volume in the 'Heidelberg Series in South Asian and Comparative Studies'. Professor Mitra launched this series in response to the fact that much of the scholarship on India produced in Europe and North America does not reach the academic community in India due to high price or, as in the case of the special issue, due to lack of

[3] Claudia Kramatschek, *Abschied von 'spice and curry' – Indien ist überall* [Farewell to 'spice and curry' – India is everywhere], NEUE ZÜRCHER ZEITUNG (20 November 2006).

internet access. Volumes in the Heidelberg Series are modestly priced and effectively distributed in addition to being well produced.[4] I was co-editor of the special issue (with Professor Russell A. Miller of the School of Law at Washington & Lee University, USA) and agreed to serve as the volume's editor.

ACKNOWLEDGEMENTS

I am deeply grateful to Professors Mitra and Miller for helping me conceive the volume and the special issue, respectively; to Mr. Surit Mitra and Saṁskṛiti Publishers in New Delhi as well as to the GLJ's student editors at Washington & Lee Law School for their hard work in preparing these for publication; to the individual contributors and the GLJ for granting permission to reprint; and finally to Mr. Soli Sorabjee (Senior Advocate to Supreme Court of India and former Attorney-General of India) for contributing a foreword that should enhance understanding of the volume as well as the number of its readers.

Malcolm MacLaren

---

[4] STATE AND FOREIGN POLICY IN SOUTH ASIA, Vol. 1, Heidelberg Series in South Asian Studies Jivanta Schöttli and Siegfried O. Wolf eds., 2010, and THE JAINA HERITAGE: DISTINCTION, DECLINE AND RESILIENCE, Vol. 2, Heidelberg Series in South Asian Studies Julia A.B. Hegewald ed., 2010.

1

Depicting the Faces of India: An Introduction

MALCOLM MACLAREN

A. OBJECTIVE

Cohesion can be a problem for collected volumes such as this: no common thread necessarily binds them. I do not, however, think that this is the case for *The Many Faces of India*, as the contributions were solicited with a particular intent. The intent was to explore the nexus between the Subcontinent and the West, that is, the points of contact and possible influences between Indian and European/Anglo-Saxon legal and political systems.

In the event, India showed itself to be a promising locus for comparative legal scholarship. Colonial influences have made the country's rules and institutions relatively familiar and accessible to Western-trained scholars,[1] though these operate in a very different social context. Considered substantively, how India deals with unity and diversity, its foreign and native heritage, its growing international power and developing country status etc. are not only of interest in themselves. Developments in Indian law and politics also have a significance and can be the basis for insights beyond the country's borders.

The volume should appeal to teachers and students in India above all as an stimulating exercise in comparative law. Comparative law is of increasing importance for everyone concerned with cross-border legal activity. More specifically, readers in India should

[1] This accessibility is enhanced by the fact that law and politics in India are largely conducted in English.

be interested in the chapters both as first-order and as second-order investigations in comparative law. In terms of the former, the subject matter offers learn effects as to the similarities and differences between legal and political systems.[2] In terms of the latter, the scope, purpose, utility and methodology of the exercise are bound to be scientifically contested.

B. CONTENTS

In the present volume, scholars from around the world have attempted to realize something of the potential of Indian law and politics for comparative scholarship. They are an eclectic blend of academics (legal and political science, established and up-and-coming, female and male, as well as native and foreign), and they bring extraordinary breadth of perspective and depth of knowledge to bear on a range of concerns from the Subcontinent.[3]

Specifically, the volume consists of the following chapters (alphabetically by contributor):

- a critique of India's policy and legislative response to global climate change by Deepa Badrinarayana (School of Law, Chapman University, USA);
- a meditation on mediation in India by Hiram E. Chodosh (College of Law, University of Utah, USA);
- a reading of sacred texts in Indian law by Donald R. Davis Jr. (Department of Languages and Cultures of Asia, University of Wisconsin-Madison, USA);
- an interpretation of the sublime codes of Manu by Piyel Haldar (School of Law, Birkbeck College, University of London, UK);
- lessons from federalism in India by Malcolm MacLaren (Law Faculty, University of Zurich, Switzerland);
- coverage of the civil code debate in India by Werner Menski (Department of Law, School of Oriental and African Studies, University of London, UK);

[2] The subject matter should also arouse natural curiosity in the form of 'what do others think about us?'.

[3] Comparative coverage of Indian corporate governance, judicial independence, electoral law, micro-finance and euthanasia was also considered.

- a definition of citizenship in light of India's colonial legacy and contemporary diversity by Subrata K. Mitra (South Asia Institute, University of Heidelberg, Germany); and
- an examination of Gandhi's concept of the political by Mahendra P. Singh (WB National University of Juridical Sciences, India).

C. MESSAGE

The volume as a whole is more than the sum of these impressive parts. As explained, the special issue and the volume sought to show India's potential for comparative scholarship. They have achieved, I feel, this objective. The special issue and the volume also say much about the 'what', 'why', 'wherefore' and 'how' of the whole comparative endeavour. The contributors cannot but bring their own conceptions of comparative law to bear: all but one writes about India from abroad for a worldwide audience.

These conceptions are of interest and importance. The relevance of comparative law has increased over the last decades as globalisation and governance processes have spread. Such studies have in turn been facilitated by advances in communication and technology. The popularity of comparative law has grown in sync. Comparative law remains nonetheless a relatively esoteric discipline in search of itself.[4] Indeed, comparatists themselves often define comparative law not according to what it is, but according to what it is not, e.g. a "discipline apart from jurisprudence or international law on the one hand, and from the social sciences and the humanities on the other".[5]

---

[4] Further regarding the contested identity of contemporary comparative law read Jennifer Hendry, *Contemporary Comparative Law: Between Theory And Practice – Review of Esin Örücü & David Nelken's Comparative Law: A Handbook,* 9(12) GERMAN LAW JOURNAL 2253-2262 (December 2008); Ralf Michaels, *Review of Annelise Riles (ed.), Rethinking the Masters of Comparative Law,* 4(4) GERMAN LAW JOURNAL 411-417 (April 2003); Peer Zumbansen, *Comparative Law's Coming of Age? Twenty Years after* Critical Comparisons, 6(7) GERMAN LAW JOURNAL 1073-1084 (July 2005).

[5] Annelise Riles, *Introduction: The Projects of Comparison,* in RETHINKING THE MASTERS OF COMPARATIVE LAW 2 (Annelise Riles ed., 2001).

I will now review the collected volume from the perspective of the comparative endeavour rather than from that of its subject matter. (A summary of the contributions' findings is to be had in the chapters themselves.) Through considering the contributors' approaches to their subject, much may be learned about the state of comparative law today. I will examine in turn what the contributions say (explicitly and implicitly) about the discipline's scope, purpose, utility and methodology.[6]

I. Scope

The diversity of the subject matter in the collected volume answers the question put by a scholar elsewhere: "[s]hould mere analyses of 'foreign law' come under the auspices of comparative law?"[7] By their choices, the contributors argue in effect that all the laws[8] of all legal systems, singly or severally, past as well as present, are fit for such scholarship. It is understood, however, that an international element is required. The investigation must involve a legal system different from that of the intended reader and better yet, of the scholar him- or herself.

Perhaps Badrinarayana offers the best example of this broad understanding of what comparative law comprises in "India's Policy Priorities - Bleak Forecast for a Global Climate Regime". Her contribution approximates a country law report. It analyzes how India has sought to reconcile national interests in encouraging prosperity, developing infrastructure and generating energy with international efforts to hinder climate change. Badrinarayana does not consider similarities and differences of law between India and other countries (let alone undertake second-order investigations). India is simply asserted to be typical of countries faced with multiple challenges of economic growth, social inequities and environmental degradation. (Readers desiring an overview of China's policies are referred elsewhere.) That the

---

[6] The following review is mine alone; it does not represent a consensus among the contributors to the volume.

[7] Hendry, *supra* note 4, at 2254.

[8] It may be noted that in contrast to the present volume, the leading European/Anglo-Saxon comparative law textbooks and treatises largely concern private law.

subject matter is of interest outside India is assumed, since the future of an effective climate regime post-Kyoto depends in part on the country's response.

Davis' contribution "Law and 'Law Books' in the Hindu Tradition" also focuses on India to the exclusion of other national legal systems, but again like Badrinarayana's contribution, it does so in an international context. Davis is interested in the effect of British colonial rule on Indian institutions and traditions relating to law. To this end, he compares the use of sacred Hindu texts in two periods of Indian legal history, the classical/medieval and the colonial/postcolonial. (A comparison of Hindu with Islamic, Jewish and Christian religious legal systems is raised at the contribution's end as a possibility for further study.) This understanding of the scope of comparative law is, however, again contested. There are scholars who object to legal history such as Davis' being considered comparative law. The focus, they argue, is on a legal system's past and not on the variety of legal systems today. Davis implicitly makes the case for a contrary understanding, namely that comparison underlies legal history as well as comparative law (narrowly defined) and that research of another legal system must include research into that system's origins and development.[9]

II. *Purpose*

Comparative law has been accused by some of busying itself with "ideas and notions that cannot be put to practical use" and that are of interest only to those "who spend their time devising them and […] quoting each other with self-satisfaction".[10] What purposes then animate the contributions in the collected volume, and how far do they confirm or contradict accusations of practical irrelevance?

[9] Further KONRAD ZWEIGERT AND HEIN KÖTZ, AN INTRODUCTION TO COMPARATIVE LAW 8 (Tony Weir trans., 1998).

[10] BASIL MARKESINIS, COMPARATIVE LAW IN THE COURTROOM AND CLASSROOM 53 (2003).

The question of purpose looms particularly large over Davis' and Haldar's contributions. Davis' purpose can be said to be the search for knowledge. Davis seeks to trace the transformative effects of colonialism in Indian legal history based on a knowledge more profound than that commonly applied (p. 63). His description of the use of sacred texts through time is intended "to further establish a responsible and accessible basis for the study of Hindu law" (p. 80). For its part, Haldar's contribution, "The Sublime Codes of *Manu:* Law and Eighteenth Century Orientalism", examines the translations of the Hindu law codes by a British judge in late eighteenth century Calcutta, that judge's understanding of the Oriental sublime and the use of such understandings in defining legal subjectivity.

Scholars in favour of limiting the scope of comparative law will likely approve of "The Sublime Codes"' concern with the interrelations of different legal systems - here Hindu law and the Common law towards a universal law - if not of its legal historical vantage point. The purpose of Haldar's contribution, like Davis', is, however, open to criticism for being 'academic' in the pejorative sense cited. The knowledge pursued is pure; its aim is not to supply solutions to 'real' legal problems. Moreover, the insights into a particular moment in the history of law are intended for and will resonate only in a small circle, regardless of how compelling they are on their own terms.

III. Utility

The question of the purpose of comparative legal scholarship is closely related to the question of its utility. Here, "The *Eighteenth Camel:* Mediating Mediation Reform in India" contrasts starkly with "The Sublime Codes", as Chodosh's contribution speaks directly to the world of practice and is eminently applicable. Chodosh draws lessons from his experience as an American expert intermediating between mediation and the Indian legal culture and seeks to provide "engaged assistance in comparative justice reform" (p. 27). His advice is explicit, detailed and targeted at legislatures, courtrooms and law offices. In offering it, Chodosh tries to supply, if not himself become, the proverbial eighteenth camel in India's deliberations on adopting mediation.

In comparative legal terms, Menski's contribution could also be considered according to its scope and purpose. "The Uniform Civil Code Debate in Indian Law: New Developments and Changing Agenda" is a detailed description of laws in a particular country, in terms of their function and efficacy, penned by a national expert. The approach to comparative law that it represents has been criticized as positivist and accordingly technical, irrelevant and outdated.[11] Putting aside – but not conceding – such criticism, I would like to consider what "The Uniform Civil Code Debate" says about the utility of comparative law. For the contribution makes a no less bold claim in this regard than it does as regards the discipline's scope and purpose.

Menski reviews the UCC debate not just as an Indian problem but as a conundrum for legal systems everywhere. Specifically, the debate as to how to handle cultural diversity through "plurality-conscious legal intervention rather than the traditional insistence on state-centric legal uniformity" (p. 137) may be instructive for European lawmakers. Menski argues that "the future of the world" lies not in trying to banish diversity through legal reform but in respecting diversity and recognizing it legally (p. 137 with 182). The contribution's most sweeping claim of utility comes in the conclusion that the post-modern Indian state can act as a "management *guru*" (p. 140) to countries facing massive migrations bringing 'ethnic implants'.

IV. Methodology

Like Menski's contribution, Mitra's analyzes India's 'experiment' for lessons that it may hold for other states. "Level Playing Fields: The Post-Colonial State, Democracy, Courts and Citizenship in India" uses India as a case study for societies emerging from colonial or communist rule that are attempting to make citizens out of subjects. Mitra's contribution is, however, distinguishable in comparative legal terms from Menski's as regards methodology. Here, the analysis is expressly set in a broader, theoretical framework (exemplary see Part B, "The Context of Research"). Mitra does not directly compare the Indian legal system with the legal systems of those post-colonial states that he has in mind (Pakistan and Sri Lanka). Instead, his contribution is intended to

[11] Further Hendry, *supra* note 4, at 2258.

open up "the analytical space for the comparative and general dimensions of the problem of citizenship" (p. 209), i.e. to facilitate further case studies.

While "Level Playing Fields" focuses on the general factors determining success in citizen making (law, politics and above all history), Mitra is not oblivious to the role that specific factors (such as religion and culture) may play (p. 209). He appropriately concludes with a call for research into features contextual to India. Such sensitivity to difference is also explicit in other contributions.[12] In its prescriptions, "The *Eighteenth Camel*" displays awareness of the awkward position of the outsider (especially American) in mediation (as process and as subject of reform), while "The Uniform Civil Code Debate"'s argument is premised on the observation that India is rejecting foreign (especially European) models of handling cultural diversity and developing "its own country-specific and situation-sensitive methods" (p. 136). Concern with the 'self' and the 'other' as well as with 'alterity' in the law is a hallmark of newer scholarship and a fault-line between those who integrate in the discipline non-posited things (such as customs, traditions and ultimate values) and those who practice comparative law as the analysis of official rules.[13]

"'Thank You India': Lessons from the 4th International Conference on Federalism, New Delhi, 5–7 November 2007" is the most considered contribution in the volume as regards comparative law: MacLaren's contribution explicitly addresses contemporary controversies regarding the discipline's scope, purpose, utility and methodology. Such was to be expected. Since MacLaren (and Miller, *supra*) conceived the special issue as an exploration of India as a locus for comparative legal scholarship, this conception informed his own contribution.

---

[12] It should be added that though sensitivity to difference may not be explicit elsewhere, none of the present contributions treat their subject matter with parochial arrogance or naïve fascination. (Further Michaels, *supra* note 4, at 414.)

[13] Further Hendry, *supra* note 4, at 2258–2260.

MacLaren undertakes both first- and second-order investigations in comparative law in critiquing the Conference claim that India's political system should be considered a model for other countries. He begins by examining the Indian experience with federalism (see the empirically oriented Part D I), then considers lessons that it may offer other democracies (see the discussion of 'best practices' and 'ground realities' in Part D II), and finishes by theorizing on the potential for general insights through comparing specific federal systems (see Part D III, where comparative law is regarded as an activity in its own right).

The final contribution to the volume is Singh's review of *Gandhi und der Begriff des Politischen* by Dieter Conrad. The review and the book under review consider Gandhi as a political thinker and compare his thought with that of European counterparts (such as Carl Schmitt, Max Weber, and Martin Luther). The comparison is neither between the 'Oriental' and the 'Occidental' nor between 'civilizations clashing' with one another; these thinkers are treated, despite their diffferent cultural settings, as partners in an ongoing universal discourse.[14] As Singh explains at the outset of his review (p. 210), the book has deep roots in European (especially German) theology and political philosophy, which are critiqued in relation to the Gandhi's views and practices, but these themselves were Western influenced. Conrad and Singh now call upon the former to learn from the latter, especially as regards how to conduct politics without violence *(ahimsa)*.

D. RESULTS

The present volume may be read as an exercise in 'doing' comparative law today. On this reading, the contributions display diverging conceptions of the discipline. Can a common thread be traced through them?

The definition of the discipline as any "intellectual activity with law as its object and comparison as its process"[15] brings together

---

[14] As is indicated alone by the choice of book's title, which is an allusion to Carl Schmitt's *The Concept of the Political.*

[15] ZWEIGERT AND HÖTZ, *supra* note 9, at 2.

these conceptions perhaps best of all those current. This definition is broad – comparative law is then in another scholar's words "a big tent, encompassing lots of different types of scholarship".[16] Arguably it must, however, be so if it is to reflect a lack of consensus about the discipline's identity among comparatists in this collected volume as elsewhere. More positively put, "it is these different possible modalities that give the discipline its depth and texture".[17]

At a more fundamental level, it may be said that all of the contributors agree on the innate importance of undertaking comparative law. None even felt the need to justify their endeavour. The present volume confirms their appraisal. Hopefully the volume will encourage similar studies of the Subcontinent in future. It is appropriate that the volume concludes with a call by Singh for *Gandhi und der Begriff des Politischen* to be translated into English so that Conrad's extensive research and profound insights are more readily accessible to comparative scholars around the world, especially in India.

[16] David Kennedy, *The Methods and the Politics, in* COMPARATIVE LEGAL STUDIES: TRADITIONS AND TRANSITIONS 345 (Pierre Legrand and Roderick Munday eds., 2003).

[17] Riles, *supra* note 5, at 6.

2

India's Policy Priorities: Bleak Forecast for a Global Climate Regime?

DEEPA BADRINARAYANA

A. INTRODUCTION

The efficacy of the global climate regime post-2012 depends ultimately on three countries: China, India, and the United States of America.[1] Although a deadlock persists concerning adopting binding international obligations for targeted reduction of greenhouse gas (GHG) emissions, all three favour action to address climate change.[2] Domestically, each country is exploring a range of policy and legislative options to retard carbon emissions, especially by promoting alternative energy options and energy efficiency.[3]

More specifically, the success of any climate endeavor will depend largely on the ability of growing economies, which are faced by multiple challenges of economic growth, social inequities, and environmental degradation, to align their competing domestic policies and then to translate them within an international regime. This chapter presents India as a case study in policy and law making in this context. The first part of the chapter lays out the economic and climate challenges of the Subcontinent. The second part reviews India's policy and legal response to the emerging

[1] *Spotlight on China and India as delegates gather for U.N. global warming summit in Bali*, INTERNATIONAL HERALD TRIBUNE (1 December 2007).

[2] C. Boyden Gray (U.S. Ambassador to European Union), Foreign Press Center Briefing, Washington D.C. (18 December 2007).

[3] For an outline of U.S. policy read U.S. Environmental Protection Agency, U.S. Climate Policy and Actions. For an outline of China's policy read Yang Zhang and Yongnian Zheng, *New Development in China's Climate Change Policy*, UNIVERSITY OF NEW SOUTH WALES FACULTY OF LAW RESEARCH SERIES (2007).

challenges. The third and final part looks at Indian and global efforts on climate change in future.

B. INDIA'S MULTIPLE CHALLENGES - ECONOMY, ENERGY AND ENVIRONMENT (CLIMATE)

In just over a decade of economic liberalization,[4] India's GDP has grown steadily at a rate of about 8% annually.[5] A recent report of the International Monetary Fund (IMF) listed India as one of the countries making the "largest country-level contributions to world growth" [6]: According to the report, India, China, and Russia accounted for one half of global growth in 2007.[7] The Organization for Economic Development and Cooperation (OECD), which is considering extending an invitation to India to become an OECD member,[8] classified the country as the third largest economy in the world in a recent survey.[9] Moreover, Indian industries have received global attention with their recent global ventures, such as Mittal Steel's acquisition of Arcelor,[10] making it the world's largest steel company, and Tata's bid for Jaguar and Land Rover.[11, 12] There has also been a steady flow of capital investment in different sectors, notably technology-based outsourcing.[13]

---

[4] VIJAY JOSHI AND I.M.D. LITTLE, INDIA'S ECONOMIC REFORMS 1991–2001 (1996).

[5] Reserve Bank of India, Press Release, RBI Increases Cash Reserve Ratio (13 February 2007). Between 2005–2007, India posted an average annual GDP growth of about 9%. IMF, *infra* note 6.

[6] International Monetary Fund (IMF), World Economic Outlook, Globalization and Inequity xi (October 2007).

[7] *Id.*

[8] OECD, OECD invites five countries to membership talks, offers enhanced engagement to other big players, Council Resolution on Enlargement and Enhanced Engagement (16 May 2007).

[9] OECD, Economic Survey of India, Policy Brief (October 2007).

[10] Anand Ghiridharadas, *Mittal's Stormy Quest for Arcelor,* INTERNATIONAL HERALD TRIBUNE (27 June 2006).

[11] Bryce G. Hoffman, *Ford Picks Tata as Top Bidder for Jaguar, Land Rover,* DETROIT NEWS (3 January 2008).

[12] Tata has also launched the world's cheapest car – approximately US$ 2500. Anand Ghiridharadas, *The Making of Tata's New Car,* INTERNATIONAL HERALD TRIBUNE (7 January 2008).

[13] However, Indian companies are now "outsourcing" the outsourced work back into the United States. Anand Ghiridharadas, *Outsourcing Works, So India Exporting Jobs,* NEW YORK TIMES (25 September 2007).

These positive developments in the Indian economy are, however, contingent upon continuing market-based reforms to sustain economic growth. Such reforms according to the OECD include lowering protective labor regulations that inhibit growth and investment in infrastructure projects.[14] The demand for construction of roads and other facilities such as water supply and sewage to accommodate a growing population and vehicular traffic is increasing.[15] Economists, political leaders, and industrialists in India have acknowledged that maximizing industrial production and agricultural output depends on an efficient supply chain, which in turn requires reliable infrastructure.[16]

Infrastructure development is directly correlated with a steady energy supply. Electricity generation, distribution, and supply are under strain, and the demand for energy in the subcontinent is spiking upwards.[17] The International Energy Agency (IEA) predicts that demand for all types of energy in India will continue to grow by an average of 3.6% by 2030.[18] Notably, energy consumption for power generation for commercial use and for industrial operations, as well as for transportation, is projected to grow rapidly. India could become the third largest importer of oil and coal by 2030, overtaking Japan.[19]

Further, India will likely increase the exploitation of its significant domestic reserve of petroleum and coal for energy supply. India has the second largest reserve of crude oil in the Asia-Pacific region – about 5.6 billion barrels, of which it produced about 845,000 barrels per day (bbl/d) in 2006 and consumed 2.65 million bbl/d.[20] The U.S. Energy Information Administration (EIA estimates that

---

[14] *Supra* note 9.

[15] The Planning Commission of India estimates that the country will require seven or more times its current electricity supply in order to sustain an annual 8–10% GDP growth through 2031. Planning Commission, Government of India, Integrated Energy Policy, Report of the Expert Committee (August 2006).

[16] World Economic Forum, India: Meeting New Expectations, India Country Report No. 07/63, India Economic Summit, New Delhi (26–28 November 2006).

[17] *Supra* note 15.

[18] International Energy Agency, World Energy Outlook 2007, China and India.

[19] *Id.*

[20] Energy Information Administration, Country Analysis Brief, India (30 January 2007).

India's registered oil demand will continue to grow at a rate of about 100,000 bbl/d.[21]

Coal reserves in the country are also substantial. As of 2003, India had 101.9 billion short tons of coal, of which it produced and consumed 443.7 and 478.2 million short tons, respectively.[22] Coal is a major source of energy in India, making it the third largest producer in the world.[23] The reduction in coal consumption in other countries may in fact be countered by growing demand in India and China. The two countries are predicted to account for 83% of the increase in global coal use by 2020.[24]

Demand for other sources of energy is also slated to increase, in particular for natural gas and liquefied natural gas. Much of the demand for natural gas as well for coal and petroleum will have to be satisfied by importing the fuels.[25] Thus, the Indian Government must, on one hand, increase domestic production, and, on the other, expand imports. Further, it must establish strategic petroleum reserves, an effort for which projects are already under construction.[26]

Global warming is obviously linked to these issues of infrastructure and energy demands. The rise in global temperatures and the consequent catastrophic impacts on climate are attributed directly to increases in anthropogenic greenhouse gas emissions.[27] Of specific concern are carbon dioxide (CO_2) emissions, by products of fossil fuel combustion, primarily petroleum, coal, and natural gas.[28] Land use shifts, particularly deforestation or permanent removal

---

[21] *Id.*

[22] *Supra* note 20.

[23] Energy Information Administration, Report DOE/EIA-O484 (2002), International Energy Outlook 2002 (26 March 2002).

[24] Energy Information Administration, International Energy Outlook 2002, Coal.

[25] *Id.*

[26] Construction of storage tanks in the coastal region of Mangalore has already commenced under the supervision of the State-controlled company, Oil Industry Development Board. *Supra* note 20.

[27] Intergovernmental Panel on Climate Change, Fourth Assessment Report, Climate Change 2007: Synthesis Report, Summary for Policy Makers.

[28] U.S. Environmental Protection Agency, Human-Related Sources and Sinks of Carbon Dioxide.

of trees from forests, not only shrinks carbon sinks, or areas where CO_2 is absorbed from the atmosphere, but also increases emissions.[29]

In its most recent report, the Intergovernmental Panel on Climate Change (IPCC) determined that failure to stabilize the increase in global temperatures at 2 degrees Celsius by 2020 will result in irreversible non-linear, exponential, impacts and feedback effects in the climate.[30] The consequences for the global climate will be catastrophic.[31]

The more specific predictions for the Subcontinent and the Asian region are similarly disturbing. The melting of the Himalayan glaciers is projected to increase flooding and landslides, which will destabilize land and water resources in the entire region.[32] The availability of fresh water in Central, South, East, and Southeast Asia could be jeopardized, just as population increases drive up demand.[33] Land use in mega deltas and coastal areas could be disrupted due to flooding. Agricultural outputs could change indiscriminately in the region – with East and Southeast Asia experiencing an increase of 20% and Central and South Asia experiencing a decrease of about 30%.[34] Endemic morbidity and diseases could grow in the entire region.[35]

Studies of the impact of climate change on India point to major changes in hydrological cycles,[36] agricultural outputs,[37] forest

---

[29] Intergovernmental Panel on Climate Change, Contribution of Working Group I to the Third Assessment Report of the Intergovernmental Panel on Climate Change 2001: The Scientific Basis.

[30] *Supra* note 27.

[31] Intergovernmental Panel on Climate Change, Contribution of Working Group II to the Third Assessment Report of the Intergovernmental Panel of Climate Change 2001: Impacts, Adaptability and Vulnerability.

[32] *Id.*

[33] *Id.*

[34] *Id.*

[35] *Id.*

[36] Rivers could either flood or recede significantly, according to studies conducted on the river basins of Krishna and Mahanadi. Read A.K. Gosain, Sandhya Rao, and Debajit Basuray, *Climate Change Impact Assessment on Hydrology of Indian River Basins,* 90(3) CURRENT SCIENCE 346–353 (10 February 2006).

[37] Short crop durations could decrease yields. Read Jayant Sathaye, P.R. Shukla

ecosystems[38] and coastal areas,[39] as well as human health concerns.[40] As such, the Gangotri glacier in the Himalayas, the perennial source for the sacred river Ganga, has reportedly receded by about 30 meters.[41] Water level rises in the Sunderbans region shared by India and Bangladesh have submerged land.[42] These catastrophic climate change consequences will not only lead to loss of life and property but also migrations both locally and regionally.[43]

Economic growth and infrastructure development are increasing India's contribution to climate change. India is the fifth largest emitter of GHGs,[44] even though its per capita contribution remains markedly lower than China's and the United States'.[45] The country's contribution to climate change will continue to increase if its dependency on traditional energy fuels continues to increase. Of particular concern are the demand trends in the urban areas – electricity for commercial and residential buildings for air conditioners and light, petroleum for increasing private

---

and N.H. Ravindranath, *Climate Change, Sustainable Development and India: Global and National Concerns,* 90(3) CURRENT SCIENCE 314–325 (10 February 2006).

[38] Damage to biodiversity hotspots could be irreversible. Read N.H. Ravindranath, N.V. Joshi, R. Sukumar, and A. Saxena, *Impact of Climate Change on Forests in India,* 90(3) CURRENT SCIENCE 354–361 (10 February 2006). See also Climate Change Impacts on Industry in India, Keysheet 8, IIM Ahmedabad Report.

[39] Extreme sea-level rise could threaten life and property in coastal regions, as could increase in cyclones. Read A.S. Unnikrishnan, K. Rupa Kumar, Sharon E. Fernandes, G.S. Michael and S.K. Patwardhan, *Sea Level Changes Along the Indian Coast: Observation and Projections,* 90(3) CURRENT SCIENCE 362–368 (10 February 2006).

[40] Malaria-carrying vectors are particularly worrisome. Read Sumana Bhattacharya, C. Sharma, R.C. Dhiman and A.P. Mitra, *Climate Change and Malaria in India,* 90(3) CURRENT SCIENCE 369–375 (10 February 2006). Read also *Health Ministry Warns of Spurt in Diseases,* INDIAN EXPRESS (16 May 2007).

[41] Emily Wax, *A Sacred River Endangered by Global Warming,* WASHINGTON POST A14 (17 June 2007).

[42] Roger Harrabin, *How Climate Change Hits India's Poor,* BBC NEWS (1 February 2007).

[43] CNA Corporation, National Security and the Threat of Climate Change 16–18 (2007)

[44] World Bank, *Little Green Data Book* (2007).

[45] German Watch, Climate Change Performance Index (2008).

transportation, and coal for cement and steel industries.[46] Infrastructure projects such as road building and electricity generation and distribution will also cause adverse land use shifts.[47]

The close link between India's economic growth, infrastructure deficits, energy requirements, and climate consequences translates into complex law and policy-making. Unless government policies and legislation balance the competing and overlapping interests, it may not be in a position to sustain its economic growth or prevent climate-related catastrophes.

C. POLICIES AND LAW—ECONOMICS, ENERGY, AND ENVIRONMENT

India's economic policies have undergone dramatic transition since the early 1990s, when India signed the General Agreement on Tariffs and Trade (GATT) and became a member of the World Trade Organization (WTO).[48] The new liberal economic policies helped stabilize the country's external debts.[49] Now, the Government's focus is on increasing the country's share of global merchandise and employment opportunities.[50]

The Foreign Trade (Development and Regulation) Act (1992) not only enforces India's obligations under GATT, but also limits the application of some exceptions to free trade provided under the agreement, such as restrictions on non-tariff trade barriers to protect the environment or human health.[51] The objective of the

---

[46] P.R. Shukla, Rajesh Nair, Manmohan Kapshe, Amit Garg, S. Balasubramaniam, Deepa Menon, and K.K. Sharma, *Development and Climate: An Assessment of India*, Indian Institute of Management, Ahmedabad (2003) (on file with author).

[47] Sathaye, *supra* note 37.

[48] National Council of Applied Economic Research, Economic and Policy Reforms in India (2002) (on file with author); JOSHI, *supra* note 4.

[49] IMF, India: 2006 Article IV Consultation—Staff Report, Staff Statement, and Public Information Notice on the Executive Board Discussion, IMF Country Report No. 07/63 (February 2007).

[50] Foreign Trade Policy, 1 September 2004–1 March 2009, Notification No. 1 (RE-2006)/2004–2009 (7 April 2006) effective 1 April 2006.

[51] *Id.*

1992 Act is to reduce red tape and trade restrictions. It has been successful in promoting trade in coal and petroleum products.[52] As a result of the legislation and the Government's trade policies, major trade arrangements have been established with almost every region, including Africa, Americas, Asia, Europe, and the Middle East.[53]

The Government has also adopted policies and legislation to promote infrastructure development. A major step has been the deregulation of relevant sectors – power, roads, airports, and ports – to attract foreign direct investment (FDI).[54] For example, the administration is promoting policies that would encourage domestic oil production. The New Exploration License Policy, adopted in 2000 by the Ministry of Petroleum and Natural Gas, permits foreign companies to hold 100% equity in oil and natural gas projects, even though the corresponding companies, such as the Indian Oil Corporation (IOC) and the Oil and Natural Gas Corporation (ONGC), are State-owned.[55, 56]

The Government is facilitating the expansion of exploration and production activities abroad by its corporations. ONGC reportedly holds interests in about 25 projects in 15 countries, including Sudan and Russia.[57] The supply side of the oil sector has been deregulated, allowing private refiners to directly enter the market to provide petroleum products to their customers.[58] The new Market Determined Price Mechanism (MDPM)[59] allows

---

[52] Ministry of Commerce and Industry, Annual Report 2004–2005.

[53] *Supra* note 49.

[54] FDI has been facilitated by a series of policy measures. For an overview of FDI in India read Secretariat for Industrial Assistance, Department of Industrial Policy and Promotion, Department of Industry and Commerce, Manual of Foreign Direct Investment in India, Policy and Procedures (May 2003).

[55] *Supra* note 20.

[56] To date, however, no international oil company owns major equities in any project. *Id.*

[57] India has also started several new projects for importing natural gas, including projects to construct pipeline with Iran-Pakistan, Turkmenistan-Afghanistan-Pakistan, and Myanmar. *Supra* note 20.

[58] *Id.*

[59] MDPM replaces the Administered Price Mechanism (APM), under which the Government determined the prices. *Id.*

market pricing of fuel, and subsidies are slowly being phased out as fuel prices rise.[60]

Energy policies to catalyze and sustain economic growth are supplemented by legislation to promote infrastructure development. The Indian Electricity Act of 2003, a consolidation of earlier legislation, is aimed at stimulating private investment, domestic and foreign, to boost the power sector.[61] The new law seeks to upgrade the domestic grid system by 2012. If properly implemented, the legislation will support efforts to supply electricity to nearly 40% of the population currently without access to power.[62] The legislation also seeks to cut losses faced by State Electricity Boards by establishing irrevocable letters of credit and escrow accounts to ensure proper management of the resources.[63]

Legislative activity to support construction projects is also on the rise. For instance, the National Highway Act permits "build-own-transfer" projects to expand and improve the highway system in India.[64] A special Airport Economic Regulatory Authority to oversee the modernization and construction of airports is being established.[65] A range of targeted policies have been adopted to attract FDI for marine ports, telecommunications and real estate development projects.[66]

---

[60] Heather Timmons, *Citing Oil Prices, Asia Starts Reducing Fuel Subsidies*, NEW YORK TIMES (2 November 2007). However, the Government continues to subsidize fuels for consumers, driving several private refiners such as Reliance Petroleum to export their products. *Supra* note 20.

[61] Electricity (Amendment) Act, 2003, No. 57 of 2003.

[62] Measures to spur investment include a fixed return of 16% on investment, removing licensing requirements to operate and maintain power-generation stations, participation in distribution and transmission with license from a newly created Central Electricity Regulatory Commission (CERC), provision for selling power directly without government intervention, and the creation of a separate Appellate Tribunal for Electricity. Read Mark J. Reidy and Andrew Kurth, *Project Finance India*, 1587 PRACTICING LAW INSTITUTE 143 (2007).

[63] Nandan Nelivigi, Doug Peel, and Christopher Krishnamoorthy, *Infrastructure Project Finance in India: Recent Developments*, 1587 PRACTICING LAW INSTITUTE 133 (2007).

[64] *Id.*

[65] Reidy and Kurth, *supra* note 62.

[66] *Id.*

In addition to the above legislation, cumbersome regulations that slow down infrastructure development are under review for change. A special committee – the Govindrajan Committee – was set up to identify laws and policies that hinder fast growth and to provide recommendations to resolve the issue. Among others, the Committee identified environmental impact assessment regulation as a major hurdle to infrastructure improvement and recommended a single window procedure to expedite regulatory clearances.[67]

Legislation to speed infrastructure development and expand energy supply is complemented by policies and laws to achieve energy efficiency. The Energy Conservation Act of 2001 was passed to promote efficient use and conservation of energy as part of the effort to provide electricity to all citizens by 2012.[68] The Bureau of Energy Efficiency created under the Act comprises a Governing Council representing all energy-related ministries.[69] The Council advises the Central Government on energy conservation policies and coordinates the implementation of corresponding action. The Appellate Tribunal for Energy Conservation adjudicates disputes arising from both Central and State Government orders on energy conservation.[70]

The Bureau has initiated several projects to promote sustainable energy use, starting with an evaluation of government buildings for efficiency. It is also consulting key industries through the Indian Industry Programme for Energy Conservation, which brings together task groups representing the textile, cement, paper and pulp, fertilizer, and aluminum industries. They share

[67] Government of India, Report on Reforming Investment Approval and Implementation Procedures, Part-I (Investment Approval Procedures – Government and Public Sector Projects) (May 2002).

[68] Section 1, Energy Conservation Act, 2001, No. 52 of 2001, Gazette of India Extraordinary 3.

[69] These include the Ministries of Power, Petroleum and Natural Gas, Coal, Non-conventional Energy Sources, Atomic Energy, Consumer Affairs, Central Electricity Authority, Commerce and Industry of Kolkata, Central Mine Planning and Design Institute, Bureau of Indian Standards, and Central Power Institute of Karnataka. *Id.*, Section 4.

[70] *Id.*, Sec. 30.

best practices and establish voluntary targets and benchmarks towards energy efficiency, to set up workable efficiency programs and strategies.[71] In the pipeline are projects such as energy standard-setting, labeling, green building codes, energy certification, accreditation programs, school education, and supply side conservation projects.[72]

The work of the Bureau is complemented by the Ministry of New and Renewable Energy, which explores alternative energy sources such as solar, wind, hydropower, and biogas.[73] The Ministry's target is to ensure that 5–6% of all energy will be derived from renewable energy sources by 2032.[74] Notably, the Government of India is presently exploring civilian nuclear energy options, having recently decided to negotiate an agreement with France,[75] and working on another with the United States.[76]

India's climate change policy and law primarily flow from global arrangements. India acceded to the Kyoto Protocol in 2005,[77] but due to low per capita emissions it has a surplus of emission rights.[78] India, unlike Annex I countries such as Australia, Japan, Canada, and Europe, is not legally required to reduce its emissions

---

[71] *Id.*

[72] For an overview of the powers and functions of the Bureau *see* http://www.bee-india.nic.in.

[73] The Ministry began life as the Department of Non-Conventional Energy Sources within the Ministry of Energy, which was established in the 1980s to ensure energy security after the oil crisis in the 1970s. The Department became a separate Ministry of Non-Conventional Energy Sources in 1992 and was renamed the Ministry of New and Renewable Energy in 2006. Ministry of Renewable Energy, Annual Report 2005–2006, read also Government of India, Administrative Circular Notification, No. 24/1/1993-Admn.II (20 October 2006).

[74] *Id.*

[75] *India, France to Sign Nuclear Deal,* BUSINESS STANDARD (26 January 2008).

[76] Jim VandeHei and Dafna Linzer, *U.S., India Reach Deal on Nuclear Cooperation,* WASHINGTON POST A1 (3 March 2006).

[77] Clean Development Mechanism of India.

[78] Per capita emission is defined in terms of total emissions (excluding land-use) Units – thousands metric tones of carbon dioxide consumption per capita per 1000 population, see Center for American Progress, The world's Top emitters 21 september 2007. For a list of countries with high per capita emissions see CO_2 Emissions (per capita) (most recent) Nation Master, For a list of countries in order of per capita emissions Union of Concerned Scientists.

by a specific target date.[79] Further, Annex I countries can invest in clean development mechanisms (CDM) and other emission reduction projects in India and receive credits towards meeting their own reduction targets under the Protocol.[80]

The Government has established a National Clean Development Mechanism Authority (NCDMA) within the central Ministry of Environment and Forests (MoEF) to coordinate CDM projects.[81] NCDMA has developed interim procedures for granting approval to project proposals, and it supervises the project implementation.[82] However, poor infrastructure, market viability, and intellectual property regimes that inhibit transfer of low-carbon technologies into India limit the efficacy of CDM undertakings.[83]

Specific policies and legislation to mitigate or adapt to climate change are, however, absent. A special committee, the National Council on Climate Change established by the Prime Minister of India, is finalizing a draft policy.[84] The report, scheduled to be released in December 2007, may not be out until June 2008.[85]

As matters now stand, efforts to conserve energy are driven more by concerns of meeting growing economic demands than by a desire to arrest climate change.[86] Supplementary, and not

---

[79] Annex I countries are required to reduce their GHG emissions by specific percentages below their 1990 levels under Art. 2, Kyoto Protocol to United Nations Convention on Climate Change, 10 December 1997, in 37 International Legal Materials 32 (1998).

[80] *Id.*, Art. 12.

[81] The Authority was established by an order the Joint Secretary, as required under UNFCCC. Read Ministry of Environment and Forests, Order (16 April 2004), S.O. 515 (E), F.No. 4/5/2003-CCC, issued by R.K. Viash, Joint Secretary.

[82] National CDM Authority, CDM India: Designated National Authority.

[83] Energy and Resources Institute and Institute of Development Studies, University of Sussex, UK-India Collaboration to Identify the Barriers to the Transfer of Low Carbon Energy Technology, (October 2006) (on file with author).

[84] Prime Minister of India's Office, PM's Council on Climate Change constituted, Press Release (5 June 2007).

[85] Aasha Khosa, *Draft Climate Change Report This Month,* BUSINESS STANDARD (20 February 2008).

[86] Former President of India Abdul Kalam noted the importance of energy efficiency to energy independence, stating "Energy independence [was] the lifeline of [the] nation", but not referring to the nexus with global warming. Address at the Inauguration of The South Asian Conference on Renewable Energy, New Delhi, 18 April 2006.v

entirely successful, efforts such as conservation of forests are incidental to and part of ongoing efforts that were launched in the 1980s.[87] In fact, these initiatives may be adversely affected by the country's drive to increase production of biofuels as an alternative source of energy.[88]

The Government has not taken any step to reduce carbon dioxide emissions under its pollution control law nor are there any plans to do so imminently.[89] If experience is any indication, the Government may not undertake such measures voluntarily: critical pollution controls have in past been motivated by judicial intervention.[90] The administrative structure to address environmental concerns is, as such, inadequate to address most problems, and climate change is no exception.[91]

Adaptation policies and law are also subject to the recommendation of the National Council on Climate Change and to consultations

---

[87] In 1988, the Ministry of Environment and Forests adopted the National Forest Policy under the Forest (Conservation) Act, 1980 and launched a series of afforestation and reforestation programs through community partnerships – the Joint Forest Management Programs. However, much remains to be done in terms of preserving species and gene pools as well as drawing up comprehensive forest management plans. Read Armin Rosencranz, Edward Boenig, and Brinda Dutta, *The Godavarman Case: The Indian Supreme Court's Breach of Constitutional Boundaries in Managing India's Forests,* 37 ENVIRONMENTAL LAW REPORTER 10032 (January 2007).

[88] Jayalakshmi K., *Biofuels and the Need for Caution,* DECCAN HERALD 3 (29 May 2007). The Government's interest in promoting biofuels is evident in its efforts to establish a National Mission on Biofuels by 2011–2012. Read Preety Bhandari, *India's Pragmatic Approach to Climate Change,* SCIENCE AND DEVELOPMENT NETWORK (31 August 2006).

[89] India's reluctance to adopt pollution-reduction measures was articulated by Prime Minister Manmohan Singh recently. In an address, Singh assured that India's per capita emissions would not surpass that of industrialized countries, implying that no emissions control measures would be taken. See Krittivas Mukherjee, *India's Climate Change Roadmap to be ready in June,* REUTERS UK (7 February 2008),

[90] The Government adopted the Euro Emissions II standards for all road vehicles following litigation at the Supreme Court of India. Read *M.C. Mehta v. Union of India and Others,* WP 13020/1985 (1999.04.06). Litigation, however, may not be the answer to many of the concerns either. R.K. Pachauri, *Clearing the Air: Many Roadblocks on the CNG Route,* TIMES OF INDIA (1 September 2001).

[91] Ministry of Environment and Forests, India's Initial Communications to the United Nations Framework Convention on Climate Change (2004).

with the Global Environment Fund.[92] Until proper adaptation strategies are designed, citizens will have to be resilient, as in past, when catastrophic events occur.[93] In the alternative, courts may be approached. However, access remains problematic,[94] despite the Indian judiciary's liberal interpretation of constitutional rights.[95]

In sum, India is progressively aligning its policy and legislation to sustain its economic growth and infrastructure development, but has yet to adopt a comprehensive climate change policy that would address mitigation and adaptation concerns without interfering with economic and ancillary growth.

D. CONCLUSION: LOOKING AHEAD

India's kaleidoscope of policies and laws is steadily focused on economic growth. The policies and laws clearly promote energy use, and much of this will have to come from traditional sources that have high emissions. Environmental laws are lax and are being deregulated to promote infrastructure development. As a barometer of the country's participation in the global climate regime in future, these policies do not indicate any major shift from the current position.

The Government is determined to push for economic growth and to expand its share of global energy consumption. Its only concession to climate change relates to the Government's push to alternate and efficient energy use. Other efforts such as policies for adaptation remain indeterminate. Given the Government's thrust

---

[92] The Government is exploring insurance and technology solutions to address the issue. Surya P. Seth, Energy Planning Commission, Climate Change Dialogue India Country Presentation (May 2006) (unpublished).

[93] Prime Minister of India's Office, PM Reviews India's Response to Tsunami, Press Release (24 December 2005).

[94] Y.K. Sabharwal, Speech at the Inauguration of the Joint Conference of Chief Justices and Chief Ministers (11 March 2006), Dr. Jayaprakash Narayan, *Judicial Reforms – Need of the Hour*, LOKSATTA RESEARCH PAPER.

[95] S.P. Sathe, *Judicial Activism: The Indian Experience,* 6 WASHINGTON UNIVERSITY JOURNAL OF LAW AND POLICY 38 (2001). The author thanks Prof. Richard L. Ottinger, Pace Law School, and Professors Daniel Bogart and Denis Binder, Chapman Law School, for their inputs.

and the general lack of concern, the forecast for the global climate regime remains bleak. At the very least, emission reduction targets may not be a good platform for engaging India in negotiations for a legally binding treaty.

3

The *Eighteenth Camel*: Mediating Mediation Reform in India

HIRAM E. CHODOSH

A. INTRODUCTION

In western India, on the edge of the Thar Desert, a wealthy camel herder died, leaving his seventeen camels to his three sons. His final wishes distributed the camels among them in specific proportions: one-half to the eldest, one-third to the middle son, and one-ninth to the youngest. The sons quickly appreciated the immediate obstacle in fully complying with their father's wishes. How could they make this specific distribution? They could not wait for the camels to breed; nor did they want to sell them off and share the proceeds because herding camels was all they had ever known. Accordingly, they decided to consult the village elders from the local panchayat. Seemingly uncertain of the appropriate solution, one of the five elders suggested that the sons accept a loan of one of his camels, go home, think it over again, and return the camel to him on the very next day. Disgruntled by the ostensible futility of his advice, they returned to their tent, cursing under their breath the stupidity of the old man.

As they shook their heads over tea, the youngest suddenly rose in excitement. "Brothers," he exclaimed, "we now have eighteen camels." "So?!?," the eldest mocked him, "we will have seventeen only tomorrow. What good will that do, you fool?!?" "But bhaya, with eighteen camels, we can divide them up according to the wishes of our papa: you get nine; our brother gets six; and I get two. That makes seventeen. We divide the herd, and give the eighteenth camel back to our elder!"[1]

[1] The "18th Camel", a fable from the Middle East adapted here, is well known to the mediation community and many other areas of discourse. Further LYNN SEGAL, THE DREAM OF REALITY (1986).

Of the many anecdotes and fables that have informed over a decade of work and observations on mediation reforms in India, the *Eighteenth Camel* stands out for the author. First, it illustrates the powerful technique of integrative bargaining.[2] Second, and more importantly, it captures a goal of outsiders in controversial legal reforms: to become *essentially superfluous*. Engaged assistance in comparative justice reform teaches the "expert" to appreciate the frequently superficial nature of legislative pronouncements, the nearly insuperable obstacles to institutional reform, the conflicts within the legal and broader community about the nature of reform itself, the pressing need for applied techniques to help resolve that higher-level social conflict, and the necessarily limited role of foreign expertise in that domestic conversation. From the author's time in India (and elsewhere), it was concluded that the optimal role for external expertise and coordination is to help supply, if not to become, the proverbial *Eighteenth Camel*.

Accordingly, this essay seeks to draw lessons from the author's work and observations as an intermediary in the encounter between mediation and the Indian legal culture. Section B. summarizes mediation reform in India to date, including the assessment upon which mediation reform proposals were initially based, a brief history of the legislation, and the Supreme Court's framework for exploring questions of implementation. Section C. explores the value of *specific* mediation negotiation and communication tools, draws attention to a daunting set of reform obstacles, and suggests some strategies for overcoming them. Section D. advances two critiques of foreign (primarily American) involvement in Indian mediation reform. The first critique focuses on American conceptual assumptions about mediation that frustrate the adaptation of mediation tools to the Indian legal context. The second critique isolates special problems encountered by outsiders in advancing local reforms. Finally, Section E. illuminates an unforeseen application of mediation in India, namely tools that may assist in resolving conflict over the mediation reform itself. Based on this discussion, the Conclusion

---

[2] Integrative bargaining involves the investment of external resources in the resolution of a conflict or solution to a difficult problem.

explains why the *Eighteenth Camel* may be instructive for future forms of American (or other foreign) assistance in Indian and possibly other national justice reform efforts.

B. ORIGINS OF MEDIATION REFORM IN INDIA

I. *Introduction to the Indian Legal Process*[3]

The Indian justice system resembles its common law counterparts of British origin. The system features a coordinate, pyramidal structure of judicial authority, emphasizes formal procedural justice dominated by litigants of equal status engaged in adversarial processes, and provides binding, win-lose remedies. A politically independent judiciary applies both federal and state law under a unified federal system and administers the formal civil justice process. The Supreme Court sits at the apex of the federal system; the High Courts, one per state, serve as the highest state *fora* in both civil and criminal matters. Every state is subdivided into several districts, each with a District Court (sometimes called a Sessions Court) designated as the principal civil court of original jurisdiction, under which sit a number of lower courts, including *panchayats*, whose powers differ greatly from state to state.

Generally, the civil justice process is governed by the Code of Civil Procedure of 1908 (or CPC, itself a derivation of the British Judicature Acts) and subsequent amendments. A typical civil proceeding consists of several adversarial, party-controlled stages, including pleadings, a determination of jurisdiction, trial, judgment and decree, appeals (including revision and review), and execution.

II. *The Assessment*

Despite the salient strengths of the Indian civil justice system and its proactively independent judiciary, inefficient court administration systems, judicial passivity in an adversarial legal process, and limited alternatives to a protracted and discontinuous

[3] Further Hiram E. Chodosh, *Indian Civil Justice Reform: Limitation and Preservation of the Adversarial Process,* 30 NEW YORK UNIVERSITY JOURNAL OF INTERNATIONAL LAW AND POLITICS 1–78 (1998).

full trial frustrate several goals of the adversarial process itself. Inefficiency in court administration denies timely access to legal dispositions. Excessive party control places those seeking legal redress in an unequal position because respondents can abuse and delay the resolution procedures with impunity. Finally, the unavailability of alternatives to litigation clogs the system. Many cases awaiting judgment are no longer contentious and long-awaited judgments are often difficult to enforce.

As both a daunting symptom and aggravating cause, widespread and profound backlog and delay[4] undermine the fundamental priorities of a law-based society. Protracted delays erode public trust and confidence in legal institutions and act as significant barriers to India's chosen path to social justice and economic development. The inability to enter final legal decisions within a reasonable time renders state action functionally immune, turns obligations to perform contractual duties into effective rights to breach with impunity, and devalues remedies eventually provided. In sum, the inability to resolve disputes in a timely manner eviscerates public and private rights and obligations.

In the daily operation of the civil litigation process, records of new filings are kept by hand, and documents filed in the court house are frequently misplaced or lost among other paper. Lawyers crowd the courtroom and wait for their cases to be called. Even when called, judicial attention is frequently deferred by innumerable adjournments: the witness is not available, the party is not present, the lawyer has not arrived, or a document is not yet available. When the case is heard, a judge orally summarizes testimony for a court reporter. There is little likelihood that this judge will be the same one to issue a decision because judges are transferred more quickly than legal dispositions are made. Judges are so under-paid and over-worked that they often adjourn and delay the preparation of a case to put off the demands of reaching a decision.

---

[4] Robert Moog, *Delays in the Indian Courts: Why the Judges Don't Take Control*, 16 JUSTICE SYSTEM JOURNAL 22–30 (1992). Moog cites various structural constraints, including a three-year judicial rotation system and a power imbalance between judges and attorneys in favor of the attorneys, as the major impediments to case management approaches in India.

Streamlining procedures that enable the judge to frame the issues are rarely effectuated. Likewise, sanction power to impose costs for frivolous conduct is seldom exercised. Interim injunctive relief is routinely granted, but long delays in hearing the contentions of those enjoined persist. Commonly made interlocutory appeals fracture the case into many parts and effectively stay the trial. The absence of alternatives to litigation makes a full, discontinuous trial necessary, regardless of how long it may take. Once a judgment is reached, the truly hard work of enforcement and execution begins.[5]

III. Procedural Reform

Such concerns were first expressed in a study led by Chief Justice A.M. Ahmadi in the spring of 1997, when Parliament promulgated (in 1999) several amendments to the Civil Procedure Code of 1908.[6]

---

[5] Adapted from Chodosh, *supra* note 3.

[6] The Code of Civil Procedure (Amendment) Act, No. 46 of 1999; India Code (1999).

[7] INDIA CODE CIV. PROC. § 89(1)–(2), describing and directing court to utilize dispute resolution mechanisms, including arbitration, conciliation, judicial settlement, judicial settlement through lok adalat, or mediation:

> (1) Where it appears to the court that there exists elements of a settlement which may be acceptable to the parties, the court shall formulate the terms of settlement and give them to the parties for their observations and after receiving the observations of the parties, the court may reformulate the terms of a possible settlement and refer the same for—
>
> (a) Arbitration;
> (b) conciliation;
> (c) judicial settlement including settlement through Lok Adalat; or
> (d) mediation.
>
> (2) Where a dispute has been referred—
>
> (a) for arbitration or conciliation, the provisions of the Arbitration and Conciliation Act, 1996 (26 or 1996) shall apply as if the proceedings for arbitration or conciliation were referred for settlement under the provisions of that Act;
>
> (b) to Lok Adalat, the court shall refer the same to Lok Adalat in accordance with the provisions of sub-section

Among these, Section 89[7] and Order X (1A)[8] provided for court-annexed alternative dispute resolution (ADR). Under the new provision, the court directs the parties to choose among several ADR mechanisms, including *lok adalat* (people's court), arbitration, conciliation, and mediation. Section 89 contemplates that the judge (presumably the judge assigned to the case) should first determine whether there exist "elements of a settlement which may be acceptable to the parties". If so, the court "shall

---

> (1) of section 20 of the Legal Services Authority Act, 1987 (39 of 1987) and all other provisions of that Act shall apply in respect of the dispute so referred to the Lok Adalat;
>
> (c) for judicial settlement, the court shall refer the same to a suitable institution or person and such institution or person shall be deemed to be a Lok Adalat under the provisions of the Act;
>
> (d) for mediation, the court shall effect a compromise between the parties and shall follow such procedure as may be prescribed.

[8] INDIA CODE CIV. PROC. Order X, describing and directing court to utilize dispute resolution mechanisms, including arbitration, conciliation, judicial settlement, judicial settlement through *lok adalat,* or mediation:

> Direction of the court to opt for any one mode of alternative dispute resolution.
>
> 1A. After recording the admissions and denials, the court shall direct the parties to the suit to opt either mode of the settlement outside the court as specified in sub-section (1) of section 89. On the option of the parties, the court shall fix the date of appearance before such forum or authority as may be opted by the parties.
>
> Appearance before the conciliatory forum or authority.
>
> 1B. Where a suit is referred under rule 1A, the parties shall appear before such forum or authority for conciliation of the suit.
>
> Appearance before the court consequent to the failure of efforts of conciliation.
>
> 1C. Where a suit is referred under rule 1A, and the presiding officer of conciliation forum or authority is satisfied that it would not be proper in the interest of justice to proceed with the matter further, then, it shall refer the matter again to the court and direct the parties to appear before the court on the date fixed by it.

formulate the terms of settlement and give them to the parties for their observations". Finally, "after receiving the observations of the parties, the court may reformulate the terms of a possible settlement" and refer the same for arbitration,[9] conciliation, judicial settlement, including through *lok adalat*, or mediation.[10] These provisions, drawn from the conciliation provisions of the Arbitration and Conciliation Act (1996),[11] are based on the UNCITRAL model law, itself derived mainly from European practice of conciliation.

Based on widespread opposition to the amendments from the practicing bar, the amendments were suspended indefinitely. In July 2002, however, Parliament decided to put the amendments, including Section 89, into full effect. Following the effectuation of Section 89, a bar association in Tamil Nadu brought a constitutional challenge in *Salem Bar Association*. In a panel decision written by Chief Justice Kirpal in late October 2002, the Supreme Court upheld the constitutionality of the law and established a five-person committee to study the reforms and to make recommendations on the need for any amendments or additional rules to facilitate implementation of the reforms.[12]

---

[9] The statute can admittedly be read to mean that a judge might refer parties to binding arbitration without their consent. However, it would be inconsistent with the principle of consent and self-determination to compel parties to binding arbitration without their consent. The control of the parties over the outcome in each of the other proceedings reduces concern about compelling a constrained choice of an ADR technique.

[10] India Code Civ. Proc., *supra* note 7.

[11] The Arbitration and Conciliation Act, No. 26 of 1996; India Code (1996), § 73 (using language nearly identical to Section 89).

[12] *Salem Advocate Bar Association v. Union of India,* (2002) 8 S.C.C. 35, 146–52. ("With the constitution of such a Committee, any creases which require to be ironed out can be identified and apprehensions which may exist in the minds of the litigating public or the lawyers clarified.") Former Supreme Court Justice Rao and Chairman of the Law Commission headed this committee, on which former Law Minister Arun Jetley also served. The Supreme Court initially gave the Committee four months to seek comments and to report back. Rao drafted consultation papers, including rules on mediation and case management, and circulated them to the High Courts for comments; however, these papers did not reach the High Courts until late January, thus leaving insufficient time for adequate study and commentary. Rao requested an extension of the deadline until July, and organized a national conference on mediation and case management. The national conference involved Chief Justices of each of the High Courts, and two lower court judges, as well as prominent lawyers from the bar.

The Law Commission conducted a national conference in 2003 and then promulgated guidelines for the use of mediation. The decision in *Salem Bar Association* was affirmed in 2005.[13]

Conflicts among and between the bar and the bench over the role of these reforms and the impact they may have on corporate or individual professional interests has substantially delayed widespread implementation. Even with strong initiative in several important pockets of the judicial system (including the Bombay High Court in particular), the judiciary and the bar were at first ill-prepared to move the reforms forward to meet the country's challenge. Until recently, no court in the country had implemented a formal Section 89 proceeding. In other words, for several years after the major anti-delay legislation in the country, no responsive changes had taken place. Only now with the express direction of the Supreme Court and responses from several courts in Chennai, Delhi, Ahmedabad, and Bombay beginning to implement rules is any observable activity taking place.[14]

C. MEDIATION: VALUES, OBSTACLES, AND STRATEGIES

I. The Value of Mediation

An evaluation of the usefulness of mediation[15] in light of its core objectives presupposes an awareness of what it is and what specific value it offers. Further, an effective adaptation of mediation to a set of new conditions first counsels separate treatment of a wide variety of features clustered under the mediation rubric. Separate treatment of these processes and techniques underlines the view that many, if not all, of these features are severable from the rest. Severability allows for more creative designs and experiments to overcome problems encountered in the application of mediation to Indian legal disputes (especially U.S. mediation practices and theories).

---

[13] *Salem Advocate Bar Association II v. Union of India,* (2005) 6 S.C.C. 344 (including the Civil Procedure ADR and Mediation Rules).

[14] J. Venkatesan, *Apex court for early clearance to national mediation policy,* THE HINDU, 7 January 2007.

[15] Global interest in mediation is growing substantially. For example, see the newly formed International Mediation Institute at http://www.imimediation.org/?cID=about_imi.

Mediation is facilitated negotiation. Facilitation includes establishing joint communication, neutral reframing, agenda setting, acknowledgment and several other important communication strategies and tactics. Negotiation tools include distributive, interest-based, integrative, and other strategies. Specific attributes clustered together in mediation systems vary greatly. The result is always consensual, the facilitator is neutral, and the process is usually (but not necessarily) confidential, jointly participatory, interest-based, future-looking, and aimed at a durable, win-win solution. Initiation of mediation may be voluntary or compulsory (usually as one of several constrained options of other ADR techniques), court-annexed or private, position-based, or interest-based, facilitative or evaluative, and free of charge or fee-for-service.

Mediation does not come as an unchangeable recipe or rigid system. Indeed, one of its most attractive features may be its flexibility and thus its adaptability. Overly prescriptive or doctrinaire views about the *essentials* of mediation risk undermining this feature. Rigid recipes may also preclude experimentation with independently fruitful communication and negotiation tools that may be incorporated into an emerging, Indian mediation process.

Each tool may have its own considerable value or application. A brief description of available techniques will help illustrate their independent usefulness.

1. Negotiation Techniques: the Intellectual Technology

a) Position-Based Bargaining

As an example of an overly prescriptive view, many mediation experts stress the negative consequences of position-based or performative bargaining and urge that mediations should focus primarily (if not exclusively) on a determination, prioritization, and maximization of the parties' interests. Indeed, the first chapter in the seminal book, *Getting to Yes,* begins with the mandate: "Don't Bargain Over Positions."[16] Such advice may be misplaced, particularly in the early stages of developing mediation practice.

---

[16] ROGER FISHER AND WILLIAM URY, GETTING TO YES 3–8 (1983).

Performative or position-based bargaining is a frequent starting point for giving full expression to the conflict, and premature interventions to divert the emotional impulses that support it may not be productive. Further, position-based bargaining can help the parties to reach a more realistic view of the settlement value of their claims and defenses (thus narrowing their differences) and to take that settlement valuation into account as one of their many *interests.*

Let's suppose that the plaintiff and defendant are equally and completely confident of the merits of their respective claims and defenses. Let's suppose further that the claim is for $100,000. As for settlement positions, the defendant's first position is that he owes nothing, and the plaintiff's first position is that she is owed $100,000. In conducting position-based bargaining, a mediator may point out to the parties that they cannot both be completely correct in their insistence of a certain result in their favor. The parties may begin to see that there may be a modest weakness in their positions. If that weakness can be quantified as a 20% weakness, the settlement values can be recalculated.

If the parties can be convinced of a 20% weakness in their positions (a modest proposition), the settlement values to each may be recalculated as follows: plaintiff's claim has an $80,000 value (100 x 80%); and the settlement valuation for the defendant is $20,000 (100 x 20%). With this simple operation, the difference between the two parties' settlement valuations (from $80,000 to $20,000) has been reduced by a difference of $40,000 from $100,000 to $60,000.

Beyond recognition of weakness is further sensitivity to the uncertainty of the process and the determination on the merits. Even with the most predictable legal process there are uncertainties in realizing the expected result. If there is an additional 10% uncertainty (or chance from one party's perspective that the court will be in error), the parties' settlement valuations will come even closer to one another: $70,000 for the plaintiff, and $30,000 for the defendant. With these calculations, only $40,000 separates the parties' settlement estimates.

The mediator may at this point explore the expected costs of proceeding with trial. These include court costs (which can be considerable), legal fees, non-monetary costs of aggravation and stress, and opportunity costs (distraction from other valuable activities). Some of these costs are easily quantifiable, others not. Recognition of these costs, however, allows the parties to see that the final judgment is not the only indication of cost or benefit (to which these other items need to added or subtracted). The avoidance of those costs through settlement (e.g., a reduction in court costs prior to framing of issues, a reduction in legal fees having alleviated a good deal of work over many years) may be captured, indeed shared by the parties and their attorneys through position-based settlement negotiations of this type.

Finally, the time value of money may dramatically discount the settlement value to the plaintiff, especially in a system burdened with protracted delays. If under the best of circumstances a plaintiff will not recover the full amount due for a period of ten years; if the cost of an unsecured loan is 15% (9% greater than the maximum pre-judgment interest rate that might be applied (e.g., 6%), then the time value of money will reduce the present value of a $100,000 claim to approximately $40,000 (or 40% of its original value). This economic reality, though an unfortunate consequence of delay, may provide a more realistic picture for the plaintiff of the settlement value of their claim, and this means that the quantifiable differences in the parties' settlement valuations are even smaller (40% of $40,000 in our example equals $16,000) and the proportionate cost savings even greater.

b) Interest-based Bargaining

The foregoing discussion took a modest step beyond the parties' conflicting views on the legal merits of their positions. A more realistic settlement value based on weaknesses in their positions, uncertainty, hidden costs, and the time value of money may help bring the parties closer together, if not in settling the matter altogether. Surely some cases will settle with the help of these tools alone; others will not. For this latter subset of conflicts, effective mediators explore the parties' interests (beyond their legal positions).[17] For example, a plaintiff injured by an allegedly defective or harmful product may have interests beyond the $100,000 requested for (i) continuing health care, (ii) schooling for her children, (iii) a job lost as the result of an injury, or (iv) a concern about preventing similar injuries to others. (This is but a short list.) Commercial parties in a contractual dispute may have interests in a continuing business relationship. (Mediation may also be effective in helping to form new relationships from a conflict or severing lock-in relationships where exiting them is in the interest of the parties.) A separated couple has a shared interest in the best situation for their children. A family torn apart by a property partition has an interest in continuing business investments that may have been stalled by severed communication in the wake of the conflict. These interests provide potential resources for settlement that tap the additional dimensions of relationships (one legal and others not) and provide the basis to settle conflicts in the interest and according to the determinations of the parties. This requires an exploration of why parties are fighting over limited resources and whether there are benefits of particular terms of settlement that override those of even the most favorable legal outcome. A dispute between two people over the ownership of a goat, for example, presents the adjudicator with the task of finding a rule of decision: who had it first (property); who purchased it (contract); who needs it more (equity)? The arbitrator (upon not finding a rule of decision) might split the difference, awarding half to each person and ordering the slaughter of the goat. This may be in neither party's interest if they rely on the goat for milk. The mediator will instead ask the parties why each wants the goat. If one wants the goat for the milk and the other for breeding purposes, the parties may agree to hold equal rights in it and distribute the benefits accordingly. This process of interest identification and accommodation creates a win-win outcome of mutual gains for both parties, and they are unlikely to continue fighting over the distribution after it is

[17] To go beyond the parties' positions does not mean that these are no longer relevant. Experts speak in terms of knowing the best alternative to a negotiated settlement (BATNA), the worst alternative to a negotiated settlement (WATNA) and the most likely alternative to a negotiated settlement (MLATNA) (similar to BATNA, but including a factor of probability in the calculation) (together referred to as ATNA).

made (because it is consistent with their interests and because they were involved in agreeing to the particular outcome). Not every case, perhaps not even most, will resolve this easily, and may require other distributional bargaining strategies, but the exploration of interests (beyond positions) provides a powerful negotiation strategy for creating durable settlements of seemingly unreconcilable conflicts.[18]

c) Integrative Bargaining

If the parties cannot agree on how to share or cooperate, an effective mediator may explore integrative bargaining strategies. Integrative bargaining explores the investment of resources outside those at stake in the controversy. The *Eighteenth Camel* wonderfully illustrates integrative bargaining. Resources external to the dispute (in this case, one camel) are invested, the problem is solved, and the resource is returned.

Examples of integrative bargaining applied to legal conflict are many: convincing a bank not party to the dispute to finance a new business arrangement formed from a breach of conflict claim; a wealthy malpractice claimant promising to donate money to the retraining of doctors in the relevant area of practice; a landlord-tenant family repossession case where the owner gets a contractor to knock down the building and build more units for a growing family and provides a new flat to the recalcitrant tenant, or an unenforceable maintenance award in a divorce proceeding where the broader community pays the maintenance (thus alleviating the underlying source of conflict, e.g., financial pressure) and eventually brings the couple back together.

2. *The Value of Neutralizing Communications Skills*

Beyond the negotiation techniques employed by an effective mediator, several communication techniques are useful tools of facilitation. As in negotiation, none is a sure-fire way to settle a dispute. However, each one alone can bring the parties closer together by neutralizing the emotionally harsh and irrationally exaggerated behavior and perspectives of the parties and can

[18] Further FISHER AND URY, *supra* note 16.

transform the frequently self-defeating aspects of their conflict (particularly where they have an interest in preserving or enhancing a relationship) into a mutually beneficial settlement.

a) Establishing Joint Communication

Mediations reestablish joint communication between the parties in three significant ways. First, and particularly in private mediation, the parties may have to communicate about logistics for the mediation itself (e.g., timing, exchange of documents, confidentiality agreements). Second, the mediator brings the parties together and in the first joint session, they hear from one another their different viewpoints (and often those of their attorneys). Third, the parties frequently begin to speak directly to one another. Joint communication of each varied kind is obviously no guarantee to settlement; however, this one factor may be key to bringing parties together where resistance to communicating with one another further escalates the conflict.[19]

b) Establishing Tone

An effective mediator establishes a positive tone and environment conducive to settlement by behaving in a professional, confident, purposeful, open, constructive, and socially engaging manner. The mediator may set an example and encourage through body language and emotional tones the kind of behavior expected in the session. Again, this can have a neutralizing impact on the more negative, insecure, closed-minded, destructive, and resistant behavior frequently encountered in adversaries.

[19] A lawyer from Hyderabad related a story about a married couple engaged in a serious conflict. The husband had decided to donate a kidney to his ailing mother without having consulted with his wife. The wife, who had no substantive disagreement with his decision, was offended by her husband's failure to confer in advance of such an important decision. The couple grew estranged and could not speak to one another. A family lawyer asked them to come to his house. He put them in a room together and left. The couple sat silent for a long time, then began to yell at each other, and after some time began to talk (and listen). Finally, they were able to overcome their conflict. This was no mediation. The lawyer only facilitated the meeting of the couple, their joint presence, short of communication, which only came later. However, this story shows that even arranging a meeting by itself can help bring parties together to resolve their disagreements.

c) Active Listening

Both as a necessary tool for effective facilitation and as a way of acknowledging the viewpoints of each side, active listening is an essential quality of a good mediator. It allows for a more accurate comprehension of the dispute, the ability to distinguish dispositive or helpful from irrelevant or unhelpful comments, positions from interests, and lower priority interests from higher priority interests. Again, active listening also signals to the parties that what they have to say is important, and that can encourage the parties to listen actively to one another as well.

d) Acknowledgment

Acknowledgment is one of the most important communication skills in effective mediation.[20] As emphasized by Albie Sachs of the Constitutional Court of South Africa, an architect of the Truth and Reconciliation Commission,[21] acknowledgment may be the most critical means to breaking the vicious cycle of human conflict. To acknowledge a party's views is not to express judgment (either positive or negative) but to indicate that these have been heard and understood. Acknowledgment of one party by another (without apology) often defuses a conflict by allowing the combating parties to feel that their voice has been heard.

e) Neutral Restatements, Summaries, and Word Changes

Mediators listen to and use language effectively to take the edge off volatile statements and words.[22] They may reframe a statement as neutrally as possible without trivializing the viewpoint of the speaker.[23] Parties often describe the factual background in a disorderly fashion, and a mediator's role is to bring some order

[20] WILLIAM URY, GETTING PAST NO 40 (1991). ("Every human being, no matter how impossible, has a deep need for recognition.")

[21] ALBIE SACHS, SOFT VENGEANCE OF A FREEDOM FIGHTER (2000).

[22] Further Gregg F. Relyea, *The Critical Impact of Word Choice in Mediation,* 16(9) ALTERNATIVES TO THE HIGH COST OF LITIGATION 137–146 (1998).

[23] Take, for example, the statement, "My husband is a pathological liar! I hate him!" The effective mediator may reframe it as: "I can understand why you would be so angry if you feel that your husband was not truthful." Here no judgment, only acknowledgment has been expressed in a neutral way without losing the substance of what was stated.

to confusing statements.[24] Finally, an effective mediator will be careful in the choice of words. "Damages" may become "bills or expenses". "Liability" may become "responsibility". "Your side of the story" may be restated as "factual background". By rephrasing more neutrally, the mediator defuses the language of its explosive impact without changing the core meaning. The mediator may thereby encourage the parties themselves to speak with fewer offensive or conflictual phrases and words that make the other side defensive.

f) Sequencing Agenda Setting, Deferring, Redirecting

Effective mediators control the sequencing of what is discussed by setting the agenda, deferring, and redirecting. They may postpone the discussion of positions until they explore the parties' interests. They may advance those topics they believe are more likely to bring the parties together. For example, instead of focusing a separated couple on what led to their conflict, a mediator might ask them to describe their children. The ability to adjust the sequence provides the mediator with enormous flexibility to move in fruitful directions based on input from the parties.

g) Changing the Messenger

In conflictual relationships, even close ones, suggestions by one party are automatically discounted by the other. The very same suggestion may come from a third party and be far more readily accepted. Mediators can solicit ideas from one side and communicate those suggestions to the other without attribution and thus without any reactive discounting by the recipient. Changing the messenger can advance acceptance of the message, and confidential private caucusing allows the mediator to play this important role of a go-between.

---

[24] For example, if the litigant stated: "And then she left for the hospital, but before she got back she took out money from our joint bank account, which did not belong to her, and then she went shopping with it, for shoes, but that was before she went to the hospital or so she said; she is always doing stuff like that, lying, taking money, not going where she says she's going." An effective mediator might reply, in a more neutral and structured summary: "You appear upset about two things: first, you feel that your wife should not have taken money out of your joint bank account; and second, you feel that she does not tell you what she's going to do."

II. *Obstacles to Mediation Reform*

The growth of mediation does not necessarily follow from these tools and their perceived advantages. Mediation is not self-effectuating; indeed, it faces resistance from a variety of sources. In many systems, at least initially, mediation poses a perceived threat to important values and individual incentives of key actors in the system. Moreover, issues arise from the implementation of the current statutory framework for mediation. Finally, even when actors are convinced of the value of mediation in theory, they may have difficulty applying those processes to current legal conflicts.

Judges and lawyers are understandably apprehensive about the relationship between mediation and the formal judicial process and deeply skeptical about the application of mediation to a wide variety of Indian legal disputes (particularly outside the commercial area). The courts are still searching for an operational case management trigger (e.g., under Section 89 or Order X of the CPC)[25] for referring cases to mediation. The explicit terms of Section 89 (calling for a form of judicial conciliation by the trial judge) may be incompatible with subsequent referrals to mediation under that provision. Trained mediators in most courts are not yet available. In advance of a more comprehensive exposure and engaging national debate over these important concerns, some opinion leaders have formed prematurely strong opinions about the limited role of mediation. Finally, despite these obstacles, a series of short-term incentives (judicial evaluation schemes, lawyer compensation methodologies, litigants in defense of dispute resources) further motivate resistance to mediation, thereby producing a social dilemma in which critical actors view their professional or personal short-term interests as potentially inconsistent with the system's long-term objectives.

---

[25] INDIA CODE CIV. PROC., *supra* note 7; INDIA CODE CIV. PROC., *supra* note 8; *Salem Advocate Bar Association, supra* note 12; *also* Law Commission Consultation Paper on ADR and Mediation Rules 1 (2003) (calling for a Section 89 proceeding "after recording admissions and denials at the first hearing of the suit under Rule 1 of Order X"); Law Commission Consultation Paper on Case Management, Rule 4, 9 (2003).

How might these issues and perceived threats be persuasively addressed?

1. Judges

Judges may see mediation as potentially undermining their authority to make public judgments and normative pronouncements. Professional incentives may also discourage judicial support for mediation. For example, judges may feel they will lose the professional satisfaction of issuing judgments if cases settle and they may be evaluated on the number of "legal" dispositions that they reach, excluding settlements.

Judges quickly see, however, that effective mediation depends on, while complementing, the core function of adjudication. Without normative standards, the parties have much greater difficulty negotiating according to their alternatives, and thus mediation alone is unlikely to bring justice to a law-based society. As a complement to the formal process, mediation may alleviate the burdens placed on the courts, transmit norms more effectively to society, increase compliance with the law, prevent parties from pursuing extra-legal strategies (i.e., crimes) to resolve their disputes, and improve the communication skills used *within* the courts. Further, many judges will take as much satisfaction, some even more, from settling difficult cases, particularly in ways that please both parties (rather than only one, as in litigation). Finally, methods of evaluating judicial performance can be adjusted to take the relative value of settlements into account, if that is an impediment to support for mediation.

2. Lawyers

Lawyers may be understandably concerned that mediation threatens their livelihood by reducing the number of matters they handle or fees they charge. If more disputes are to be mediated, lawyers might view ADR as nothing more than an "alarming drop in revenues". They may encounter pricing problems in how to charge for their role in a particular mediation. Additionally, they may wonder about the value of their own role in a party-dominated process and about how they will act as zealous advocates when their parties do not want to settle and engage in a process that calls for cooperation (which may be a sign of weakness in trial).

Attention to the unmet need for legal dispute resolution in society, the underlying economics of litigation, the need for integrated legal expertise in mediation, and the professional opportunities to represent litigants in mediation, as well as to serve as mediators, tend to allay these initial concerns.

First, in any society, but particularly where using the legal system is costly (in terms of money, time, or uncertainty), many legally cognizable disputes are not brought to court. Legal injuries are internalized or "lumped", and many lawyers are not consulted for their advice. When either those costs decrease or superior conflict resolution services are provided, a significant subset of those potential litigants will consult a lawyer, if not file a claim. Just as better roads bring more cars to the city; better conflict resolution processes bring greater need for legal services, even when it does not necessitate work in court. Further, legal mediation provides another venue in which legal services can be valuable to litigants, thus creating new opportunities for law practice and for lawyers to serve as neutrals.

Second, the time value of money dramatically discounts the *actual* value of claims filed in the courts. From an economic perspective, legal fees are a function of the difference they make in extracting social or economic value from the legal process. If delays in the system discount this value, the fees that lawyers can charge will be significantly less. Consider the following example. If a litigant approaches a lawyer who suggests that he or she can make on average a 20% difference in the outcome of the litigation, and the litigant and the lawyer agree to split that value between them, the lawyer would be justified economically in asking for approximately 10% of the value of the case in fees. If, under the best case scenario, an injured party cannot collect a claim for ten years (especially when both observations of delays are much more devastating, e.g., fifteen years in Ahmedabad to twenty-five years in Mumbai), the difference between the cost of money for an unsecured loan (e.g., 15%) and the highest pre-judgment interest rate (6%) may discount the value of that claim by some 60%. That is, a claim for $100,000 may be discounted to a value of $40,000. With these calculations, a plaintiff would be (economically) justified in paying the lawyer $4,000 (not $10,000) in fees. This means that a more economically efficient system may translate into higher fees for lawyers. If the value of their service to the client increases due to the results they can achieve, their fees may rise accordingly.

Finally, after an initial adjustment, when engaged in the process of mediation, with its own set of special practices and incentives, lawyers have no difficulty in adapting their modes of representation, and may find a wider range of skills upon which to draw to provide valuable service to their clients outside formal court settings.

3. *Private and Public Litigants*

Private litigants too may harbor anxiety about mediation as an alternative to the court system. Afraid of exploitation, distrustful of private proceedings, comforted by the familiarity of the court system, insecure about making decisions about their own interests, or interested in vexatious litigation or delaying the case for economic reasons, some litigants may prefer the lawyer-dominated, public, formal, and evaluative judicial process.

First, mediation will not frustrate the preferences of such litigants; indeed, their right to trial is fully preserved under the Indian reforms. An effective mediation process can quickly allay these fears. Litigants involved in the process are much less likely to be exploited. They will quickly understand that the mediator has no power or social control over them or their resolution of the dispute. Second, effective mediators will gain their trust over time. Third, if the parties still feel the need for an evaluation of the legal issues, the mediation can be accordingly designed to deliver that service. At times, litigants can better save face with members of their family, community, or organization, if they can put responsibility for the result on a neutral third party, and for this group, a strong evaluative process may be appropriate. Surveys of litigants find that mediation receives the highest satisfaction ratings of any dispute resolution process, the reason for which lies in the valuable features of the process explicated above. For vexatious litigation, mediation, unlike trial, can get beneath the surface of the filed dispute to address the underlying conflict that motivates a frivolous lawsuit.

Finally, the conventional view that incentives for settlement for one of the parties will be low, thus frustrating the likelihood that mediation will succeed, is based on an unexamined and false assumption. Naturally, the defendant in the example of the $100,000 claim has a weak incentive to settle the claim *for that amount*. Indeed, the claim by the plaintiff does not represent its real present value, if the defendant can delay for fifteen years before facing his responsibilities. Once the plaintiff realizes that the true value of that claim may be as low as one-tenth of its stated value, the defendant's incentives to settle the case with a more realistic plaintiff will suddenly become stronger. Note that it is not the availability of mediation that reduces the value of the claim but delays in the formal system. Settlement negotiations merely take account of that unfortunate reality.

Public litigants may present a less permeable set of barriers, at least in the early growth of mediation. Cases against the government may be difficult to settle for several reasons. Private caucusing with government litigants may seem improper. Officials may be reluctant to settle cases for fear that they will be accused of differential treatment, will undermine government policy, or will bring a flood of additional claimants seeking compensation. For these reasons, officials participating in the mediation may not have sufficient authority to settle. Overcoming these barriers requires considerable ingenuity. Mediators may shape the proceedings to be transparent and public (forsaking private caucusing). They may have to innovate ways to join all relevant cases together in one mediation to avoid the risk of inequitable results, uneven policies, or a new flood of litigation. Alternatively, if these adaptations are initially unworkable, the expansion of mediation services to cases against the government may be deferred until mediation is sufficiently developed in private litigation.

4. *Concerns about the Statutory Framework of Section 89*

In addition to the foregoing questions about the acceptance of mediation by different actors in the legal process, many arise from a critical reading of Section 89.[26] This provision contemplates that

[26] Enforcing confidentiality and ensuring that the Section 89 process does not prolong the trial process are additional concerns.

the judge (presumably the judge assigned to the case) should first determine whether there exist "elements of a settlement which may be acceptable to the parties". If so, the court "shall formulate the terms of settlement and give them to the parties for their observations". Finally, "after receiving the observations of the parties, the court may reformulate the terms of a possible settlement" and refer the same for arbitration,[27] conciliation, judicial settlement, including through *lok adalat*, or mediation.[28]

These provisions, drawn from the conciliation provisions of the Arbitration and Conciliation Act (1996),[29] itself based on the UNCITRAL model law, raise several questions. First, the timing (after written statement, when parties are examined, before framing of issues, or as a precondition to an application for ad interim relief) of Section 89 through a case management proceeding of some kind remains unsettled. An answer to that question depends on an assessment of when the perceived incentives for settlement are highest (as a function of a sense of jeopardy or the early mutual gains of saving costs).

Second, it is unclear how the judge will determine whether there are *sufficient* elements of a settlement to justify the investment of time. Every case has elements of settlement, but these are difficult to identify without reviewing the case and questioning the parties about their underlying interests. This difficulty may be resolved either by using Order X (1a)[30] as a primary and *independent* mechanism for triggering a choice of ADR venues or by sequencing the types of cases in which Section 89 processes will be employed as a matter of course (rather than discretion).

Third, if the Section 89 judge is the same one who presides over the trial, the parties are unlikely to share observations that would

---

[27] *Supra* note 9.

[28] INDIA CODE CIV. PROC., *supra* note 7.

[29] Arbitration and Conciliation Act, *supra* note 11 (using language nearly identical to Section 89).

[30] Order X may solve this and other problems raised in the context of Section 89, including the question of timing. Further INDIA CODE CIV. PROC., *supra* note 8, at 1.A. ("After recording the admissions and denials, the court shall direct the parties to the suit to opt either mode of the settlement outside the court as specified in sub-section (1) of section 89.")

narrow their differences. There is no Section 89 provision for the confidentiality of these observations, and even if there were, the parties would be understandably reluctant to admit shortcomings in their positions or to suggest compromise for fear of appearing weak to the other side. Assignment of a special Section 89 (or settlement) judge within the court and ensuring the confidentiality of the party observations may alleviate these concerns.

Finally, it is unclear what impact the specific terms defined by the judge will have on a subsequent settlement through mediation or other techniques. If the settlement discussions lead the parties away from or beyond the specified terms, they may worry about the enforceability of the settlement agreement. In contrast, if they constrain their negotiations to the specified terms, the likelihood of settlement may be significantly diminished. Again, instead of the judicial conciliation process contemplated by Section 89, treating Order X (1a) as an independent provision for triggering Section 89 ADR *options* (a-d) may provide a quicker, cleaner, or more versatile bridge to mediation and other Section 89 alternatives that promote settlement.

5. *Adaptation Concerns*

In addition to these concerns, many lawyers and judges wonder about the applicability of these techniques to the specific nature of the diverse Indian caseload. Will mediation work effectively beyond commercial disputes in family matters, property partitions, landlord tenant, industrial disputes, cases containing elements of a crime, and, as noted, claims against the government? Theoretically, mediation may be very effective in dealing with the complex social relationships that make formal trials so difficult. Its reliance on orality may be better suited for the undereducated litigant or the litigant that does not speak the language used in the court proceedings. Mediation may be able to get beneath the surface of frequently vexatious litigation by addressing the underlying conflicts. Mutual gains and distributional bargaining techniques may help resolve partition cases. Integrative negotiation (including investments by those not engaged in the dispute) in landlord-tenant cases may allow for reconstruction and expansion of currently limited space. Deeply embedding mediation in the community may alleviate underlying causes of conflict and even some forms of criminal activity (e.g., assault). Notwithstanding the theoretical benefits in these applied contexts, however, these questions cannot be answered in the abstract. Mediation must be tried and tested, lessons learned, and adjustments made. In a phrase, the proof will be in the pudding, and early signs of mediation practice in Ahmedabad, Mumbai, and Chennai indicate early success in many of these important areas of legal conflict.

6. *Building Capacity: Next Steps*

The preceding list is far from exhaustive. Several implementation questions will be raised and addressed: how to make mediation economically desirable, how to cultivate a larger number of mediators available to the courts, and how to promote and improve educational exposure and training methodologies throughout the country, including those under the direction of the High Courts.[31] These capacity-building issues also demand attention and intellectual investment. More specifically, how should mediation attract litigants from a purely economic point of view? Who will serve as neutrals in mediation? How will mediation be initiated (for which cases) and concluded? Which attributes of mediation are most likely to be effective in different litigation contexts? How should the courts establish quality controls (including ethics and discipline) over the emerging practice of mediation? How should the courts build both internal and external capacity without incurring unaffordable costs? How should negotiation and mediation be taught in Indian law schools? Finite answers to these questions would be premature. Practice and experience will guide the emerging response.

III. Available Strategies

All of this may give the understandable, yet potentially false, impression that mediation reform is doomed to failure in India. Troubling issues and perplexing questions may be solved or answered, however, through a set of creative approaches. Here are some starting points.

---

[31] Rule 7, Consultation Paper on ADR and Mediation Rules, *supra* note 3, at 5.

First, the early economics of mediation may be critical to its long-term growth. Developing a pro bono commitment of neutrals (at least beyond high stakes commercial disputes, where parties are already paying for mediation services) may be necessary. If facing costs additional to court fees, litigants will be reluctant to enter mediations. Further, ensuring that Section 89 or Order X proceedings take place before the framing of issues would maximize any applicable court fee reduction rules. Working with lawyers on structuring fee arrangements for cases that settle (e.g., splitting in half the expected total fees from full blown trial and appeal before lawyers have completed even close to half the work, thus sharing the savings with clients) will be equally necessary.

Second, the potential pool of mediators should be as large as possible, so as not to foreclose the application of invaluable human resources, even from unexpected subsets of professionals. In addition to judges (as specialists within court), retired judges, lawyers (both junior and senior), and academic experts in ADR in collaboration with law students in legal services clinics, non-lawyers (including doctors, accountants, engineers, family psychologists) should be considered.

Third, coordination of the mediation process with the trial system will need to be further developed. In particular, a specific trigger for mediation must be chosen. Court-annexed mediation through Section 89 or Order X requires a case management event to give life to the rule. The chief judges of courts will have to designate the official responsible for triggering the process (whether a judicial officer, registrar, or special administrator), and case event tracking mechanisms must ensure continuing oversight of the annexed ADR process to ensure that unsettled cases return to the trial track without undue delay (e.g., within two months) or are dismissed upon full settlement. Ways to capture the benefits of "unsuccessful" mediation by allowing the parties to narrow the issues clarified by the mediation can also be explored.[32] Whether the choice of ADR technique is obligatory or voluntary, the specific timing of that choice, and the cases subjected to the process (old or new, family or commercial) are additional questions to be resolved.

---

[32] Chodosh, *supra* note 3, at 9.

Fourth, the specific attributes (the negotiation techniques, the communication skills, or the structure and sequence) of Indian mediation will be selected in the context of a wide range of legal disputes. Open questions remain. Will these processes be primarily evaluative or facilitative in the longer run, employ a community model or private caucusing once trust is developed, and embrace confidentiality or publicity (in cases of public interest)? Each answer will require special attention to the specific nature of the controversies to which mediation will be applied. It is important here to avoid dogmatic perspectives about foreign models (whether wholly positive or negative), to resist the view of any specific configuration as necessary to the essentials of mediation, and to urge experimentation and pragmatism in order to maximize the values of the great array of techniques offered by mediation practices.

Fifth, ways to achieve oversight (without excessively regulating and thus stiffening mediation) will be equally important. Evaluating mediators through surveys of litigants and lawyers, continual review of panels and periodic retraining will be critical to the integrity of the system. In addition, the determination of ethical norms (self-determination, impartiality, disclosure of conflicts of interest, competence, confidentiality, and overall quality of service) and disciplinary mechanisms (ethics hotlines, calibrated sanctions) to enforce them are a few of the tools available for effective oversight.[33]

Sixth, Indian law schools, which are required by the Bar Council to teach ADR, only have the capacity to teach arbitration as part of the basic curriculum. Mediation programs are sprouting; however, they are almost always special certificate courses outside the formal degree programs. Further, the tools for teaching negotiation and mediation are limited by class size, lecture-orientation, as well as training in interactive and simulation methods. To overcome these hurdles, the addition of negotiation and mediation to the basic curriculum must be studied by the Bar Council and materials, interactive videos, and in-class pedagogies developed.[34]

---

[33] *Id.* at 6-13.

[34] HIRAM E. CHODOSH AND JAMES R. HOLBROOK, ADR EDUCATION IN LAW SCHOOLS (2007).

Finally, the courts will seek ways to build human resources and administrative capacity for mediation as a complementary institution. Stategies include building court units (with internal staff or external panels of trained neutrals) to perform mediation services or to act as clearing houses. Legal educators are also exploring ways to enhance a growing set of graduate diploma courses, experiential mediation education, and training methodologies, particularly for young lawyers. Here, there is much opportunity for exchange and collaboration in pursuit of common goals.

D. THE LIMITS OF FOREIGN EXPERTISE

I. Foreign Nature of External Expertise

With these conditions in mind (the value, obstacles, and available strategies), is there any role for American assistance in developing effective mediation systems?

The large industry that now supports rule of law or access to justice reforms abroad risks overlooking Professor John Henry Merryman's admonishments. He wrote forty years ago of something disturbingly apt today: U.S. reformers tend to be unfamiliar with foreign systems, lack a respectable theory, are unaccountable to the consequences of reform failure, and have a tendency to impose their uninformed views and foreign values on legal communities in distress.[35] Without attention to Merryman's admonishments and the exploration of reconstructive responses, reformers may fall victim to an inescapable intellectual pendulum in which the folly of the imposed approach is intermittently exposed and then quickly forgotten.[36] Consequently, U.S. reformers appear to swing

[35] John Henry Merryman, *Comparative Law and Social Change: On the Origins, Style, Decline & Revival of the Law and Development Movement,* 25 AMERICAN JOURNAL OF COMPARATIVE LAW 481 (1977). For a more recent critique of U.S. foreign assistance read THOMAS CAROTHERS, AIDING DEMOCRACY ABROAD: THE LEARNING CURVE (1999) (noting lack of humility, superficial assessment, simplistic modeling, misplaced emphasis on ends instead of process, and weak evaluative tools and commitments).

[36] Further David M. Trubek and Marc Galanter, *Scholars in Self-Estrangement: Some Reflections on the Crisis in Law and Development Studies in the United States,* 4 WISCONSIN LAW REVIEW 1062–1102 (1974).

back and forth between arrogance insulated by ignorance on one extreme, to embarrassment, disillusionment, and self-criticism on the other. The choice between equally undesirable starting points is unsatisfactory: either foreign assistance is indispensable or it is useless. Reaching a different plane of interaction will require both candor about the limitations of the reforming system and creativity to find new starting points for reform-directed, cross-national relationships.

1. Unfamiliarity

Unfamiliarity with local conditions can sabotage efforts of American experts engaged in mediation reforms abroad. To take India as one example, insistence on purely facilitative forms of mediation may underestimate the need for independent evaluations from well-respected sources of authority. Proposing mediation as a fully continuous process (i.e., one sitting) may undervalue the need for individuals to consult people not involved in the dispute (e.g., an older brother or patriarch) for their approval of the settlement. Advising that the judge who conducts mediation should not be the same as the trial judge ignores the fact that many local courts in the country have only one judge per rural district. Mediation processes derived from or designed for complex commercial disputes in which the participants have full settlement authority may not be as effective in cases against the government, which officials are extremely reluctant to settle for fear of allegations of bribery, concern about making inconsistent policy decisions, or due to insecure authority.

The actual operation of legal systems is complex, and an understanding of legal process dynamics, including the incentives and behavioral responses to them, is elusive, even with prolonged study. Any foreign advice therefore carries a very high probability of error. Errors derive from false assumptions about what is happening and why. In addition, faulty reform proposals may rely on simplistic comparisons between different social contexts (e.g., between the United States and the foreign country or between dramatically contrasting rural and urban contexts within a single national jurisdiction).

2. Questionable Theories

The proper role of mediation in the legal system is hardly a matter of empirical proof or settled theory. The most frequently cited justification for mediation is that it reduces backlog and delay, but this justification is based on a questionable, and particularly instrumental, theory. First, there is still little empirical evidence that mediation alone substantially reduces backlog and delay. It is hard to determine, for example, whether reforms setting predictable, early trial dates have had a greater impact on settlement than those that supply rigorous mediation services.

Second, attempts to reduce backlog may paradoxically increase them. Throughout most societies, many people have legally cognizable claims that they do not bring to court because they do not expect to get justice. Often this occurs when the price of justice in time and money is more than they can afford. If that category of potential litigants gets the signal that there is now a chance to extract some value through partial settlements of their claims, a larger number of them may file, thus increasing the number of cases to be managed by the courts. For example, highway expansions aimed at reducing traffic in densely populated areas may actually increase traffic. Bringing more people with unattended claims into the courts is not necessarily a bad thing, depending on the available alternatives that aim to prevent the conflicts in advance; however, attempts at diversion or expansion of court services do not necessarily translate into a reduction of backlog and delay.

Finally, if too narrowly or exclusively drawn, such instrumental theories can distract attention away from and thus stunt intellectual investments in exploring the intrinsic value of mediation processes. An emphasis on the internalization of neutralizing communication skills or on interest-based bargaining may do more to relieve an overburdened system by placing conflict-prevention tools in the hands of society, instead of forcing society to seek access to remote and expensive public processes.

3. Unaccountability and Conflicts of Interest

Determining the role of mediation in society is the responsibility of the reforming community. Foreign experts do not suffer the consequences of bad decision-making and are, thus, ultimately unaccountable for their influence. The aggressive posture of foreign experts or foreign or international organizations can also backfire by giving the appearance that the reforms are motivated by values or interests external to, and potentially inconsistent with, the society's. Foreign experts carry the affiliation of their sponsor or source of funding (e.g., a foreign government or international institution). This affiliation reflects, and sometimes even commands, institutional influence, ranging from mild allegiance to contractual obligation. Depending on the reputation of that foreign or international entity, the credibility of the expert may be undermined.

In addition, foreign experts often suffer conflicts of interest that are difficult to manage. Non-profits, for example, are necessarily interested in their own survival as well as in their service mission. When presented with a conflict between the constraints of available funding sources and what is truly best for the society in which they work, they may find it difficult to prioritize the society's interest when their financial livelihood is at stake. Consultants, too, often see a conflict between their own self-interest in the continuation or expansion of their assignments on one hand and their willingness to critique or publish their work on the other. This is not a purist attack on mixed motives, for there is nothing wrong with paying experts for their expertise. However, recognition of limits imposed by the business models of foreign experts (working as corporate entities or individuals) is important to developing a more effective and ethical role, if any, for outsiders. Ultimately, only national decision makers can resolve the policy questions raised by mediation reforms.

4. *Imposition of Values*

Foreign experts are also unaccountable for the implicit valuations they express in promoting the use of mediation in particular forms. For example, many U.S. proponents of mediation working abroad emphasize settlement. The author was astonished several years ago when one of America's most experienced advisers declared: "A bad settlement is better than a good judgment." What is troubling about this view? In short, it is packed with value judgments about the purpose of the judicial process and its more consensual complements.

First, emphasis on settlement alone may be inconsistent with justice and other aims. Knowing *only* that a case settled is hardly a source of comfort. The fact of disposal indicates nothing about the terms upon which the case settled. Did the parties actually maximize their interests and at what benefit or cost to their legal rights and obligations? Did they preserve and enhance their relationship, internalize the healthy process of direct communication, or get a sense of deep satisfaction from the participatory process? The limited fact of settlement sheds no light on these important considerations. Indeed, political pressure to settle large numbers of cases, which has occurred in the *lok adalat* movement in India, leads to coercive activities, such as judges pressuring lawyers to settle and encouraging fraud on the numbers. An example of this type of fraud is putting cases that would settle on their own into the favored and promoted *lok adalat* system. Alternatively, some courts may count as settlements technical, unilateral dismissals of cases that are subsequently re-filed. Further, without properly trained mediators and the incorporation of legal advice, settlements may be unjust; a fact that might be compounded by the lack of recourse to subsequent challenge or review. Finally, an absolute emphasis on settlement may undermine two important purposes of the justice system: publicity and normativity. As settlements are confidential, people who violate their obligations can thereby keep such violations out of the public's view. Settlements also produce no normative pronouncement upon which others in society can order their behavior.

Second, the implicit assumption that mediation is cheaper and quicker, and thus better or more efficient, is not necessarily correct. Mediation in routine cases may be inexpensive and speedy, but so would many other techniques. Mediation in the most difficult cases (e.g., complex family or business disputes, high stakes intellectual property claims, or cases against the government) may be both costly and time-consuming, particularly when done properly. The issue of efficiency is not about cost or speed alone, but whether the time and resources invested in a particular dispute are worthwhile, measured by the social product generated by the process employed. Even if one process is cheaper and quicker than another, the social outcome must be included when assessing the efficiency of the process. Therefore, the role of mediation and the policy issues it raises require a substantial set of value choices by the society in which it is to operate.

II. Inapplicability of Foreign Assumptions

How does the experience of foreign mediation experts in India reflect these common propensities? What in particular are the ways in which foreign expertise can actually inhibit the growth of mediation in India?

Having delivered and participated in innumerable programs on mediation in India, including presentations by U.S. mediation experts from areas of the country that have evolved forms of mediation practice, the author has identified a set of commonly expressed postulates about mediation that may hinder its development in India.

The first postulate is that mediation is a *system.* In the U.S., the United Kingdom, and Australia, where mediation has grown within legal processes similar to that of India, mediation has developed into a complex system of court-referred or annexed mediation and private mediation (often conducted by mediation companies, some even publicly traded on the open stock market). The sophistication and regularity of mediation processes have produced an alternative to the court system that is well financed and structured. Presentations on mediation in these countries frequently focus on the administrative foundation of their systems: the procedure for court referrals or judicial mediation, the training and certification of mediators, the integration of mediation into case management, the ensurability of confidentiality, and more recently, the growth of mediation ethical systems. This emphasis on mediation as a system, while well intended, poses difficulties (both intellectual and political) for Indian reformers.

Understanding such a system requires a great deal of empirical exposure to mediation systems as they operate abroad. This exposure is certainly useful in envisioning what an advanced mediation system would look like, but it is expensive and that money may not be well spent. For the cost of a couple of senior

Indian judges traveling to the U.S. for a week to gain this systemic understanding, a local mediation center in a mid-sized city may be run for a whole year. Time spent on the administration of a mediation system is time not spent on the intrinsic (or arguably instrumental) values of the specific tools falling under the mediation rubric. Therefore, focusing on mediation as a system (and its consequential and opportunity costs) distracts from core issues of how mediation will be practiced in different contexts with potentially diversely adapted features.

The second common view emphasizes that mediation is not position-based, but is exclusively *facilitative.* Facilitative mediation may be optimal in theory; it is important, however, to acknowledge that even *facilitative* mediation involves evaluations by the mediator, including settlement valuations that the parties themselves solicit. Beyond the false claim of absolute facilitation in well developed systems, litigants involved in newly developing mediation processes are likely to seek the opinion of the neutral rather than presume that they are capable themselves of resolving the controversy consensually.

Third, many foreign experts emphasize that the mediator exercises *no control* over how the dispute is resolved. Even the most facilitative mediator surely exercises subtle influences over its outcome. Mediators are trained to make decisions about the process itself that facilitate settlement (itself a value judgment about what the parties should do). In generating options, making suggestions, admonishing parties that certain ways of proceeding, thinking, or acting may not be in their interests, mediators get intimately involved in the outcome. Such involvement is arguably necessary, even potentially positive. To pretend otherwise relieves the mediator of any ethical obligation to exercise care in the influence that is exercised.

Fourth, to reinforce the needs for the independence of any dispute resolution process, experts stress that mediators are necessarily *impartial* (free from favoritism, bias, or prejudice). A pre-existing relationship between the parties and the mediator is just one example of potential bias in mediation proceedings. In well developed systems, mediators chosen by repeat players must counter the perception and leanings of any favoritism against single players. In newly developing systems, where trust between the parties and the mediator is critical and is frequently based on a prior relationship, insisting on norms of social neutrality may prove harder.

Fifth, many mediation experts create the impression that mediation requires private caucusing. This is problematic in legal cultures exhibiting widespread corruption. Where levels of trust are low, seemingly authorized *ex parte* communications may actually corrode trust. In addition, it is unlikely that governmental officials will expose themselves to the claim, however unfounded, of impropriety during a private caucus.

Sixth, mediation experts presume that the process is necessarily *confidential*. This feature, if universally observed, would eliminate the opportunity for public mediation, which itself may be necessary in claims against the government in order to alleviate some of the obstacles in settling such cases.

Seventh, many foreign mediation experts advise that mediation should be conducted in a *continuous* process and involve only parties with the *authority to settle* the case. This assumes that litigants are necessarily autonomous in their decision-making, a misleading assumption in certain social settings. Many litigants have to consult a parent or elder brother or sister before they decide whether to settle. Thus, they often lack the full autonomy necessary to finalize the settlement in one continuous session. Firdosh Kassam, who has conducted more mediation proceedings in India than any other professional, often takes several sessions to complete a mediation.

Finally, as an instrumental justification for mediation, many experts claim that it *reduces backlog and delay*. Aside from the normative objection to mediation as a docket-clearing device noted above, if mediation is really successful, more people may flock to the courts in search of some measure of justice for which they deem the current process futile. This can put unforeseen pressure on the courts that is successful in bringing more justice to society, yet "*unsuccessful*" in reducing congestion.

III. Conclusion

In sum, foreign experts have two common limitations. First, their substantive theories on mediation itself may not be as strong as they presume. Second, their expertise is, in a word, *foreign*. They may have expertise in mediation within their own system, but this does not mean that they can communicate the value of their experience in different contexts. They may be proud of their own achievements, yet unaware, if not ignorant, of the host system.

In view of this critique, is there any role for U.S. assistance in foreign mediation reform? If so, what would it be? How would reformers overcome the problems Merryman identified long before mediation was considered an American export? Candor toward the limits of foreign assistance is surely a good first step, but where can we find creative approaches to manage, if not surmount, these limitations?

Faced with the dizzying array of American interventions in foreign legal cultures (e.g., conditionality, aid, technical assistance, and exchange), a process of self-training and engagement may help transcend these impediments. By self-training, the author means that those of us engaged in institutional justice reform abroad should take stock of our ignorance, manage it well, and try to overcome it by educating ourselves about the assumptions we carry and by thinking hard about why these may be falsely applied to contexts that we do not fully understand. By engagement, the author does not mean the mere exchange of information, foreign visits, recitation of theory, provision of funds, or the suspension of competing values. Engagement means a process of intense social interaction between foreign and domestic legal communities, experts and non-experts, proponents and opponents, top officials and lower-level actors, leaders and followers. This interaction seeks insight into the nature of the problems, the value of the specific tools, and the applicability of those tools in different combinations to identified problems. Insight necessitates asking before telling, explaining before advising, considering trade-offs before determining, experimenting before insisting on proof, and challenging before accepting assumptions. Engagement therefore requires becoming familiar with the legal system and the society in which it functions, thinking deeply about the embedded comparative theories in alternative reform proposals, explicating interests when they may conflict, and deliberating transparently over value choices that underlie support or rejection of a specific technique or proposal.

As the number of Americans involved in local rule of law development and justice reforms grows, we should recall the story of a British expert in East Africa. He travelled every year to a particular village struggling with land erosion. For over ten years, he advised the villagers to plant trees. Each year, he returned to find that they had not followed his advice, so each year, he made his pitch more strenuously - always to no avail. His posting eventually took him elsewhere, and it was twenty years later that he visited the village again. Happy to see their old friend, the villagers took the foreign expert to a place where there was a single tree and a bench with his name engraved on it. He inquired about the meaning of this special gesture. They explained that they had planted a tree in his honor to thank him for his concern for their village and its problems. But why, he asked then, had they not followed his advice? One village elder reluctantly explained that they could not plant trees for they had tried this many times before his first visit. The trees had attracted birds, and the birds had eaten their crops.[37]

The author hopes that we can learn and retain the lesson of the British expert. He never asked his hosts why there were no trees or which birds ate which crops. Thus, he could never explore the alternatives that might have both protected the crops and prevented erosion. Had he tested his assumptions against the realities of their environment and engaged his values with their sensibilities, how many more mouths might he have helped feed?

E. MEDIATING MEDIATION REFORM IN INDIA

I. Mediating Mediation

In making critical choices about how best to navigate around these obstacles, issues, and trade-offs inherent in India's attempt to adopt mediation, India is engaged in a national discussion that

---

[37] Further HIRAM E. CHODOSH *Local Mediation in Advance of Armed Conflict,* 19 OHIO STATE JOURNAL ON DISPUTE RESOLUTION 213–228 (2003).

seeks to resolve conflicting views and positions on mediation within the Indian justice system. Given the conflicts yet to be resolved over the scope, substance, and speed of mediation reform in India, their facilitated negotiation is a kind of mediation itself.

II. The Eighteenth Camel

The role of participant is an awkward one for an outsider, for the following reasons as well as for those just outlined. Although the author was a student of the Indian civil justice system, unlike Indian colleagues, he is no expert. Although he is an academic with special interest in conflict resolution and justice reform processes, unlike Indian friends, he is neither a judge nor (any longer) a practicing lawyer. Although the author has a strong emotional and personal connection to the country through his wife's family, unlike his Indian relatives, he does not work and live in the system. The ultimate determinations of these difficult issues are thus beyond his full competence, experience, or privilege. So what role could an outsider like him possibly play in this process?

The answer came to him suddenly in May 2003 in Jodhpur, where the author was conducting a two-day workshop with Niranjan Bhatt, a trial lawyer with over forty years of experience in the city civil court of Ahmedabad and the founding trustee and director of the Ahmedabad Mediation Center. He told Niranjan of his discomfort with his own role (as an outsider). As they were reflecting on it, the author realized that in conducting workshops and engaging the stakeholders they were acting as mediators: establishing a tone conducive to settling the issues, acknowledging conflicting viewpoints, reframing them more neutrally, and helping judges, lawyers, businesspeople, government officers, and civil leaders bargain over them. Then it struck him: "the outsider is just trying to become the eighteenth camel."

4

Law and "Law Books" in the Hindu Tradition

DONALD R. DAVIS, JR.*

A. INTRODUCTION

It is by now widely recognized that British colonialism in India transformed or invented many Indian institutions and traditions. Questions as to how the transformation occurred, the extent of Indians' participation in it, and how to measure its scope are still, however, hotly debated by scholars. This area of law has recently become a productive intellectual site for historians interested in describing the transformative effects of colonial governance.[1] Unfortunately, few of these studies are informed by more than a superficial knowledge of classical and medieval legal traditions in India.

The deep history of law in India is inextricably linked with questions about the place of religion and religious texts in both legal theory and practice. In this essay, the author compares the role of sacred Hindu texts in the realm of Indian jurisprudence

* This chapter was originally written for a thematic issue on sacred texts. It appeared as *Diritto e "testi giuridici" nella tradizione hindu*, 6 DAIMON: ANNUARIO DI DIRITTO COMPARATO DELLE RELIGIONI 97–114 (2006). Since then, it has been slightly revised and updated.

[1] For excellent accounts of various aspects of colonialism and cultural change in India, especially with reference to transformations of law, read BERNARD S. COHN, AN ANTHROPOLOGIST AMONG THE HISTORIANS AND OTHER ESSAYS (1988); BERNARD S. COHN, COLONIALISM AND ITS FORMS OF KNOWLEDGE: THE BRITISH IN INDIA (1996). For useful studies of colonial impact on law in India read RICHARD SAMAUREZ SMITH, RULE BY RECORDS: LAND REGISTRATION AND VILLAGE CUSTOM IN EARLY BRITISH PANJAB (1996); RADHIKA SINGHA, A DESPOTISM OF LAW: CRIME AND JUSTICE IN EARLY COLONIAL INDIA (1998); INDRANI CHATTERJEE, GENDER, SLAVERY, AND LAW IN COLONIAL INDIA (1999).

by contrasting two "periods" of Indian legal history, the classical and the colonial/postcolonial. These "periods" are too simplistic for other purposes, but they are employed here heuristically. The contrast highlights a perhaps surprising difference in the legal appropriation of sacred Hindu texts, namely that traditional legal systems of India rarely used sacred texts *directly* in the administration of law, while British colonial courts and modern courts in India regularly made a direct, but superficial use of sacred texts as sources of law.

B. SACRED TEXTS IN CLASSICAL AND MEDIEVAL HINDU LAW

I. *Śruti – Revelation*

To speak of sacred texts in Hinduism is to speak in the first place of the *śruti* (lit. "what is heard"), the collections of liturgical materials, ritual exegeses, and esoteric speculations dating from circa 1500 B.C. to 600 B.C.[2]

The most famous portions of the *śruti* are the Vedas and the Upanishads, which represent the earliest and latest strata of the *śruti* literature respectively. The sacred and foundational quality of these texts is beyond question[3] because they are considered the repositories of eternal (nitya) and "beyond-human" (apaurusheya) knowledge. Considered normatively, however, it is a disconcerting fact that "strictly speaking the Vedas do not even include a single positive precept which could be used directly as a rule of

[2] V. Narayana Rao, *Purāna,* in THE HINDU WORLD 104 (Sushil Mittal and Gene Thursby eds., 2004); S. Caldwell and B.K. Smith eds., *Who Speaks for Hinduism?*, 68 JOURNAL OF THE AMERICAN ACADEMY OF RELIGION (SPECIAL ISSUE) 705 (2000). STEPHANIE JAMISON, THE RAVENOUS HYENAS AND THE WOUNDED SUN: MYTH AND RITUAL IN ANCIENT INDIA 7-26 (1991) Thomas Coburn, *"Scripture" in India: Towards a Typology of the Word in Hindu Life, in* RETHINKING SCRIPTURE: ESSAYS FROM A COMPARATIVE PERSPECTIVE 106 (Miriam Levering ed., 1989).

[3] 2.10, MANU'S CODE OF LAW: A CRITICAL EDITION AND TRANSLATION OF THE MĀNAVA-DHARMAŚĀSTRA (Patrick Olivelle ed./Suman Olivelle trans. 2005).

conduct."[4] Law does not emanate directly from the injunctions of the *śruti*. Yet, all later Hindu legal texts (collectively known as Dharmaśāstra[5]) agree that the Vedas are the "root of dharma", or one's religious, legal, ethical, and social duties.[6] Given that the connection of religious and legal duties with the *śruti* is not direct, the connection should be imagined as one of inspiration. The *śruti* is held to be the spirit of the law in Hinduism.

II. Smriti - Tradition

The theological and jurisprudential tradition of Dharmaśāstra belongs to a second genre of sacred texts in Hinduism called *smriti* (lit. "what is remembered"). The most famous Dharmaśāstra text is the well-known *Laws of Manu,* dating approximately to the second century AD.[7] Other famous Hindu texts such as the manual of statecraft known as the *Arthaśāstra,*[8] the epics *Mahābhārata* and *Rāmāyana,* and the sacred narratives of the Purānas also belong to the *smriti* genre.

All *smriti* texts are sacred, though less so than *śruti*. In India, sacredness is not like an on/off switch, either wholly or not at all sacred. There can be degrees of sacredness that are ranked hierarchically. The most famous instance of such a hierarchy is the Indian caste system, which theoretically classifies society into four groups.[9]

---

[4] ROBERT LINGAT, THE CLASSICAL LAW OF INDIA 8 (1973). Ludo Rocher, *Hindu Conceptions of Law,* 29(6) HASTINGS LAW JOURNAL 1293 (1978).

[5] Further J.J. MEYER, ÜBER DAS WESEN DER ALTINDISCHEN RECHTSSCHRIFTEN UND IHR VERHÄLTNIS ZU EINANDER UND ZU KAUTILYA (1927). Meyer insists that Dharmaśāstra texts are "Zauberbücher", by which he seems to mean something close to a sacred text.

[6] *Supra* note 3.

[7] *Id.* At 19–25 (detailing the problems related to dating this and other ancient Sanskrit texts).

[8] For commentary on how the tradition of Arthaśāstra was co-opted early on by the Dharmaśāstra tradition and how the usual subject matter of Arthaśāstra, the *dharma* of rulers (*rājadharma*), was first incorporated into the *Mānava-Dharmaśāstra, Id.* at 46–50. Although it is difficult to consider the *Arthaśāstra* as a sacred Hindu text due to its contents, this text is important for the history of law in India, because the Arthaśāstra tradition introduced important innovations into Hindu juriprudence, most notably the eighteen titles of law.

[9] For a classic discussion of caste and hierarchy *see* LOUIS DUMONT, HOMO HIERARCHICUS: THE CASTE SYSTEM AND ITS IMPLICATIONS (1980).

With respect to the sacred texts on law, the measure of sacredness corresponds to the degree of epistemological authority (*prāmānya*) that a text has. For example, the most sacred *śruti* texts constituted a direct and perfect means of knowing one's sacred duty while the derivative *smriti* texts, along with the scholastic tradition built upon them, provided a reliable, though less authoritative means of knowledge. In theory, where rules conflicted, the less sacred text must be dismissed. However, the kinds of rules found in the *śruti* differ to such a degree from those in the *smriti* that conflict was practically speaking very limited.[10]

Further, the dharmas, or rules of religious and legal duty, in each genre had distinct and separate scopes.[11] It is therefore the genre of *smriti* that served as the foundation for Hindu jurisprudence and, much less directly and frequently, as a source of positive law. The *smriti* texts' authors understood the spirit of dharma, and thus of the law, to come from the *śruti*.

III. Scholastic Commentaries

Commentaries and digests, which comprise the scholastic tradition that interpreted and elaborated on the *smriti* texts, constitute the final genre of texts that must be considered here in order to complete the initial typology of sacred texts influencing law in Hindu traditions. Commentaries (bhāsya) take the form of linguistic exegeses, hypothetical examples, and theoretical disquisitions on a single Dharmaśāstra text. In contrast, digests (nibandha) collect a variety of opinions from the *smriti* texts and group them into topics, still interspersed with exegesis, example, and theory as before.

The distinction between the two is not absolute as many commentaries incorporate myriad outside opinions in the manner of a digest. The authority of the commentaries and digests is derivative in the sense that it is based on the authority of *smriti*

---

[10] Albrecht Wezler, *Dharma in the Veda and the Dharmaśāstras,* 32 JOURNAL OF INDIAN PHILOSOPHY 629–54 (2004).

[11] For a technical discussion of Hindu legal reasoning, including the technique of "establishing the scope" (*vivayavyavasthā*), Donald R. Davis, Jr., *Maxims and Precedent in Classical Hindu Law,* 33 INDOLOGICA TAURINENSIA 33–55 (2007).

texts themselves. These scholastic works provide, however, an essential interpretive framework for the *smriti* genre and in many cases, offer original insights on old problems. The most explicit jurisprudential discussions of Hindu law are to be found in the medieval commentaries of the Dharmaśāstra tradition

C. SACRED HINDU TEXTS AND LEGAL PRACTICE IN CLASSICAL INDIA

I. Ācāra - Customary Law

The difference between the subject matter of *śruti* and *smriti,* especially the Dharmaśāstra, has been noted. More should be said now about the origins of the latter. Whereas the injunctions of *śruti* (mostly concerned with ritual sacrifice) are held to be eternal and therefore without origin, the primary source of the *smriti* rules is customary law *(ācāra)*.[12] The *smriti*s are, however, not *coutumieres,* or mere collections of customs. "[T]he Dharmaśāstra represents an expert tradition and, therefore, presents not a 'record' of custom but a jurisprudential, or in Indian terms, a śāstric *reflection* on custom. Custom is taken here to a second order of discourse."[13]

If Dharmaśāstra was a second order of discourse, the first order of discourse for dharma and law was customary law in the form of well-known local standards and localized religious and legal systems. More specifically, the first order of practical legal discourse in classical and medieval India was *ācāra,* not *dharma* and Dharmaśāstra.[14] The sacredness of *ācāra,* however, was preserved by certain checks that *theoretically* ensured that only the customary law of those educated in the Vedic tradition, i.e. knowledgeable about the *śruti* and *smriti,* should be considered valid. The close connection between person and text in India was significant in the realm of law as well, for it meant that the written law alone enjoyed little authority without the force of a

---

[12] Richard W. Lariviere, *Dharmaśāstra, Custom, "Real Law", and "Apocryphal" Smritis,* 32 JOURNAL OF INDIAN PHILOSOPHY 611–622 (2004); Wezler, *supra* note 10.

[13] *Supra* note 3, at 62.

[14] DONALD R. DAVIS, JR., THE BOUNDARIES OF HINDU LAW: TRADITION, CUSTOM, AND POLITICS IN MEDIEVAL KERALA (2004).

personal authority to corroborate and guarantee the text's value. The sacredness of texts in classical India depended largely on the sanctity of people.[15]

II. Textual Norms in Theory and Practice

The hierarchy of the three sources (*śruti, smriti, ācāra*) is clear in theory.[16] In cases of conflict, the theoretical jurisprudence of Dharmaśāstra declares that no rule of *ācāra* can be accepted over a textual rule from *śruti* or *smriti*. In practice, the contents and concerns of the *smriti* differ from those of the *śruti* to such an extent that a conflict between the two is unlikely or rare. Similarly, the scope *(visaya)* of *ācāra* differs in such a way that normative contradiction is minimized.

Thus, conflict between *ācāra* and the textual sources of *dharma* seems more a hypothetical than a real problem. Although *ācāra* is the principal source of rules of Dharmaśāstra, the scope of neither *ācāra* nor dharma is exhausted by the Dharmaśāstra. In practice, local law (*ācāra*) informed by the theoretical jurisprudence of Dharmaśāstra – and to a lesser extent its substantive and procedural rules – constituted the core of the Hindu law tradition in classical and medieval India.[17] Textual norms were accepted, rejected, and modified for use in the myriad regional and local legal systems of early India.[18] Unfortunately, little historical evidence remains for the reconstruction of these diverse legal

---

[15] WILFRED CANTWELL SMITH, WHAT IS SCRIPTURE? A COMPARATIVE APPROACH 142–43 (1993).

[16] Another source of *dharma, ātmatutustI,* "what pleases oneself", is listed in *Mānava-Dharmaśāstra* 2.6 and *Yājñavalkya smriti* 1.7. This source never receives much elaboration or examination in the *dharma* texts. Read *supra* note 3, at 244 (for an understanding different than mine of how this source of *dharma* is closer to "personal preference" than "individual conscience").

[17] For a description and definition of Hindu law in practice in medieval Kerala read DAVIS, *supra* note 14, at 11–18.

[18] For an alternate description of local law in the sixteenth century court of Aintab in Ottoman Anatolia read LESLIE PEIRCE, MORALITY TALES: LAW AND GENDER IN THE OTTOMAN COURT OF AINTAB (2003). Peirce's nuanced case study shows in great detail how Islamic *shari'a* and Ottoman imperial laws were locally interpreted and concretized in the resolution of disputes and the transaction of legal affairs. The case study serves as an instructive parallel to draw on in imagining the practical life of Hindu law in classical and medieval India.

systems.[19] The available evidence, however, seems to support a claim that localized systems were influenced by the sacred texts of the Dharmaśāstra tradition, not in the manner of a code but rather in the realms of legal education, legal reasoning, and jurisprudence.

In general, the explicit use of sacred texts in classical Hindu law in practice was very limited.[20] Practical law, or positive law, did not depend upon appeals to written authority, whether sacred or not. Interestingly though, the positive law of classical and medieval India was circumscribed and imbued with a jurisprudence that emanated more or less directly from Dharmaśāstra. Sacred texts in the Hindu tradition imparted a technique and a way of thinking about law that had myriad practical consequences. In this way, Hindu law does depend on sacred texts, primarily Dharmaśāstra.

III. Mīmāmsā - Legal Hermeneutics

In order to discern the role of sacred texts in the practical law of classical and medieval India, one must recognize the limitations, or at least the ambiguities, of the Western categories law, legal text, and sacred text. In the Hindu tradition, sacred texts of many kinds,[21] but especially Dharmaśāstra texts, were used to educate Hindus in orthodox jurisprudence, and this jurisprudential knowledge and methodology was relied upon in many practical legal contexts. There was in early India a significant distance, both intellectually and institutionally, between the production and learning of sacred texts and the implementation of law on the ground. A mutual influence between the two nevertheless existed.

---

[19] For discussions about the practical side of law in classical and medieval India read J.D.M. DERRETT, RELIGION, LAW, AND THE STATE IN INDIA 171-224 (1968); INGO STRAUCH, DIE LEKHAPADDHATI-LEKHAPAÑCĀŚIKĀ: BRIEFE UND URKUNDEN IM MITTELALTERLICHEN GUJARAT (2002); Donald R. Davis, Jr., *Intermediate Realms of Law: Corporate Groups and Rulers in Medieval India,* 48 JOURNAL OF THE ECONOMIC AND SOCIAL HISTORY OF THE ORIENT 92-117 (2005).

[20] Ludo Rocher, *Law Books in an Oral Culture: The Indian Dharmaśāstras,* 137 PROCEEDINGS OF THE AMERICAN PHILOSOPHICAL SOCIETY 254-267 (1993).

[21] Legal categories, reasoning, and rules are to be found in Hinduism's sacred texts, including the Vedas, Mīmāmsā, the epic texts *Rāmāyana* and *Mahābhārata,*

In this realm of jurisprudence, the connection between sacred texts and law is to be found in the tradition of hermeneutics known as Mīmāmsā. In order to see fully the influence of sacred literature of classical and medieval India on the law, the notion of "sacred text" must be expanded. One could reasonably argue that Mīmāmsā texts are not "sacred" in any usual sense. They are not part of a liturgy; they do not recount sacred mythological narratives; and they are not the central religious texts of any Hindu sect. It would be harder, however, to argue that Mīmāmsā as a system of hermeneutics was not central to the bearers and transmitters of Hindu theology.[22] In this expanded sense, therefore, Mīmāmsā and the form of legal reasoning it offers must be considered part of the sacred textual corpus of Hinduism, as well as the theoretical and practical jurisprudence of Hindu law.

Mīmāmsā is a system of hermeneutics designed to facilitate correct interpretation and performance of the ritual injunctions of the Vedic texts, the *śruti*. Authors of Dharmaśāstra texts applied the same hermeneutical rules used for understanding religious texts for interpreting legal rules in their works.[23] Mīmāmsā accepts certain presuppositions that established a distinctive religious and legal cosmology within which authors of the Hindu law tradition worked.[24] The presuppositions include: 1) the aforementioned eternal and unauthored nature of the Vedas, 2) a denial of any creation or creator of the world, 3) the elevation of the ritual act above the gods, 4) the eternal connection of words and their meanings, and 5) the consonance of all authoritative injunctions of *dharma*.

Two important legal consequences result from these presuppositions and their implied cosmology. First, the morally and

---

and the Purānas. The interpenetration of religion and law in Hinduism is profound. For a discussion of the relevance of law to Hinduism from the perspective of religious studies read Donald R. Davis, Jr., *Hinduism as a Legal Tradition,* 75 JOURNAL OF THE AMERICAN ACADEMY OF RELIGION 241 (2007).

[22] Further PATRICK OLIVELLE, THE ĀŚRAMA SYSTEM: THE HISTORY AND HERMENEUTICS OF A RELIGIOUS INSTITUTION (1993).

[23] For a thorough treatment of the use of Mīmānsā in Dharmaśāstra read P.V. KANE, (5) HISTORY OF DHARMAŚĀSTRA 1152 (1962–75).

[24] For a treatment of legal cosmology read REBECCA FRENCH, THE GOLDEN YOKE: THE LEGAL COSMOLOGY OF BUDDHIST TIBET (1995).

academically educated and disciplined man (*śiksa*) becomes the central figure in both the proper interpretation of religious and legal texts and in the extension or application of the spirit of those texts to contemporary situations. Secondly, a flexibility and realism with respect to legal questions obtains a theological justification in a rhetoric that generally censures variability, contradiction, and change but permits them nevertheless.[25]

The important point to remember in the context of surveying the relevance of sacred texts to the law in Hinduism is that the hermeneutics of religion and law were precisely the same. Religious and legal texts were not distinguished in any way. Moreover, the rules and interpretive cosmology of Mīmāmsā established a framework for both the theoretical and practical solution of legal problems.

IV. Summary

To grasp the influence of sacred texts on law in the Hindu tradition, we should look to the use of sacred texts in schools more than in courts. While the sacred literature of Hinduism did incorporate a great quantity of normative legal rules that were occasionally put into practice, the texts more importantly cultivated in the educated classes a jurisprudence and legal cosmology that shaped the intellectual and moral stance, the "hermeneutic situation" in Gadamer's sense,[26] from which legal decisions and institutions developed in local contexts. Sacred texts were not normally sources of positive law, but rather of jurisprudential training. A failure to recognize the nature of the sacred texts on religion and law in the Hindu tradition, particularly the nature of Dharmaśāstra as both text and tradition, led to numerous misconceptions and misappropriations of the classical Hindu law tradition during and after the British colonial period in India. It is to this specific use of sacred texts in the Anglo-Hindu and modern Hindu law traditions that we turn now.

---

[25] Donald R. Davis, Jr., *A Realist View of Hindu Law,* 19 RATIO JURIS: AN INTERNATIONAL JOURNAL OF JURISPRUDENCE AND PHILOSOPHY OF LAW 287 (2006).

[26] HANS-GEORG GADAMER, TRUTH AND METHOD 301 (1989).

D. COLONIAL AND POSTCOLONIAL LEGAL APPROPRIATIONS OF HINDU SACRED TEXTS

I. Theoretical Considerations in the Study of Hindu Law

The baseline for describing changes and transformations in India's legal traditions from the "precolonial" to "colonial" to "postcolonial" periods has typically been a brief and stereotypical presentation of law in India, based on either secondary descriptions of the Dharmaśāstra texts or colonial observers' remarks about the predominance of "customary law" in the practical law of India. On one hand, the study of Dharmaśāstra has been the province of Indological specialists with a good knowledge of Sanskrit, a fact that isolates it from mainstream legal studies. On the other, labeling any legal system "customary" has often proven fatal to any further interest in the law of that area.[27] Linking Hindu law with either or both, therefore, has dissuaded most scholars from pursuing a deeper understanding about law in India prior to the British colonial period as a way of enhancing claims about the transformative impact of colonialism, i.e. Hindu law was like that, now it is like this. Instead, as early as 1877, J.H. Nelson could seriously ask, "Has such a thing as 'Hindu Law' at any time existed in the world? Or is it that 'Hindu Law' is a mere phantom of the brain, imagined by Sanskritists without law and lawyers without Sanskrit?"[28] Such sentiments have been rejuvenated from a different rhetorical and interpretive position in recent "invention of tradition" studies on Indian institutions, including Hindu law. As with the debates surrounding the colonial construction of Hinduism itself,[29] the question of whether Hindu law was

---

[27] For discussions of the problematic category of "custom" and "customary law" read MARTIN CHANOCK, LAW, CUSTOM, AND SOCIAL ORDER: THE COLONIAL EXPERIENCE IN MALAWI AND ZAMBIA (1983); SALLY FALK MOORE, SOCIAL FACTS & FABRICATIONS: "CUSTOMARY" LAW ON KILIMANJARO, 1880–1980 (1986); CLIFFORD GEERTZ, *Local Knowledge: Fact and Law in Comparative Perspective, in* LOCAL KNOWLEDGE: FURTHER ESSAYS IN INTERPRETIVE ANTHROPOLOGY 167–234 (1983); Sally Engle Merry, Law and Colonialism, 25 LAW & SOCIETY REVIEW 889 (1991).

[28] J.H. NELSON, A VIEW OF HINDU LAW AS ADMINISTERED BY THE HIGH COURT OF JUDICATURE AT MADRAS 2 (1877).

[29] BRIAN PENNINGTON, WAS HINDUISM INVENTED? BRITONS, INDIANS, AND THE COLONIAL CONSTRUCTION OF RELIGION (2005).

created *ex nihilo* by the British as part of their desire to administer indigenous law to the Indians hinges on one's use of and understanding of analytic categories. A primary stumbling block for some in the argument that Hindu law predated the British presence in India is the fact that neither word in the label "Hindu law" has any clear translation in an Indian language. This sort of linguistic determinism, whether crude or sophisticated, is a paralyzing academic game that has been played before in discussions of whether Africans have "law",[30] whether Indians practice "religion"[31] and whether indigenous societies have "science".[32] For present purposes, it is sufficient to suggest that the primary continuity between classical and modern Hindu law is an interest in and connection to the scholastic tradition of Dharmaśāstra. That continuity does not preclude the introduction of sweeping changes in the understanding and practice of Hindu law from the late eighteenth century to the present day.

2. *Two Views of the Impact of Colonialism on Hindu Law*

Two basic positions have been established regarding the "displacement of traditional law" in India. The first position, put forth by Derrett, Rocher, Galanter, Jain, Dhavan, Washbrook, and Lariviere among others,[33] argues for a significant rupture and disjunction between classical and modern Hindu law. While there

---

[30] Further Max Gluckman, *Concepts in the Comparative Study of Tribal Law, in* LAW IN CULTURE AND SOCIETY 349 (Laura Nader ed., 1969) (reviewing the debate between Gluckman and Paul Bohannan on the question of folk versus analytic categories in the description of African legal systems that dominated legal anthropology for a time, but has had little lasting effect).

[31] Further S.N. BALAGANGADHARA, "THE HEATHEN IN HIS BLINDNESS...": ASIA, THE WEST, AND THE DYNAMIC OF RELIGION (1994) (for a provocative, yet difficult work on the intractable connections of the term "religion" to particular institutional forms in Christianity).

[32] EMILE DURKHEIM AND MARCEL MAUSS, PRIMITIVE CLASSIFICATION (1963) (for their attempt to show the continuities between "primitive classification" and modern science and the connection of both with social forms). The notion that science is the preserve of industrialized, First World societies is still commonplace.

[33] Further DERRETT, *supra* note 19; MARC GALANTER, LAW AND SOCIETY IN MODERN INDIA (1989); M.P. JAIN, OUTLINES OF INDIAN LEGAL HISTORY 590 (1990); Ludo Rocher, *Indian Response to Anglo-Hindu Law*, 92 JOURNAL OF THE AMERICAN ORIENTAL SOCIETY 419-24 (1972); David A. Washbrook, *Law, State, and Agrarian Society in Colonial India*, 15 MODERN ASIAN STUDIES

are disagreements within this group about, for example, whether the British intended to disrupt traditional legal processes,[34] all group members agree that tremendous change did occur. The second position, advocated in different ways by Fuller and Menski,[35] is both more provocative and more challenging. It contradicts received wisdom, but in doing so may point to some overlooked continuities in both professional and ordinary legal contexts that would temper the radical rupture posited by some. Ultimately, the author sides with the first position because the evidence seems overwhelming that a major transformation in the practical operation of law in India did occur in the British period and has been continued after Indian independence in 1947.

E. AN EXAMPLE: SACRED TEXTS IN MODERN HINDU LAW

The use of sacred texts in modern Hindu law[36] demonstrates both the major changes seen in the last two centuries and the persistence of ornamental vestiges of traditional Hindu law after the structural rupturing of legal process in India.

I. *The Consensus View*

The standard interpretation, with specific focus on modern Hindu law, was set forth by Derrett as early as 1957.[37] The decision of Hastings, Governor of Bengal, in 1772 to administer the personal laws of Hindus and Muslims to those communities in

---

649–721 (1981); Richard W. Lariviere, *Justices and* Panditas: *Some Ironies in Contemporary Readings of the Hindu Legal Past,* 48 JOURNAL OF ASIAN STUDIES 757–69 (1989); Rajeev Dhavan, Dharmasastra *and Modern Indian Society: A Preliminary Exploration,* 34 JOURNAL OF THE INDIAN LAW INSTITUTE 515–40 (1992).

[34] Lariviere, *supra* note 33, at 759.

[35] Further WERNER F. MENSKI, HINDU LAW: BEYOND TRADITION AND MODERNITY (2003); C.J. Fuller, *Hinduism and Scriptural Authority in Modern Indian Law,* 30 COMPARATIVE STUDIES IN SOCIETY AND HISTORY 225–48 (1988); Donald R. Davis, Jr., *Traditional Hindu Law in the Guise of "Postmodernism"*: A Review Article, 25 MICHIGAN JOURNAL OF INTERNATIONAL LAW 735–49 (2004).

[36] A distinction is usually made between the Anglo-Hindu legal system during the British Raj and the modern Hindu law, more or less fixed by the series of Hindu Code bills in the mid-1950s. Following Fuller, the author will concentrate on the use of sacred texts in the modern Hindu law of India.

[37] J.D.M. DERRETT, HINDU LAW PAST & PRESENT (1957).

India spurred the creation of the early British digests of Sanskrit Dharmaśāstras and subsequent translations of key texts by Colebrooke, Borrodaile, Sutherland, and others. The very limited knowledge of British judges regarding the proper interpretation and practical use of these texts was not much ameliorated by the presence of court pandits, assigned to assist them in determining the applicable law from the Dharmaśāstra. The whole language of "applying the Dharmaśāstra" is, as we have seen, inappropriate in the context of classical Hindu law and, by itself, constitutes a major departure from the traditional use and influence of this branch of Hindu sacred literature in the law.

Derrett points out that the weak and highly mediated understanding of Dharmaśāstra possessed by nineteenth-century British judges has led to a situation in which "a surprising amount of 19th-century case-law is only partly competent, or even, frankly, bad. The student [of modern Hindu law] should not look at any pre-1930 case in Hindu law which is not mentioned in this book; and even where one is cited he should approach it with reserve."[38] In other words, the British misappropriation of Dharmaśāstra, as the key sacred corpus dealing with law in the Hindu tradition, innocent though it may have been in many respects,[39] was the basis for an ill-formed body of case-law that, with the dismissal of court pandits in 1864, resulted in the "death" of Dharmaśāstra as a "living and responsible science."[40] After 1864, this case-law was considered sufficient to provide judicial guidance for questions of Hindu law and formed the basis for the enactments of the modern Hindu Code bills of the 1950s.

The multiple layers of misunderstanding in the development of modern Hindu law make arguing for continuity extremely difficult. British judges were generally[41] ill-equipped to make informed use of and references to Dharmaśāstra, much less

---

[38] J.D.M. DERRETT, INTRODUCTION TO MODERN HINDU LAW 6 (1963).

[39] Lariviere, *supra* note 33, at 763–64.

[40] DERRETT, *supra* note 19, at 250.

[41] Exceptional British and Indian judges in the nineteenth and twentieth centuries, owing to their profound knowledge of Sanskrit and Mīmāmsā, did occasionally offer brilliant traditional interpretations on points of Hindu law. Mastery of two legal systems was rare, however, and could hardly be expected of most judicial appointees.

to discern a legal relevance for other sacred texts of the Hindu tradition. Accordingly, the frequent citations of Dharmaśāstra rules in Anglo-Hindu and modern Hindu law created not only a morass of radically different interpretations of śāstric positions from those in traditional sources but also a precedent for a direct appropriation of sacred texts in the law that had not existed in the same way before. Such direct application and consideration of sacred texts was new in the Hindu law tradition.

II. An Alternative View

Against this more or less canonical position, Fuller makes an intriguing case for the continuation of traditional values and interpretive strategies in the use of and reference to Hindu sacred texts in several leading cases of modern Hindu law. Fuller argues that in these cases the Supreme Court of India has repeatedly undertaken the direct interpretation of sacred texts for gleaning legal rules pertaining to Hindu law. Referring to the well-known *Seshammal*,[42] *Venkataramana*,[43] and *Satsang*[44] cases, for instance, Fuller examines the justices' use of Hindu texts such as the Āgamas, the Vedas, and the *Bhagavad-Gītā* as sources of law. He concludes that "if their decisions seem to contradict a textual prescription, the courts will justify their rulings by acting as textual interpreters."[45] More importantly, though less convincingly, Fuller claims that the legal reasoning used by the justices in these cases mirrors traditional Dharmaśāstra/Mīmāmsā hermeneutics such that this set of modern judgments "issues from a method of reasoning that is almost entirely consistent with classical precedents" and "reveals a continuity with the modes of reasoning of traditional pandits."[46] From these two arguments, Fuller concludes that the sharp demarcation between traditional and modern law in India must be blunted in favor of seeing real continuities between the two systems.

---

[42] (1972) 3 S.C.R. 815.
[43] A.I.R. 1958 S.C. 255.
[44] A.I.R. 1966 S.C. 1119.
[45] Fuller, *supra* note 35, at 234.
[46] *Id.* at 241, 246.

While Fuller has demonstrated very clearly that Hindu sacred texts are being and have been directly used as sources of law for certain kinds of cases in the Supreme Court – a point of considerable importance for this chapter – there are two fatal problems in Fuller's larger argument concerning the alleged continuities of traditional and modern Indian law. First, Fuller's claim for continuity suffers by not establishing a plausible baseline for traditional Hindu legal practice against which to compare modern Supreme Court decision-making. Fuller accepts uncritically that classical Hindu law directly used sacred texts for making decisions.[47] Classical Hindu law depended upon Dharmaśāstra, and other sacred texts to a lesser extent, but not in the manner presumed by Fuller. Direct appropriations were rare, as I tried to show above. Thus, Fuller's clear demonstration of the explicit reliance on sacred texts in certain Supreme Court decisions undermines ironically his larger argument for continuity between traditional and modern law in India: it shows the new and different manner in which legal decisions might be based on the direct use of sacred texts and their interpretation.

Second, Fuller fails to substantiate fully his claim that the type of reasoning employed in the Supreme Court is a form of theological-cum-legal hermeneutics that emanates directly from traditional Hindu modes of reasoning. It is important to remember that Dharmaśāstra and Mīmāmsā are best understood in the first place as part of a scholastic tradition.[48] In constrast, the work of modern judges has an immediate practical purpose that is missing from the traditional hermeneutic system. A theoretical solution is not always practicable or enforceable. Although it is important not to draw too sharp a division between the hermeneutic labor necessary for the scholiast and the judge, the difference must still be acknowledged.[49] Specifically, these Supreme Court decisions make only superficial use of categories and logic from the Mīmāmsā tradition, so crucial to Dharmaśāstra interpretation. Lariviere has called this "Dharmaśāstra as window dressing".[50]

[47] *Id.* at 226, 247 (invoking Dharmaśāstra explicitly in claiming a similarity between past and present notions of "scriptural authority").

[48] For a discussion on this underappreciated point made repeatedly in the works of Ludo Rocher and Patrick Olivelle read, e.g., *supra* note 3, at 64–65.

[49] GADAMER, *supra* note 26, at 324–41 (discussing with great insight this problem of drawing too sharp of a division).

[50] Lariviere, *supra* note 33, at 764.

When Fuller assimilates traditional and modern modes of reasoning, he overestimates the depth of the similarities. The author believes that the superficial connections Fuller notices between the interpretive strategies of the modern justices and traditional pandits are barely more than the similarities that exist between all modes of legal reasoning, i.e. the shared logic that distinguishes certain forms of reasoning as "legal".[51] There is little indication of any peculiarly Indian or Hindu element in the justices' reasoning in these decisions. It is telling that even Ayyar's book, which is dedicated to explaining the use of Mīmāmsā in Hindu law, can only adduce a single decision in which a Mīmāmsā principle is directly referenced.[52] Justice Kumaraswamy Sastry wrote, "The principles of Atidesa where by principles laid down with reference to one case are applied to other analogous cases were recognised [...] in Mimamsa". Each of the other ten cases Ayyar offers as evidence of "Mīmāmsā" thought in modern Hindu law speaks only of "analogy".[53] Without describing the complex nature of atideśa (better thought of as "transfer"),[54] we may say that Ayyar, like Fuller, reduces jurisprudence to a vague sense of analogy for the modern period and fails to consider any specific Mīmāmsā rule concerning the restricted bases for transfer or analogy in word, context, syntax, etc.[55]

Put another way, the legal cosmology presupposed in classical Hindu law has been lost and replaced with a very different legal cosmology in modern Hindu law. One would expect a deep engagement with traditional reasoning as a continuation of that tradition to manifest in more obvious and explicit uses of, and perhaps even acknowledgments of, the categories, axioms, maxims, and logical rules of Mīmāmsā and Dharmaśāstra. A

---

[51] For an example of one of Ganeri's writings on "case-based reasoning" in Indian philosophy read Jonardon Ganeri, *The Ritual Roots of Moral Reason*, in THINKING THROUGH RITUALS: PHILOSOPHICAL PERSPECTIVES 207–33 (K. Schilbrack ed., 2004).

[52] I.L.R. 41 (Mad.) 44 (containing the *Subramaniam v. Ratnavelu* decision).

[53] A.S. NATARAJA AYYAR, MĪMĀMSĀ JURISPRUDENCE 77–81 (1952).

[54] For a more plausible comparison of Mīmāmsā and modern legal reasoning read FRANCIS X. CLOONEY, THINKING RITUALLY: REDISCOVERING THE PŪRVA MĪMĀMSĀ OF JAIMINI 88–93 (1990).

[55] For a thorough discussion of *atideśa* read KANE, *supra* note 23, at 1321–24.

profound engagement with the classical Hindu law tradition is not evident in the decisions of India's Supreme Court. Instead, the justices have performed or utilized modern interpretations of Hindu sacred texts, notably those of the philosopher and former Indian President Radhakrishnan,[56] which differ in both form and content from the ways in which sacred texts influenced classical Hindu law in practice.

III. *Affirming the Consensus View*

Both of Fuller's principal arguments appear therefore improbable when one scrutinizes his problematic description of the use of sacred texts in classical Hindu law in practice and the alleged continuities of legal reasoning over time. The mainstream position, which postulates a historically complicated, but distinct rupture in the operation of Hindu law during and after British colonialism, is affirmed. Sacred texts were used for the first time as direct sources of law in this modern period, but their use was largely shallow and ornamental because the bases for legal reasoning in India had shifted dramatically toward a strongly precedential case-law and the interpretation of parliamentary legislation. The modern uses of sacred texts in Hindu law differed significantly from the indirect influence that such texts had in the practical administration of law in earlier times.

F. CONCLUSION

By examining the Hindu materials from different eras, we have learned that sacred texts have generally not been central to the positive law in any period of Indian history, either because their impact was in the realm of jurisprudence and legal education — i.e. at a considerable remove from the positive law — or because their use was an ornamental overlay on legal decisions arrived at by other means. However, it should not inferred that sacred texts, represented primarily by the Dharmaśāstra here, were not and are not taken seriously in Indian society and in Indian legal contexts. On the contrary, we can imagine, following Dhavan, that the legal

[56] Fuller, *supra* note 35, at 236.

cosmology of Dharmaśāstra has always been a primary factor in civil society.[57]

In this world beyond the state and the economy, Dharmaśāstra and its theological jurisprudence exerted and, to some extent, still exerts a tremendous hold on the moral imagination of Hindu society.[58] As such, a consideration of Dharmaśāstra remains crucial for understanding India's legal history and the evolution of the Hindu law tradition. First, it permits us to establish a better historical view on law against which to judge recent changes and second, it opens us to another system of religious law that might be compared with cognate traditions in Islamic, Jewish, and Christian religious legal systems. "Thicker" descriptions of precisely how and to what extent Dharmaśāstra ideas and rules impacted the practical realm of law are still needed, but we have surveyed here some of the basic contours of the connections and disconnections in order to further establish a responsible and accessible basis for the study of Hindu law.

•

[57] Dhavan, *supra* note 33.

[58] Further LEELA PRASAD, POETICS OF CONDUCT: ORAL NARRATIVE AND MORAL BEING IN A SOUTH INDIAN TOWN (2006).

5

The Sublime Codes of *Manu*: Law and Eighteenth Century Orientalism

PIYEL HALDAR

A. INTRODUCTION

The first disquisition on the concept of the sublime, written by the anonymous Greek Pseudo-Longinus, famously mourns the passing of the pagan relationship between gods and men.[1] In his essay on Pseudo-Longinus's work, the French poet Michel Deguy stated that "the question of the sublime was doubtless first of all an attempt to measure the decline of the Orient, to measure the author's distance from the time of gods and heroes."[2] For Deguy, the Longinian tradition of emphasising the sublime as a key feature of rhetoric must be regarded as an attempt to establish some hope of a truly exalted discourse at a time in which man moves further and further away from his sacred relationship to the highest of origins. Such nostalgia obviously colours each cycle of secularisation; from paganism to Christianity to modernity and beyond. If each cycle generates a more worldly state of affairs, it also produces a Longinian longing for a more vertical axis to explain our mortality.

[1] Pseudo-Longinus, *Of the Sublime*, available at http://classicpersuasion.org/pw/longinus/.

[2] Michel Deguy, *The Discourse of Exaltation, in* OF THE SUBLIME: PRESENCE IN QUESTION 6 (Jeffrey Librett ed., 1993).

This chapter addresses one such Longinian moment as it arises at a particular moment in the history of law. More specifically, it examines the work of Sir William Jones, a high court judge of the *puisne* courts in Calcutta at the end of the eighteenth century, whose translations of the Hindu codes of law were both an attempt to understand those laws as they cohered the relevant section of Indian society and an attempt to infuse the common law with the same spirit of the sublime that he discerned in the writings and reception of Hindu law. What will be argued is that for Jones, the category of the sublime is not simply nostalgia for a period of natural justice. It must instead be understood in two senses. First, the category of the sublime is a means of sublimating, containing and controlling what was perceived to be the excesses of the Orient. In this sense, the understanding of the mystical aspects of Hinduism might be seen as an essential aspect of the Orientalist project uncovered so critically by Edward Said.[3] Second, the concentrated focus on the Oriental sublime was symptomatic of, and reveals, a more general juridical approach to questions of legal subjectivity. It is at this level that we might begin to comprehend why the category of the sublime seems to be locked into every generation of secularism.

B. JONES AND ORIENTAL SCHOLARSHIP

Before turning to Jones's specific projects relating to law, some context should be provided on scholarship on India during the eighteenth century, when a significant portion the Subcontinent came to be administrated by the East India Company. Under the administration of Warren Hastings in the eighteenth century, scholars such as Charles Wilkins and Nathaniel Halhed initiated studies into the Indian past. Having established the first printing press in India, Halhed published his *Grammar of the Bengali Language* and Wilkins published the first translation of the *Bagavad Gita*. Such works were ostensibly issued to inform Englishmen interested in India and to "conciliate the affection of the natives".[4]

---

[3] EDWARD SAID, ORIENTALISM: WESTERN CONCEPTS OF THE ORIENT (1995).

[4] NATHANIEL HALHED, A CODE OF GENTOO LAWS, OR THE ORDINATIONS OF THE PUNDITS ix (1776).

In fact, there was more to these works, and the desire for exotic knowledge betrayed a deeper obsession with India that centred around the remoteness and sublime nature of its antiquity and the origins of its culture, religion, and law. Orientalist scholars, spurred on by such discoveries as the ancient cave temples of Elephanta, turned to the East in an attempt to calculate the origins of all culture. The Elephanta caves, for example, were not simply dark, mysterious and terrifyingly colossal. Their sublimity also resided in the suspicion that they predated any known culture. The implication was that somewhere in the East existed the cradle of civilization and that the clues as to its precise location were to be found in ancient Sanskrit texts.[5] Contained in this literature was a history that went back further in time than Christianity or even the immemorial origins of English common law!

> I, who cannot help believing the Divinity of the Messiah, from the undisputed antiquity and manifest completion of many prophesies, especially those of Isiah, am obliged of course to believe the sanctity of the venerable books to which that sacred person refers as genuine (the books of Moses); but it is not the truth of our national religion, as such, that I have at heart - it is truth itself; and if any cool unbiased reasoner will clearly convince me that Moses drew his narrative, through Egyptian conduits, from primeval fountains of Indian literature, I shall esteem him as a friend for having weeded my mind from a capital error, and promise to stand among the foremost in assisting to circulate the truth which he has ascertained. [...] I am persuaded that a connexion subsisted between the old idolatrous nations of Egypt, India, Greece and Italy.[6]

---

[5] JOHN DREW, INDIA AND THE ROMANTIC IMAGINATION 199 (1998).

[6] William Jones, *On the Divine Inspiration of the Jewish Scriptures*, in MEMOIRS OF THE LIFE, WRITINGS AND CORRESPONDENCE OF SIR WILLIAM JONES 280-281 (John Shore (Lord Teignmouth) ed., 1804). Read also William Jones, Ninth Discourse on the Origin and Families of Nations, in 3 THE WORKS OF SIR

Nature and the antiquity of the Orient are simply two forms of excess that excited the Orientalist scholar. As Voltaire suggested, the Brahmin had sublime ideas about the supreme being and the peculiar theocracy of Hinduism prompted Orientalist speculation on the sublime location of divine power.[7]

These appropriately disparate forms of the sublime stimulated the work of the Welshman Sir William Jones, who was regarded as perhaps the most obsessed of all early scholars. Biographical details about Jones (1746–94) suggest that his life was almost wholly devoted to Eastern scholarship.[8] His biographers never fail to repeat that, even before traveling to East, he had published his *Grammar of the Persian Language* (1771)[9] and *Poems, consisting chiefly of Translations from the Arabic Languages* (1772).[10] Any residual scholarly commitments outside this exotic field were dedicated only to the more mundane study and practice of law as a judge on the Welsh circuits.[11] Even so, it was recognition of Jones's talents as an Orientalist by Hastings that earned him an appointment as a *puisne* judge in the presidency of Bengal.

In Calcutta, the judge devoted much of his time to studying various Oriental cultures, stating that "my daily studies are now, what they will be for six years to come, Persian and law, and whatever relates to India."[12] Such studies elicited a sense of pleasure that often seemed to border on the sublime and that is expressed in hymn-like prose: "as the thirsty antelope runs to a pool of sweet water, so I thirsted for all kinds of knowledge, which was sweet

---

WILLIAM JONES IN 13 VOLUMES 176 (Garland Cannon ed., 1993). A range of eighteenth century English works suggested the influence of Brahminism on ancient religious life in Britain. For a discussion read DREW, *supra* note 5, at 50–51.

[7] Voltaire, *The Good Brahmin*, in THE PORTABLE VOLTAIRE 436–458 (Ben Ray Redman ed./various trans., 1977).

[8] MICHAEL J. FRANKLIN, SIR WILLIAM JONES (1995).

[9] WILLIAM JONES, GRAMMAR OF THE PERSIAN LANGUAGE (1771).

[10] WILLIAM JONES, POEMS, CONSISTING CHIEFLY OF TRANSLATIONS FROM THE ARABIC LANGUAGES (1772).

[11] FRANKLIN, *supra* note 8. Franklin suggests, however, that Jones may have also initiated the society of the "Druids of Cardigan".

[12] WILLIAM JONES, 1 THE LETTERS OF SIR WILLIAM JONES 362 (Garland Cannon ed., 1970) (Letter to Viscount Althrop); *Id.* at 449 (Letter to John Macpher

as nectar."[13] Again, the pleasure of Orientalist study is sometimes expressed as "infinite pleasure":

> If envy can exist with an anxious wish of all possible entertainment and reputation to the person envied, I am not free from that passion, when I think of the infinite pleasure which you must receive from a subject so new and interesting [as Sanskrit]. Happy should I be to follow you in the same track.[14]

Even the justification for Jones's studies was Orientalised, and his scholarly appetite was determined by and surrendered to a more despotic cause: "the *Mahomedans* have not only the permission, but the positive command, of their law-giver, *to search for learning even in the remotest parts of the globe*."[15] However, this compulsive obsession with studying as many things Oriental as he could commanded a certain price: "I do not expect, as long as I stay in India, to be free from a bad digestion, the *morbus literatorum*, for which there is hardly any remedy, but abstinence from too much food, literary and culinary."[16] Jones was to die from an inflammation of the liver in Calcutta.

In addition to his judicial tasks, Jones founded the Asiatic Society of Bengal in 1784. Modeled on the Royal Society, its aims were to "furnish proof to our posterity, that the acquisition of [Indian wealth] did not absorb [our] attention, and that the English laws and English government, in those distant regions, have sometimes been administered by men of extensive capacity, erudition and application."[17] Jones himself, the gentleman scholar-administrator, undertook full scale studies in the history,

---

son, stating "By rising before the sun, I allot an hour every day to Sanscrit, and am charmed with knowing so beautiful a sister of Latin and Greek").

[13] *Id.* at 464 (Letter to Earl Spencer). The lines are Jones's translation of a stanza from a Sanskrit poem.

[14] *Id.* at 391 (Letter to Charles Wilkins).

[15] William Jones, *Second Anniversary Discourse*, in 1 ASIATIC RESEARCHES 22 (1784).

[16] JONES, *supra* note 12, at 382 (Letter to Patrick Russell).

[17] William Jones, *Presidential Address*, in 1 ASIATIC RESEARCHES 221 (1784).

religions, customs, manners, geography, chronology, zodiac, mystical poetry and pastoral drama of India[18] and is recognised as having founded modern philology.[19] He assiduously gathered a portfolio of icons, drawing images of Hindu Gods and symbols that would later haunt the gothic imagination of writers such as Thomas de Quincey.[20] Broad and eclectic though his research was, its determining influence on imperial manners should not be underestimated. His research shored up respect for a fundamentally inaccessible set of cultures and informed policy on the treatment of Muslims and Hindus. Jones's research engaged with Oriental knowledge in the broadest terms. However, it also betrayed a desire to accumulate a different sort of wealth than the financial wealth pursued by the East India Company men. Knowledge of the Orient, in other words, provided cultural rather than material capital. It may be that, as Said argued, early Orientalism laid down a cultural foundation that enabled the establishment of colonial power. Information was to be managed so as to be understood and controlled. At the same time, it ought to be remembered that the acquisition of knowledge was always inherent in the idea of imperialism. In classical terms, the colonised world was to be understood as what had "fallen under inquiry", and the antecedents of Roman law implied the empire to be a source of knowledge.[21]

It is evident that the study of the Orient was a source of pleasure. A distinction must be drawn, however, between the pleasure of study and the affective quality of the object studied. India was the source of the sublime for Jones, as for the other Orientalists. But this claim, repeated in the following passage that employs images and expressions of the sublime, follows a trajectory that runs from

[18] For a fuller overview of the range of Jones's research interests read FRANKLIN, *supra* note 8.

[19] GARLAND CANNON, THE LIFE AND MIND OF ORIENTAL JONES: SIR WILLIAM JONES, THE FATHER OF MODERN LINGUISTICS (1991).

[20] THOMAS DE QUINCEY, SPECULATIONS LITERARY AND PHILOSOPHIC 236 (1862).

[21] ANTHONY PAGDEN, LORDS OF ALL THE WORLD: IDEOLOGIES OF EMPIRE IN SPAIN, BRITAIN AND FRANCE, C.1500-C.1800 19 (1998) (citing Polybius).

a state of being attracted to the Oriental sublime to a state where that sublime is somehow contained and articulated:

> When I was at sea last August, on my voyage to this country, which I had long and ardently desired to visit, I found one evening, on inspecting the observations of the day, that India lay before us, and Persia on our left, while a breeze from Arabia blew nearly on our stern. A situation so pleasing in itself, and to me so new, could not fail to awaken a train of reflections in a mind, which had clearly been accustomed to contemplate with delight the eventful histories and agreeable fictions of this eastern world. It gives me inexpressible pleasure to find myself in the midst of so noble an amphitheatre, almost encircled by the vast regions of Asia, which has ever been esteemed the nurse of sciences, the inventress of delightful and useful arts, the scene of glorious actions, fertile in the productions of human genius, abounding in natural wonders and infinetly diversified in the forms of religion and government, in the laws, manners, customs, and languages, as well as the features and complexions of men. I could not help remarking, how important and extensive a field was yet unexplored, and how many solid advantages unimproved, and when I considered, with pain, that in this fluctuating imperfect, and limited conditions of life, such inquiries and improvements could only be made through the united efforts of many, who are not easily brought, without some pressing inducement or strong impulse, to converge in a common point, I consoled myself with a hope, founded on opinions, which it might have the appearance of flattery to mention, that if in any country or community, such an

> union could be effected, it was among my countrymen in Bengal, with some of whom I already had, and with most desirous of having, the pleasure of being intimately acquainted.[22]

The phrases and metaphors used by Jones consciously engage with the themes of romantic sublime. The "inexpressible pleasure" in the face of unexplored territories directly transferred onto the Orient Burkean ideas of ignorance inciting the sublime passions. Typical of romantic sensibilities, the sublime Orient is expressed through the feminised descriptions of Asia – "nurse of the sciences, inventress of the delightful arts"– and directs our attention to the formlessness and excesses of femininity. Elsewhere, Jones was more explicit and suggested that "[the mythology of] the Hindus and Arabs are perfectly original; and to my taste their compositions are sublime",[23] for the Indians are those "who receive the first light of the rising sun".[24] That the study of the Orient produced such an "infinite pleasure" was due not to the nature of study as study, but to the nature of the object of those studies. What is even more interesting about the above passage, however, is the shift away from the feminine and unexplored sublime to the more mundane descriptions of a society of acquaintances. "Inexpressible pleasure" turns into expressible pleasure as Jones seeks artistic reward by means of sublimation. The hidden, undiscovered and excessive forms of the East provided the initial motor propelling "the delightful and glorious arts" and became the condition of the tamer pleasures of societal research and of mastery through knowledge. This trajectory alerts us to the Orientalist agenda of converting the excess of the sublime into something more manageable and governable.

---

[22] William Jones, *A Discourse on the Institution of a Society, for Inquiring into the History, Civil and Natural, the Antiquities, Arts, Sciences, Literature of Asia, by the President,* 1784, in 3 THE WORKS OF SIR WILLIAM JONES IN 13 VOLUMES, *supra* note 6, at 2.

[23] JONES, *supra* note 12, at 445 (Letter to Robert Orme).

[24] William Jones, *Third Anniversary Discourse,* 1786, in 3 THE WORKS OF SIR WILLIAM JONES IN 13 VOLUMES, *supra* note 6, at 42–44.

This simultaneous attraction to and utilisation of the sublime can be traced throughout all disciplines that form objects of Orientalist study. The architectural ruins of India, for example, were a key motif in the sublime imagination. A leading Company artist of the time, William Hodge, excelled in depicting the supernatural atmosphere of India so that both mundane and exotic aspects, e.g. the terror of *sati*, are set in front of gloomy architectural ruins.[25] In the words of Jones, relentlessly pursuing connections:

> the remains of architecture and sculpture in India, which I mention here as mere monuments in antiquity, not as specimens of ancient art, seem to prove an early connection between this country and Africa; the pyramids of Egypt, the colossal statues described by PAUSANIAS and others.[26]

Indeed, India itself was characterised as the ruins of ancient and sublime civilizations, and a common argument in contemporary literature was that they were the result of Moghul mismanagement.[27] Yet, the architectural remains and the ruins of India were an excuse to dominate and rebuild the land. The suspicion that the Oriental ruler embodied a limitless capacity of enjoyment, coupled with the unpredictable nature of alien manners, provoked the need to reconstitute a sense of order fashioned according to prim European standards.[28] It was by controlling the mysterious sublime of the Orient that colonialism was to pave the way for a strategy of rule based on the management of pleasures. Colonialism may be characterised in this sense as the attempt to dominate, control and assimilate the dangerous excesses of enjoyment.

---

[25] WILLIAM HODGES, TRAVELS IN INDIA DURING THE YEARS 1780, 1781, 1782 AND 1783 (1794).

[26] JONES, *supra* note 13, at 221.

[27] For an overview of this argument MICHAEL EDWARDS, BRITISH INDIA 1772–1947 (1999).

[28] PIYEL HALDAR, LAW, ORIENTALISM AND POSTCOLONIALISM (2007).

The use of the Oriental sublime can be traced in Jones's own compositions and is exemplified in his *Hymn to Ganges*.[29] Here, Jones located the British within the sublime time of ancient Indian history. British imperialism is characterised as inevitable and as part of India's destiny. As prophesied by a mythological Brahmin, the British would arrive in India in order to rule by "good laws well administered". Again, in the *Ode to the Surya*, Jones composed a mythical scene that employs all the common-places of the romantic sublime (the obstructed caves, the pure fountains, the obscure paths). What is prophesied on this occasion is the arrival of Jones himself.

> From the bosom of your silver isle,
> Where skies more softly smile,
> He came; and, lisping our celestial tongue,
> Though not from *Brahma* sprung,
> Draws Orient knowledge from its fountains pure,
> Through caves obstructed long, and paths too long obscure.[30]

In this ode, Jones submitted himself to a sublime landscape that is larger than he, and he is a mere recipient of a language that pre-exists his own existence. Yet it is precisely his status as a foreigner that allows him to be the gift bearer, to return to the Indians what was theirs in any case.

Put simply, the sublime provided the pivot that both romantic speculation and imperial mastery revolved around. This irresolute attitude towards the sublime was expressed time and again in different disciplines. Jones's position was not unique, and poets and philosophers were drawn to the East in search of romantic inspiration and those elements that lent themselves to

---

[29] William Jones, *Hymn to Ganges, in* 6 THE WORKS OF SIR WILLIAM JONES IN 13 VOLUMES, *supra* note 6, at 383. For a different analysis of the *Hymn to Ganges* read TEJASWINI ṆIRANJANA, SITING TRANSLATION: HISTORY, POSTSTRUCTURALISM, AND THE COLONIAL CONTEXT 19 (1992).

[30] William Jones, *Ode to Surya, in* 6 THE WORKS OF SIR WILLIAM JONES IN 13 VOLUMES, *supra* note 6, at 348.

sublime feelings.[31] At the same time as submitting to it, this aspect of Orientalism, this process of sublimating the excess, yielded and mythologised British authority and was crucial to the control and management of the East and its potential subjects.

C. THE SUBLIME ORIGINS AND FORCE OF THE LAW

I. Menu Sat Reclined, with His Attention Fixed on One Object, the Supreme God; When the Divine Sages Approached Him[32]

The colonisation of the Oriental sublime must be understood foremost as a symptom of jurisprudential thought. Sublimation is after all the transference or reassignment of excess enjoyment into something more socially acceptable, and so it operates as a form of prohibition. It is therefore not surprising to find the same jurisprudential concerns centred around Jones's projects to translate Hindu laws. Just as he found "infinite pleasure" in the study of Sanskrit and Hindu mythology, the study of Indian laws became an equally romantic past-time. "Do you not agree", he wrote to Schultens as early as 1774, "that nothing should be more pleasant or noble than the study of native and universal law?" Yet again, it was the object of study itself that satisfied the romantic desire for, and submission to, the sublime. As Jones observed "a spirit of sublime devotion [...] pervades the whole work [of Hindu law]."[34] On a more mundane level, however, these translations differed significantly from others such as his translation of Kalidasa's plays. In being directly applicable, this was a form of Orientalism that constituted the text as an object of knowledge while also creating the "Indian", a subject of law. The totality of this exercise would have included

[31] In literature, obvious examples include Byron, Shelley, Moore and Coleridge. In philosophy, the influence of the Indian sublime is most notable and direct in the works of Goethe, Herder and Schlegel. Andrew Rudd, *Romantic Period Writing and India*, 1 LITERATURE COMPASS 1-5 (2004).

[32] William Jones, *Preface to the Institutes of Hindu Law; or the Ordinances of Menu according to the Gloss of Culluca comprising the Indian System of Duties, Religious and Civil*, in 2 THE WORKS OF SIR WILLIAM JONES IN 13 VOLUMES, *supra* note 6, at 91.

[33] JONES, *supra* note 12, at 93 (Letter to Henry Albert Schultens).

[34] Jones, *supra* note 32, at 76.

> six or seven law books believed to be divine with a commentary on each of nearly equal authority; these are analogous to our Littleton and Coke, next Jimut Bahur, the best book on inheritances; and above all a digest of Hindu law in twenty-seven volumes precisely in the manner of the original digest.[35]

The project was never completed by Jones. What survives are the Laws of Manu, translated in 1794 as *The Institutes of Hindu Law: or, the Ordinances of Menu*.[36]

What was so sublime to Jones's mind about the Hindu laws of Manu in particular was that they were revealed and written down rather than composed and invented: "It was not MANU who composed the system of law, by the command of his father BRAHMA, but a holy personage or demi-god, named BHRIGU who revealed to men what MANU had delivered at the request of him and other saints or patriarchs."[37] Menu, or Manu, was not simply the hand or the amanuensis, he was, as it were, the first hand and the holiest of amanuenses! The law descends, having been promulgated "in the beginning of time by MENU, son of BRAHMA, or, in plain language, the first of created beings, and not the oldest only, but the holiest of legislators."[38] So old are these laws, "the laws [of Menu] are considerably older than those of SOLON or even LYCURGUS",[39] that Jones declared himself to be "lost in an inextricable labyrinth of imaginary astronomical cycles, *yugas, mahayugas, calpas, and menwantaras,* in attempting to calculate the time when the first MENU, governed this world, and became the progenitor of mankind."[40]

---

[35] JONES, *supra* note 12, at 447 (Letter to C.W. Boughton Rouse). Rouse was then Secretary to the Board of Control for India.

[36] WILLIAM JONES, THE INSTITUTES OF HINDU LAW; OR THE ORDINANCES OF MENU ACCORDING TO THE GLOSS OF CULLUCA COMPRISING THE INDIAN SYSTEM OF DUTIES, RELIGIOUS AND CIVIL (1825).

[37] William Jones, *On the Gods of Greece, Italy and India*, 1784, in 3 THE WORKS OF SIR WILLIAM JONES IN 13 VOLUMES, *supra* note 6, at 344.

[38] Jones, *supra* note 32, at 76.

[39] *Id.* at 78.

[40] *Id.* at 76-7.

While obviously interesting for an Orientalist, why did Jones *as a lawyer* wish to allocate any legal authority to a high Hindu text such as Manu? Various reasons, simultaneously practical and ideological, are advanced by Jones, his contemporaries and modern commentators. It is important to analyse these in order to reveal the way in which they hang on the idea of the sublime and on the process of sublimation.

II. A "Best Practicable System of Judicature"[41]

At one level of analysis, the codification of the original texts of Indian laws arranged according to the scientific method simply facilitated decision making by the Calcutta Supreme Court. Judges other than Jones were unwilling to learn Sanskrit and were consequently ignorant of the laws they were applying to Indian subjects. They had to rely on the written opinion of local lawyers, and translations of particular laws were provided only when required.[42] The inefficiency of this process of discovering and applying Hindu, or Muslim, law was exacerbated by the lack of trust afforded to the relevant court officials; "pure integrity is hardly to be found among the Pandits and Maulavis".[43] Copies of the work enabled British judges to avoid relying on these intermediaries and to detect any misinformation that these pandits and maulavis might have provided in the courts.[44] In this sense, Jones's attempt to translate the law was symptomatic of the training of all common law lawyers. The process of translating the Hindu and Muslim laws might be regarded as equivalent to that of legal education in the Inns of Courts and simply provided direct access to what was hidden in the depths of an esoteric language. The secular lawyer assumed the mantle of the priest as guardian of a sacred text and of its meaning. Whether written in a foreign tongue or in English, training on legal priesthood was, and remains, necessary in order to unlock the mysteries of legal knowledge (*arcana juris*).[45] The hieroglyphic nature of law

[41] WILLIAM JONES, *Best Practicable System of Judicature, supra* note 12, at 387 (Letter to Edmund Burke).

[42] *Id.*

[43] JONES, *supra* note 35.

[44] JONES, *supra* note 41.

[45] PETER GOODRICH, READING THE LAW: A CRITICAL INTRODUCTION TO LEGAL METHOD AND LEGAL TECHNIQUE (1986).

was regarded as universal. Translation enabled the lawyers of the supreme courts to access legal wisdom without the intermediation of the pandits and maulavis.

In strict doctrinal terms, however, the idea that a translation of indigenous laws would ease the judicial process of determining rules to be applied elides a more substantial point somewhat. It remains unclear as to why Hindu laws should be used in place of the common law given that in 1608 the English courts had stated firmly that "if a Christian king should conquer the kingdom of an infidel [...] the laws of that kingdom are abrogated".[46]

Several reasons were given for keeping intact the laws of the "native" subject. For Halhed, it was a matter of following the precedent of the Roman empire:

> [The Romans] not only allowed their foreign subjects the free exercise of their own religion and the administration of their own civil jurisdiction, but sometimes, by a policy still more flattering, even naturalized parts of the mythology of the conquered, as were in any respect compatible with their own system.[47]

The reason provided by James Forbes, another eighteenth century East Indian Company official, recognised, however, the limits of imperial authority.

> It is impossible to separate the political tendency of laws from the genius of government from which they emanate. The spirit of the English constitution assigns to the mass of the people an extensive control over the exercise of public authority; and deems the executive government to be the

[46] PETER GOODRICH, LANGUAGES OF LAW: FROM LOGICS OF MEMORY TO NOMADIC MASKS 212 (1990), quoting from SIR JOHN FORTESQUE, DE LAUDIBUS LEGUM ANGLICAE (1773 ed.).

[47] HALHED, *supra* note 4.

> representative of the public will. This spirit pervades the whole body of its laws; these laws necessarily reflect back and reproduce the principles from which they spring; and it is a matter of grave reflection should, that if this species of reaction should ever be produced in India, from that moment it is lost to this country for ever. The efficient protection of our native subjects in all the rights which they themselves consider to be essential to their happiness is certainly the most sacred and Imperious of all our duties. [...] It is not the question, whether the English or the Hindoo code of religion and jurisprudence be entitled to the preference; but whether the Hindu law and religion [...] are, or are not to be, maintained, or whether we are at liberty to invade both.[48]

According to Forbes, the "invasion" of Indian law and its replacement with the common law did not form part of British imperialism. Such an agenda would have compromised the spirit of liberty that was essential to the jurisprudence of the common law. Jones continually emphasised the same. In his recommendations to Edmund Burke for the "Best Practicable System of Judicature",[49] Jones observed that the replacement of Indian laws would have entailed a violent imposition of one institution upon another and would have implied that the English assume the despotic attributes of intolerance which they were necessarily opposed to:"A system of *liberty*, forced upon a people invincibly attached to opposite *habits*, would in truth be a system of cruel *tyranny*."[50] The spirit of liberty implied that the very system and set of institutions on which it depended could not be transferred to and imposed upon other cultures. However, the real paradox and irony of this sentiment was that for these

---

[48] JAMES FORBES, 2 ORIENTAL MEMOIRS: A NARRATIVE OF SEVENTEEN YEARS RESIDENCE IN INDIA 317 (1834).

[49] JONES, *supra* note 41.

[50] *Id.*

Hindu and Muslim subjects the enjoyment of their own laws had to be sanctioned and determined by a foreign system, a foreign institution, and foreign legislation.

> [A] legislative act [is needed] to assure the Hindu and Musselman subjects of Great Britain, that the private laws, which they severally hold secret and a violation of which they would have thought the most grievous oppression, should not be superseded by a new system, of which they could have no knowledge, and which they must have considered as imposed on them by a spirit of rigour and intolerance.[51]

This rhetoric of liberty, in other words, disguised the constitutional theory that there was *posited* a non-Indian geographical location of authority; the seemingly autonomous survival, existence and application of Indian laws hung upon a set of instructions relayed from London to Calcutta. Behind this legislative authority lay an ulterior imperial motive, namely buying the respect and affection of the Bengalis. These additional and superficial reasons for the preferential use of Hindu and Muslim laws given by Jones in his letter to Burke point to mercantile interests and the importance of maintaining good relations between the English (or in Jones's case, the Welsh) and the subjects of Bengal:

> Any system of *judicature* affecting the natives in *Bengal,* and not having for its basis the old *Mogul* constitution, would be dangerous and impracticable. [...] The natives must have an *effective* tribunal for their protection against the *English,* or the country will soon be rendered *worse than useless* to Britain.

Holding back on the application of the common law was part of an established code of behaviour that sought to ensure the happiness and respect of "the natives [who] are charmed with the idea of

[51] JONES, *supra* note 12, at 485 (Letter to the Marquis of Cornwall).

making their slavery lighter by giving them their own laws."[52] Jones's reification of the spirit of liberty thus masks a motive for maintaining imperial authority through the judicial system: "The Hindus are incapable of civil liberty; few of them have any idea of it; and those who have do not wish it. They must (deplore the evil, but know the necessity of it) they must be ruled by an absolute power."[53]

Further, the translation of a sacred Hindu text into English ensured the manipulation of that text. Sanskrit texts had their untranslatable words and contained forms of signification and meaning unthinkable in an English idiom. Indeed, all projects of translation put signification and the status of the original into question. Translation necessitates mistranslation and glosses over the remnants of enigmas and puzzles that are impossible to solve. Where, to subvert Gayatri Spivak's original argument, did Sanskrit end and English begin?[54] Translating a legal text into English in order that its rules may be enforced in a court erases that text's ability to speak in its own language, i.e. in a language other than the British court system's. Hindu or Mohammedan laws were translated and tailored to fit British conceptions of justice. According to John Strawson, Jones's project of translating the *Al Sirajiyyah*, Islamic law of inheritance, was given legitimacy only "by reference to European criteria which are taken almost as fact".[55] Legal Orientalism thus denied and obscured the diverse literary traditions of both Hindu and Islamic jurisprudence.

What is at stake at this (practical/ideological) level of analysis is the use of the courts and the process of translation to manoeuvre and contain the law. It might be supposed that Hindu law was to

[52] JONES, *supra* note 12, at 558 (Letter to 2nd Earl Spencer). Consider too his remark that the "three excellent things, which the ancients feigned to be the daughters of their supreme God, a good system of laws, a just administration of them, and a long peace will render this country a source of infinite advantage to Great Britain." *Id.* at 397 (Letter to William Pitt the Younger).

[53] *Id.* at 443 (Letter to Patrick Russell).

[54] Gayatri Chakravorty Spivak, *Translator's Preface, in* JACQUES DERRIDA, OF GRAMMATOLOGY (Gayatri Chakrovarty Spivak trans 1976).

[55] John Strawson, *Islamic Law and English Texts*, 6 LAW AND CRITIQUE 33 (1995).

be kept as a mark of difference. Nations might be defined according to their laws and their systems of interdiction and so a Hindu was to be kept in his place and differentiated according to the law to which he appealed. The Hindus are Hindus by virtue of their laws. The point is certainly implied by Forbes in his criticism of early attempts by the English to abolish the practice of *suti*: "If we are to govern Hindoos by their own laws, why do we tear them up by their roots, they are no longer Hindoos if they are subject to innovation."[56]

III. The Sublime Universality of Laws

There was more, however, to this process of translation than the control and manipulation of positive laws. For Jones, and here his attitude was symptomatic of contemporary jurisprudential concerns, there was a genuine recognition of the spirit of Hindu law that actually refers him to similarities and connections between Eastern and Western notions of legality. Or, put slightly differently, the spirit of Hindu law refers to the other face of European legality that Jones and common law lawyers such as Blackstone had been trying to recuperate throughout the eighteenth century. In what seems like typical apologia, linking a legal system to the manners and civilization of its people, the following passage introduces Jones's recognition and obsession with the idea of legal sublimity.

> It is a maxim in the science of legislation and government that *laws are of no avail without manners*, or, to explain the sentence more fully, that the best intended legislative provisions would have no beneficial effect even at first unless they were congenial to the disposition and habits, to the religious prejudices, and approved immemorial usages, of the people, for whom they were enacted; especially if that people universally believed that all their ancient usages and established rules of conduct had the sanction of an actual revelation from heaven.[57]

[56] FORBES, *supra* note 48, at 318.
[57] Jones, *supra* note 32, at 75.

While this idea of antiquity and sublime revelation is a feature of Hindu law, it also resonates with the reflections on the original time and place of the common law that had been rattling around its own lawyers' minds. Eighteenth century doctrinalists frequently used the category of the sublime to describe the complexity, disorder and obscurity of the common law. For Blackstone in particular, this irregular form of the law was founded in an idea of nature from which England was to derive the law of the land.[58] Like the sublime ruins of gothic castles, churches and abbeys, the law was magnificent, venerable, winding, difficult, inspiring and at times neglected. Far from rendering it defunct, the idea of neglect simply meant that common law contained latent, undiscovered perfections. It was because of its sublime nature that the law was capable of evolving new and beautiful solutions to problems: "my system is formed; and I did not carry it to the law, but found it in the law."[59] A second level of analysis, beyond the practical concerns of authority, has to be considered. Here, the focus is on similarity rather than difference. That both Hindu law and common law shared ideas about their beginnings and celebrated their obscurity in similar ways might seem like a weak comparison, but to Jones and other Orientalists of the Asiatic Society it implied that both systems may well have emerged from the mists of a common time immemorial and from a common place. It is at this mystical and sublime moment, whose precise date was lost in the labyrinth of astronomical cycles, that Jones saw the familial connection between Eastern and Western sources of law: "the Hindus believe [their law] to be almost as old as creation. It is ascribed to MENU, the MINOS of India, and like him, the son of JOVE." [60]

In this respect, eighteenth century jurisprudential claims that English law was to boost its legitimacy if it "conformed to the norms of a community of legal systems" have to be remembered.[61]

---

[58] Further DANIEL J. BOORSTIN, THE MYSTERIOUS SCIENCE OF THE LAW: AN ESSAY ON BLACKSTONE'S COMMENTARIES (1996).

[59] JONES, *supra* note 12, at 383 (Letter to Earl Spencer).

[60] *Id.* at 440 (Letter to Patrick Russell). Read also *Id.* at 464 (Letter to Earl Spencer, in which Jones described Menu as "the first created man, many millions of years old").

[61] BOORSTIN, *supra* note 58, at 45.

Familial connections were essential to the iconic unity of the English law. As Jones put it: "The great system of jurisprudence like that of the Universe, consists of many subordinate systems, all of which are connected by nice links and beautiful dependencies."[62] Correspondences were even sought and found between the laws of Manu and Justinian's *pandectae*:

> If we had a complete digest of Hindu and Muhammedan laws, after the model of Justinian's inestimable Pandects, compiled by the most learned of native lawyers, with an accurate verbal translation of it into English; and if copies of the work were reposited in the proper offices [...] of the Supreme Court, that they might occasionally be consulted as a standard of justice, we should rarely be at a loss for principles at least and rules of law applicable to the cases before us. [...] The great work, of which *Justinian* has the credit, consists of texts collected from law-books of approved authority, which in his time were extant at Rome; and those texts are digested according to a scientifical analysis; the names of the original authors, and the titles of their several books, being constantly cited with references even to parts of their works, from which the different passages were selected; but although it comprehends the whole system of jurisprudence [...] that vast compilation was published, we are told, in three years; with all its imperfections, it is a most valuable mine of juridical knowledge; it gives law at this hour to the greatest part of Europe; and though few English lawyers dare make such an acknowledgement, it is the true source of nearly all our English laws that are not feudal in origin. It would not be unworthy of a British government to give the

[62] WILLIAM JONES, AN ESSAY ON THE LAW OF BAILMENTS 173 (1998).

> natives of these Indian provinces a permanent security for the due administration of justice among them, similar to that which Justinian gave to his Greek and Roman subjects. The labour of the work would also be greatly diminished by two compilations already made in Sanscrit and Arabick, which approach nearly in merit and in method, to the Digest of Justinian. [...] The *Vivadarnava [Bridge over the Sea of Litigation*] consists, like the Roman Digest, of authentick texts, with the names of their several authors regularly prefixed to them, and explained where an explanation is requisite, in short notes taken from commentaries of high authority.[63]

Even at the mundane level of individual rules of contract or inheritance, familial connections between the common law and other legal systems had to be sought and found.[64] As Boorstin, commenting on Blackstone, noted: "the ancient or foreign rule is first used to explain, and then to justify the English institution." Jones provided the following example:

> That the Hindus were in early ages a *commercial* people, we have many reasons to believe; and in the first of their sacred law-tracts, which they suppose to have been revealed by MENU many *millions* of years ago, we find a curious passage on the legal *interest* of money, and the limited state of it in different cases, with an exception, which the sense of mankind approves, and which commerce absolutely requires, though it was not before the reign of CHARLES I that our own jurisprudence fully admitted it in respect of maritime contracts.[65]

---

[63] JONES, *supra* note 12, at 485 (Letter to Lord Cornwall).
[64] BOORSTIN, *supra* note 58, at 44.
[65] Jones, *supra* note 24.

There was, then, no clear discrimination against this foreign legal order. The word "foreign" simply meant "ancient", and "ancient" meant the possibility that at some time – beyond human memory – Hindu, Roman and common law systems were conjoined or even identical.

Further, what was to prove beneficial to the imperial enterprise was that this universal law had universal jurisdiction and applied across the whole human race irrespective of differences. That the Hindu code of laws was comparable to the codes of Roman law points to the place of the legal text in classical ideas of imperialism. These comparisons and connections appealed to Roman imperial policy according to which the essence of legal authority devolved from the textual body of its laws. Similarly, Manu was to replace the Pandects as law's *ur*-text and transfer its authority right across the globe. After all: "Legislative provisions have not the individual for their object, but the species; and are not made for the convenience of the day but for the regulation of ages."[66] Even in this age of reason, law was to be considered universal, beyond mere geography, and as deriving from, as well as revealed by, the gods. For Jones, "[Hooker's] idea of heavenly law is just and noble; and human law as derived from it, must partake of the phrase as far as it is perfectly administered."[67]

The universality of law, so crucial to the idea of empire, did not derive from differentiating Western from Eastern jurisprudence. It was based on their similarities, or at least a similarity in so far as both posited a mysterious and sublime cause at the center of their institutional organization.

IV. The "Dread Force of Law"

In the context of imperialism, the sublimity of Hindu laws offered the English further advantages. The sublime was connected with power, and control over the sublime would be control over

---

[66] William Jones, *Charge to the Grand Jury*, 1785, *in* 3 THE WORKS OF SIR WILLIAM JONES IN 13 VOLUMES *supra* note 6, at 3.

[67] JONES, *supra* note 12, at 516 (Letter to John Shore). The text Jones referred to is "of law there can be no less acknowledged, than that her seat is the bosom of God, her voice the harmony of the world." Richard Hooker, *Of the Laws of Ecclesiastical Polity, in Id.* at 835–836.

power: "I know of nothing sublime" stated Burke, "which is not some modification of power."[68] Or as Jean-Luc Nancy put it: "In the sublime, enjoyment touches, moves, that is also commands."[69] For Burke as well as later romantics such as Jones and Forbes, the sublime was rooted in objects that are obscured from sight; darkness, confusion, ignorance and terror are what excited romantic passions. Just as the dread of night and the fear of ghosts lay in their obscure forms, the despot was one who exercised his form of justice in private: "Those despotic governments, which are founded on the passions of men, and principally upon the passion of fear, keep their chief as much as may be from the public eye."[70] It was this inaccessible private domain, a common-place in gothic fiction, that characterised despotic enjoyment as exclusive, absolute and terrifying.

In dressing its own prehistory with a mantle of sublimity, in emphasising its obscure origins, the law was to occupy the place of the despotic potentates; the law was to inherit the exercise of power by replacing the "dread majesty"[71] of the Sultans. As Nietzsche put it, legal authority rests on "the assumption that the rationale of every law is not human in origin, that it was not sought and found after ages of error, but that it is divine in its origin, completely and utterly without a history, a gift, a miracle, a mere communication."[72] To reveal the origins of law as something positive, as opposed to divine, would be to obviate its imperative tone. "To draw up a law-book like Manu's, is tantamount to granting to a people mastership for the future, perfection for the future, – the right to aspire to the highest Art of Life. To that end, the law must be made unconscious: this is the object of every holy lie."[73]

[68] EDMUND BURKE, A PHILOSOPHICAL ENQUIRY INTO THE ORIGIN OF OUR IDEAS OF THE SUBLIME AND BEAUTIFUL 69 (1844).

[69] Jean-Luc Nancy, *The Sublime Offering, in* OF THE SUBLIME: PRESENCE IN QUESTION 52 (Jeffrey Librett ed., 1993).

[70] BURKE, *supra* note 68, at 65.

[71] Jones, *supra* note 66, at 20.

[72] FRIEDRICH NIETZSCHE, THE ANTI-CHRIST (Thomas Common trans., 1930). For a pertinent analysis read Adam Gearey, *The Fourth Book of the Legislator: Nietzsche and John Neville Figgis, in* NIETZSCHE AND LEGAL THEORY; HALF WRITTEN LAWS 165-185 (Peter Goodrich and Mariane Valverde eds., 2005).

[73] NIETZSCHE, *supra* note 72, at 56. Further WENDY DONIGER, THE LAWS OF MANU xv (1991) .

This shift from the denigration of despotic enjoyment to the use of its energies (*puissance*) in the more socially acceptable form of law can be traced through Jones's own work. Jones expressed two differing opinions on the question of despotic power. On one hand, he naturally stood opposed: "My temperament cannot stomach the arrogance of princes and nobles."[74] He reiterated the point in comparing press gangs to Oriental tyranny: "Be assured, my dear lord, that while the *illegal* power of pressing subsists, the peasantry are no more free than the people of Constantinople or Morocco. It is only a base mode of exercising cruel tyranny."[75] On the other, he saw in the process of sublimation the chance to convert the excess energy of Oriental forms into something useful. In this light, Jones's comments on using the Hindu oath in the English courts, which required witnesses to be sworn by a Brahmin in front of consecrated fire, are important. In his address to the grand jury, Jones explained at length why the phrasing of the Hindu oath is necessarily so awful:

> because, though in form it invokes the Supreme Being as a defender, yet by implication it addresses Him as an avenger; and though it openly expresses a benediction, yet it virtually implies imprecation: the expression could not be full, without raising too violent and too painful an image [...] a sublimer idea could not enter the mind of man; since it is a clear deduction of reason, that the bare suspension of the Divine energy but for a moment, would cause the instantaneous dissolution of all worlds, and the tumultuous extinction of all who inhabit them.[76]

The figure of punishment invoked by Jones bears the same features – the black complexion and the red eyes – as the terrifying gods that previous travellers had denigrated as idolatrous symbols of polytheistic excess. It is exemplary of common law jurisprudence

[74] JONES, *supra* note 12, at 93 (Letter to Henry Albert Schultens).
[75] *Id.* at 268 (Letter to Viscount Althrop).
[76] Jones, *supra* note 66, at 20.

that any such fantasies of excess come to be assimilated and monopolised rather than rejected. Jones was as easily drawn to the idea of an alien deity such as Kali as he was to the sublime powers of despotic excess:

> In general I observe, that the *Hindu* writers have exalted ideas of criminal justice, and in their figurative style, introduce the *person of punishment* with great sublimity: 'Punishment' they say 'with a black complexion and a red eye, inspires terror, but alarms the guilty only;' Punishment guards those who sleep, nourishes the people, secures the state from calamity, and produces the happiest consequences in a country where it is justly inflicted; where unjustly, the magistrate cannot escape censure, nor nation, adversity.[77]

These once terrifying figures of Oriental excess were, in other words, to inform eighteenth century jurisprudence and to provide the law with a theoretical dias from which to instruct.

V. *The Law-Givers: Manu, Solon, Tribonian, Jones*

The process of sublimation thus converted the exclusive enjoyment of the Sultans and the obscene excesses of religious idolatry into more accepted and useful forms of control. The sublime allows power to emerge and to be posited as legitimate force. However, just as superabundant enjoyment distinguished the despot from his subjects, so too sublime power conferred a similar, but more accepted, status on the judge/legislator. The Oriental despot held a particular place as a mediator and messenger of the gods. According to Alain Grosrichard, the despot had to submit to the law because submission endowed the law with universal characteristics.[78] At the same time, because the law was regarded as universal, it empowered him to act and speak imperatively.

---

[77] *Id.*

[78] ALAIN GROSRICHARD, THE SULTAN'S COURT, EUROPEAN FANTASIES OF THE EAST 92–93 (Liz Heron trans., 1998).

The law created the despot, and the despot created the law. That the despot was simultaneously subject to the law and in a unique position to create the law might be characterised in terms of a split. If so, this split is arguably what allows the charisma of authority to emerge.

This same split economy of power and of jurisdiction is discernable if we examine Jones's own position in relation to the universal jurisdiction of law. For Jones readily submitted to the sublimity of a universal law. But he did so in order to occupy a unique position of power as a law-giver. Jones maintained his submission before the law throughout his writings. In a letter to Earl Spencer, he declared his refusal to take sides in the battle between Burke and Hastings prior to the latter's impeachment. His allegiances are only to aspects of the law. Thus he has "an equity-side, a common-law-*side*, an ecclesiastical *side*, and an admiralty-*side*, but I am quadrilateral by act of parliament"[79] Jones's quadrilateral nature (Janus squared) involves his submission to a higher cause: "it is my sole duty to convey law as though a channel."[80]

Jones's subservient relationship to the law conformed to the correct manners demanded of its institution. Yet this passive position within the dogmatic structure of the law assigned Jones to a particular place that distinguished him from those other (pre) colonial subjects of law over whom he held authority. He was no mere passive recipient of the law but a messenger and conduit of an already established truth. Jones recognised the power conferred upon him over his subjects. It is a power, he freely admitted, that made him tremble: "All the police and judicial power, therefore, of this settlement, where at least half a million of natives reside, are in my hands: I tremble at the power, which I possess."[81]

The simultaneity of passivity and authority is more pertinently discernable in relation to the translations of the legal codes. For Jones was here more than a judge; "I speak the *language of the Gods* as the Brahmens call it, and am engaged in superintending

[79] JONES, *supra* note 12, at 383 (Letter to Earl Spencer).
[80] *Id.*
[81] *Id.*

a *Digest* of Indian law for the benefit of *twenty four millions* of black subjects in these provinces."[82] Jones bestowed upon himself the status of a law-giver and continually referred to himself as occupying the same position as that of Solon. Indeed, Jones admitted to a position that Solon would have envied.

> I have the delight of knowing that my studies go hand in hand with my duty, since I now read both Sanscrit and Arabik with so much ease, that the native lawyers can never impose upon the courts, in which I sit. I converse fluently in Arabik with the Maulavis, in Sanscrit with the Pandits, and in Persian with the nobles of the country; thus possessing an advantage which neither Pythagoras nor Solon possessed, though they must ardently have wished it.[83]

Given that the sublimity of law renders it universal, the law-giver need not be specifically Greek. The law-giver might take on a number of providential guises. Jones is thus able to describe himself as a reincarnation of Manu himself, who "having written the laws of BRAHMA in a hundred thousand couplets, arranged under *twenty-four* heads in a *thousand* chapters presented them to the primitive world."[84] What Manu presented to the primitive world, Jones, the modern-day amanuensis, was to present to the civilized world of European judges and governors-general. In a private letter sent from Calcutta to London in 1786 in which Jones expressed his plans for the systematic translation and compilation of Hindu and Mohameddan laws, Jones likened himself to Tribonian, the compiler of the Justinian code, and declared that the mantle of Justinian himself was to fall upon his patron, Lord Cornwallis, the governor-general of Bengal.[85] Jones's personal pundit or Maulavy, Mujdudden, is given the title *omni exceptione major* (beyond contradiction) taken from Justinian's institutes.[86]

---

[82] *Id.*
[83] JONES, *supra* note 12, at 483 (Letter to Henry Dundas).
[84] Jones, *supra* note 32, at 84.
[85] JONES, *supra* note 12, at 409 (Letter to John Macpherson).
[86] *Id.*

The category of the sublime thus clears a space to be occupied by a mediating figure. As Pierre Legendre put it: "In theology, the power of God or absolute place of the mythical Third must always pass through a mediating figure – that of the pope, the emperor or the priest – before it becomes an object of subjective attachment."[87] Similarly, in Jones's imperial jurisprudence, it is the law-giver-Manu, Solon, Justinian or Jones himself – who is to occupy that charismatic position as mediator between the Gods and his subjects.

VI. The Affect of Subjectivity

In sublimating excess enjoyment and rendering a mythological status for himself and for the British, Jones constructed a domain of affection out of the law. Face to face with the terrifying powers of the sublime, the subject has no option but to be dominated and thereby defined. For Jones, the power of the legal sublime found in the Hindu scriptures provides for a replication of Burke's theory at the level of legal subjectivity. The legal sublime renders urgent the question of devotion and belief. Consider his description of Manu. Even though it is "a system of despotism and priestcraft", or perhaps due to this, the Hindu laws of Manu, are imbued with:

> a spirit of sublime devotion, of benevolence to mankind, and of amiable tenderness to all sentient creatures, pervades the whole work; the style of it has a certain austere majesty, that sounds like the language of legislation and exerts a respectful awe; the sentiments of independence on all beings but God, and the harsh admonitions, even to Kings, are truly noble, and the many panegyrics on the Gayatri, the mother, as it is called, of the Vedas, prove the author to have adored [...] that divine and incomparably greater light, to use the words of the most venerable text in the Indian scripture, which illumines all,

[87] PIERRE LEGENDRE AND PETER GOODRICH, LAW AND THE UNCONSCIOUS: A LEGENDRE READER 262 (Peter Goodrich, Alain Pottage and Anton Schutz trans., 1997).

> delights all, from which all proceeds, to which all must return, and which alone can irradiate (not our visual organs merely, but or souls, and) our intellects.[88]

In establishing this affective domain, the sublime is used for the psychoanalytical control and institution of the subject. The terror of the sublime and the suggestion that laws derive from origins exceeding mortal man established the proper emotional attachment to the law. Sublime enjoyment revolves around the idea that man is small when he confronts the vastness of nature. It is from this standpoint that the subject is confronted with his own limits. The numerous drawings and paintings by romantic artists in India recording the microscopic detail of everyday life reflected the concern with the interiority and contours of subjective life. They were also concerned with the way in which subjective life was instituted. As James Beattie observed: "Grammarians are not agreed about the etymology of the word sublime. The most probable is that it may be derived from supra and limus; and so denotes literally the circumstance of being raised above the slime, the mud, or the mould of this world."[89]

Such a concern for circumscribing subjective life was consciously transferred into the jurisprudential sphere by Jones. The legal subject per Jones is not a self defined entity. Rather, as the author has argued, subjectivity is to be defined only in relation to the vast sublimity of law. In the context of colonial legality, the translation of the Hindu law codes and the subsequent theorization of the sublimity of law was a key moment in the colonization and cultivation of subjectivity. Faced with the sublimity of law, the legal subject has no option but to give himself up to it. What we have seen from the numerous quotations from Jones's writing is a confidence to talk now about the Hindus and Muslims as subjects. The process of sublimating excess enjoyment simultaneously

---

[88] William Jones, *Ninth Discourse on the Origin and Families of Nations*, in 3 THE WORKS OF SIR WILLIAM JONES IN 13 VOLUMES, *supra* note 6, at 62.

[89] James Beattie, *Treatise*, 1783, *quoted in* Sue Chaplin, *How the Sublime Comes to Matter in Eighteenth Century Legal Discourse – An Irigarayan Critique of Hobbes, Locke and Burke*, 9(3) FEMINIST LEGAL STUDIES 204 (2001).

converts the Oriental individual into a subject of law. Such confidence was decidedly born of the translation of the Hindu law as a sublime source of authority.

D. CONCLUSION

The sublime provides a terrifying yet empty space from which to instruct and colonise the subject. The category of the sublime allows *man* to move away from the feminine, the *gayatri*, or the formlessness towards rationality.[90] That the sublime was to be found through Orientalism and was considered relevant to Western (common law) juridical thought is significant, as it unmasks the other face of Europeanism. The application of Jones's project was not limited to the commercial interests of the East India Company. The translation of Manu was not an attempt to recreate an alternative history of the law, but to ascertain the origins of the essence of law and the secrets of its subjectivity. What was needed was an idea of universal subjection and submission not to the state or a monarch but to the law as a universal phenomenon mediated by the judge as *sublimis*. The romantic fantasy of Oriental excess uncovered the theoretical arsenal needed to establish this omni-jurisdictionality. It exposed a desire to institute a terrifying excess as the presupposition of legal universalism. In drawing out the perceived similarities between Hindu law and the common law, Jones provided a plan for a universal law in which *all* are to be subjects of the law. By the eighteenth century, Oriental excess was to provide the co-ordinates by which the legal subject was to be dominated by the law.

---

[90] Per Jones the "laws of the ancient legislator are obscure when detached, yet clear when connected." JONES, *supra* note 12, at 584 (Letter to Edward Hay). It is precisely this process of finding connections that rationalises the Oriental sublime spirit of Oriental law.

6

"Thank You India": Lessons from the 4th International Conference on Federalism,

New Delhi, 5–7 November 2007

MALCOLM MACLAREN

A. INTRODUCTION

Some words said in closing to the International Conference on Federalism in New Delhi (hereinafter 4th ICF) could not help but bring to mind the lyrics of an old pop song: "Thank you India", said George Anderson, President of the Forum of Federations,[1] echoing the well-known refrain of Alanis Morissette. In her hit single "THANK U", Morissette expresses gratitude to India for the life lessons she learned during a visit. Anderson's words provoked at least this audience member to reflect upon "Unity in Diversity" and to "learn [...] from each other", the ICF's overall theme and goal. Ironically, the lessons that the author draws are not dissimilar from Morissette's: "clarity", "consequence", and "disillusionment". For these valuable lessons the author would like to express gratitude too, namely to the Indian Government, the Conference host.

B. THE PROCEEDINGS

The 4th ICF was above all notable for its scope and ambition. It was the biggest of the triennial conferences so far,[2] bringing

[1] Most materials cited are available at http://www.forumfed.org/en/global/indiaconference.php or http://www.federalism2007.org/.

[2] The previous ICFs were held in Mont Tremblant, Canada in 1999; St. Gallen, Switzerland in 2002; and Brussels, Belgium in 2005.

together 1,300 participants from 116 countries as well as a great variety of practitioners of federalism (including elected officials at all levels of government, civil servants, academics, and community activists). The 3-day long programme consisted of 6 plenaries, 8 dialogue tables, and 24 work sessions, all held at the premier conference venue in India.[3] The Conference plenaries were occasion for welcome addresses, keynote speeches, and votes of thanks, including from the heads of government of Comoros, Ethiopia, India, and Switzerland. The dialogue tables, in parallel to one another, gave participants the opportunity to discuss four themes: "building on and accommodating diversity", "fiscal federalism", "interaction in a federal system", and "local governments in federal systems". The two sets of work sessions were dedicated to examining 12 sub-themes in the form of 24 generic questions with each question being introduced by case studies from around the world.[4]

C. THE CONFERENCE BACKDROP

The elaborate design of the programme was intended to stimulate thinking on the sweeping theme of "Unity in Diversity" and to facilitate participants' "Learning from Each Other", which was the Conference's goal. The 4th ICF's theme and goal were similar to those of the 3rd ICF, which was held under the title "Federalism: Turning diversity into harmony, sharing best practices" two years earlier in Brussels. The Conferences take place, however, in particular federal contexts, and each reflects the special culture and personality of the host country.[5] As seemingly every Indian who spoke at the Conference noted, the 4th ICF was being held in the world's most diverse country, the world's largest federation, and the world's largest democracy. India, second in population only to China, is home to an incomparable variety of languages,

[3] *Conference Programme, 4th ICF.*

[4] The author attended all the plenaries and selected to participate in the dialogue tables on "Building on and accommodating diversity" and in the work sessions 1 and 13 on the related sub-themes "Can unity and diversity be reconciled?" (introduced by examples of India, Malaysia, and South Africa) and "Can deep differences be accommodated?" (introduced by examples of Ethiopia, Iraq, and Nigeria).

[5] *Conference Reflections – Past International Conferences on Federalism.*

religions, ethnicities, and cultures,[6] which co-exist as a federation under a parliamentary democracy. It was also proudly noted that the event was being held on the 60th anniversary of the Indian Republic's founding. Unlike its neighbours Pakistan, China, Nepal, Bangladesh, Myanmar, and Sri Lanka, India is a vibrant democracy. These facts were brought together in a claim made explicitly and implicitly throughout the Conference that India's political system should be considered a model for other countries.

The justification for this claim will be the focus of the following report. It is not enough to simply note these facts about contemporary India; what to make of them is open to interpretation and debate. The author's examination of this claim will take the form of three questions of increasing generality: (1) how successful has India been in reconciling unity and diversity; (2) can the success that the country has had be repeated beyond its borders; and (3) what does a case study of India suggest about the nature of federal systems and the insights that may be gained from their comparison?

The objection may at this point be raised that the claim that India's political system is a model for other countries should not be judged too rigorously, as it was not made scientifically. The claim was made, so the argument goes, by foreigners seeking advice on good governance[7] and by locals celebrating their country's diamond jubilee.[8] Such an objection overlooks the rationale behind the Conference's location as given by the organizers[9] themselves. For example, Anderson wrote in the Forum's magazine,

---

[6] On one account, Indian society comprises 1.1 billion people, 22 official languages, and over 2000 dialects; seven religious and a dozen ethnic groups, further divided into countless sects, castes, and sub-castes; as well as some sixty socio-cultural sub-regions spread over seven geographic regions in a country the size of a continent. Ahktar Majeed, *In Indien liegt der Schlüssel zur Konfliktlösung in der Verfassung*, FEDERATIONS MAGAZINE 21 (Special Issue, 2002).

[7] E.g., Ahmed A.M. Sambi, *Statement of the President of the Union of Comoros* (5 November 2007). Sambi earnestly requested governments present at the 4th ICF to support the introduction of federalism on his diverse, conflict-ridden archipelago.

[8] E.g., Somnath Chatterjee, Speaker of Lok Sabha, *Address* 1 (5 November 2007): "India [...] now is considered to be the symbol of Unity in Diversity".

[9] The 4th ICF was organized by the Inter-State Council Secretariat of the Government of India, an inter-governmental consultative body mandated to

> [t]he world [...] has much to learn from India. Thus, it is appropriate that India will host the 4th International Conference on Federalism. [...] India's experience is highly relevant to various fragile democracies in developing countries coping with deeply diverse and often conflictual societies. [...In addition,] it is relevant for long-established democracies that are coming to terms with multiculturalism and significant religious minorities".[10]

In short, the claim asks for - and will here be given - close examination. The author comes to the conclusion that it is inadequately grounded, both theoretically and empirically. He does not have an alternative understanding to offer. Instead, the contribution that he would like to make as an academic is to help frame the public debate: he will reveal unspoken assumptions, pose questions, disseminate research, and discuss the consequences of different scientific analyses. In addition, he will offer an assessment of the conception and realization of intergovernmental learning at the ICF. It is then for national leaders and electorates to determine how to proceed, since the form of state organization is ultimately a political concern.

D. LESSONS LEARNED

There is no dearth of statements by Conference participants that could be cited to the effect that India's political system should be considered a model for other countries. The participants came from a variety of backgrounds - professional, national etc. Nonetheless, all seemed to have wholeheartedly accepted the overall theme chosen for the Conference and the rationale given

---

facilitate good relations between the Union and States, and by the Forum of Federations, an Ottawa-based IGO dedicated to promoting best practices in federal government through world-wide programmes of outreach, education, and networking.

[10] George Anderson, *What India Can Show the World*, 7(1) FEDERATIONS MAGAZINE 32 (October/November 2007).

for the Conference's location. While the political speechmaking in the plenaries was inevitably going to be one-sided in content and format, the discussions at the dialogue tables and the work sessions proved to be as well. The discussions took the form of a dialogue, but the dialogue was explicitly about the renewal and development of federalism. All the participants were practitioners from countries that are already or want to be federal, and all were interested in sharing experiences and understandings of federalism.[11] Moreover, expert papers were not presented at the Conference itself; the papers that had been commissioned were sent as background reading to participants prior to it. While this organization meant that the "exegetical or scholastic debates" that can plague academic symposia were minimized,[12] it also meant that reflection on the premises of the ICF was lacking.[13] This tendency showed itself in the way in which the three questions posed above were handled in the discussions. The buzzwords 'success story', 'best practices', and 'comparative federalism', respectively, seemed to be on everyone's lips.

Such statements and buzzwords beg to be challenged. They are too sweeping, too self-assured, and too unclear. The author does not mean to suggest that participants used buzzwords mischievously; they were more likely used as shorthand where time and language constrained discussion. Similarly, the participants' desire to engage each other constructively should not be doubted; they strongly believed in the efficacy of federalism and cooperation in resolving governance concerns, especially those regarding diversity. Indeed, the collective response to each of the questions was based more on hope than on actual experience.

---

[11] Tellingly note the participation of a representative of the Scottish but not of the Westminster Parliament. *List of Participants, 4th ICF.*

[12] Amitabha Pande, Message from the Inter-State Council Secretariat, *Conference Information Booklet – 4th International Conference on Federalism* 5. (On file with author.)

[13] At times, the proceedings took on almost an anti-intellectual tone. For example, it was claimed that" an ounce of practice is worth more than a pound of theory". (Fali S. Nariman, *Federalism in India – Emerging Trends and the Way Forward* 20.)

I. *How Successful Has India Been in Reconciling Unity and Diversity? – Or the Lesson of "Clarity"*

Many Conference participants stated that India's *goal* is to achieve unity in diversity. Indeed, the term "unity in diversity" was alleged to have been coined by the leaders of India's struggle for independence.[14] There was a consensus among the Indian politicians present that the country does not fear diversity, rather it views diversity as a defining characteristic of its civilization. For example, the President of India, Pratibha Patil, said in her closing remarks that "we, in India, have understood that Unity in Diversity is the real strength of our country. By looking after the interests of each section of our diverse population we strengthen our unity".[15] This understanding has been echoed in other fora by foreign observers. "India", Thomas Friedman recently wrote in the *International Herald Tribune*, "has a culture of diversity", its leaders – from the Muslim Emperor Akbar in the 16th century to Jawaharlal Nehru, the first Prime Minister and a Hindu – have not just tolerated but have positively embraced other peoples and ideas.[16]

In equal measure, Conference participants, especially elected officials, stated that India's *achievement* is the reconciling of unity and diversity. The Republic was founded in a situation approaching chaos (partition, the largest mass migration in history, widespread violence between Hindus, Muslims, Sikhs, etc.); India's federation seemed destined to fail (not least because the 500-odd principalities and reconstituted States lacked experience of government in common); since independence, India has faced "virtually every challenge known to politics" (from wars through domestic insurgencies to an eighteen-month long state of emergency).[17] Despite these strains and obstacles, India has experienced "success in making representative government

[14] Anna-Elisabeth Haselbach, *Statement of the Vice-President of the Federal Council of Austria* (6 November 2007).

[15] Pratibha Patil, *Valedictory Address of the President of India* (7 November 2007).

[16] Thomas Friedman, *Democracy's Root: Diversity*, INTERNATIONAL HERALD TRIBUNE (11 November 2007).

[17] Anderson, *supra* note 10.

work in a bewilderingly diverse country".[18] The measure of India's success, continues Friedman, is made plain by comparing its experience with Pakistan's (or, as various participants added, Sri Lanka, Bangladesh, and Nepal's). "[T]hey are basically the same people, they look alike, they eat the same food, they dress alike". Yet, where India's commitment to democracy, federalism, and respect for diversity has been reaffirmed, "Pakistan, right next door, is melting down".[19] A local political scientist expressed the feelings of many compatriots at the Conference: "I sincerely hope that this conference will secure, once and for all, the place of India in the comity of federal nations as a mature and robust federal union".[20]

The claim of India's success was made even more stridently at other moments during the Conference. President Patil's speech reached a climax when she stated that "Indians celebrate their varied cultures, festivals, and religions and they effortlessly unite to make India a great nation".[21] By this point in the narrative, even the relatively uninformed reader will question whether the reality matches the rhetoric. It is well known that communal, regional, and caste tensions continue to haunt Indian politics, sometimes threatening its democratic and secular ethos. President Patil's exaggerated statement seems more like an attempt to promote unity in the Indian diversity than to document it.[22]

---

[18] Mukul Kesavan *in* Balveer Arora, *Introduction to the Themes of the Conference: An Indian Perspective* § 10.

[19] Friedman, *supra* note 16.

[20] Arora, *supra* note 18, at § 5.

[21] P. Patil, *supra* note 15.

[22] The official photo that was sent out on the newswires of the Sikh Prime Minister celebrating New Year's Day with the Muslim Vice-President in a predominantly Hindu country has a similarly constitutive rather than declaratory air about it. While representatives of minority groups may go about public life without any visible anxiety about their identity and rights, the same cannot be said of members of minorities generally. In many parts of India, minorities make little show of their distinct identities, but they live "with downcast eyes". A lobby group's description of the everyday reality of Muslims in Gujarat, *in Gujarat – A la Modi*, ECONOMIST 48 (5 January 2008).

The author cannot attempt here to give a comprehensive state of the union or society in India today,[23] but can only offer some impressions. These impressions strongly suggest that while the achievement of the Republic's 60th anniversary and the contrast with neighbouring Pakistan may be cause for satisfaction and pride, other events and trends in India today are decidedly not.

- Most recently, the Hindu-nationalist chief minister of Gujarat was re-elected with a large majority, though he has been implicated in the 2002 anti-Muslim riots in the State that left 2,000 dead. Before his re-election in December 2007, Narendra Modi was "already the most controversial figure in Indian politics. He may now become one of the most influential".[24] Gujarat's chief minister is aiming to seize control of the leadership of the country's main opposition party, the Bharatiya Janata Party (BJP), with his divisive populism. Perhaps most worrisome about the State election is that Congress, India's other main, but secularist, party, avoided mentioning the riots and Modi's alleged role in them. Congress apparently feared that doing so would remind voters "why they used to like him so much".[25] Recent incidents of religious politicking elsewhere in the country could also be mentioned.[26] The larger issue is the appeasing of the Hindu majority while integrating the many minorities, especially the 150 million Muslims. It is painfully clear that this larger issue remains unresolved.

---

[23] For two recent surveys read RAMACHANDRA GUHA, INDIA AFTER GANDHI – THE HISTORY OF THE WORLD'S LARGEST DEMOCRACY (2007); MARTHA C. NUSSBAUM, THE CLASH WITHIN – DEMOCRACY, RELIGIOUS VIOLENCE AND INDIA'S FUTURE (2007). For a review of both read David Arnold, *Sixty-Year Views*, TIMES LITERARY SUPPLEMENT 10 (24 & 31 August 2007).

[24] Gujarat, *supra* note 22.

[25] *Gujarat's Election – Don't Mention the Massacre,* ECONOMIST 63 (8 December 2007). Similarly Amelia Gentleman, *Amid Gujarat Campaign, Memories of Mass Killings in 2002 Still Smoulder*, INTERNATIONAL HERALD TRIBUNE (6 December 2007).

[26] The failure of the then BJP-led Uttar Pradesh State Government to prevent Ayodhya's Babri Masjid being destroyed by Hindu nationalists in 1992 displays some unsettling parallels to the anti-Muslim riots. It also involved a complete rejection of national commitments to secularism and democracy. In contrast to the latter incident, however, the earlier incident mobilized secularists, and the State Government in Uttar Pradesh was soundly defeated at the subsequent election.

- Insurgencies remain a serious problem in India, posing an important threat to domestic security additional to the Hindu-Muslim violence.[27] Armed attacks by Maoist Naxalites in central India have, in fact, intensified in the last years. The conflict in the northeast with the separatist United Liberation Front of Assam has continued. Bombings have failed to disrupt local elections, but peace-talks have not made any progress. The long-running dispute in Kashmir has a special history and presents its own particular challenge. Nonetheless, the hundreds of thousands of lives lost in internal clashes there since independence speak to a massive failure to achieve unity in diversity through federalism.

- Social tensions have loomed large of late. Sectarian and caste tensions have led to highway blockades, mass protests, and police killings in different parts of the country. Most notably, agitation within the Sikh community in Punjab and between scheduled and non-scheduled tribes in Rajasthan threatens to break out into widespread violence.[28]

- Specifically as regards federalism, several issues are outstanding whose resolution will decide how the Indian Republic functions long term. These include the unequal size of the States, disparities in economic and social development between and within regions, and management of natural resources amid growing inter-dependence. More fundamental, and possibly most decisive, is a concern raised by the Indian Prime Minister at the ICF, namely the distortion of the national vision and collective purpose by narrow political considerations based on regional or sectional loyalties and ideologies.[29]

These examples of chauvinism, domestic insurgencies, social tensions, and federal disputes undermine claims of the success of India's federal democracy in adopting an inclusive polity; politics as it is lived everyday diverges significantly from the official statements of President Patil *et al.* These examples suggest

---

[27] "India [...] is a violent place. In each of the past two years, [...] India lost around 1,300 lives to terrorism, putting it second only to Iraq". *India – Mad and Hyderabad,* ECONOMIST 44 (1 September 2007).

[28] *India's Sikhs – Heresy and History,* ECONOMIST 55 (7 July 2007).

[29] Manmohan Singh, *Inaugural Address of the Prime Minister of India* 3 (5 November 2007).

that the political system remains vulnerable, and they caution against complacency in dealing with the diverse aspirations of the people.[30]

In this regard, contemporary India seemed better captured by an outreach festival held in parallel to the ICF. This NGO-led event sought to mirror the discussions among participants in the Conference venue by involving ordinary citizens with the issues of governance in a nearby park.[31] *Sanjha Safar* offered the public opportunities for cultural exchange as well as an interactive platform in an effort to make ideas of decentralization and participation actual and tangible to a larger audience. Starting from the premise that the concept of federalism has yet to be duly recognized and realized within India, it celebrated the "fruits" of a federal form of state organization – namely "diversity, empowerment and interconnectivity" – and engaged citizens in a dialogue about how phrases like unity in diversity and citizen-government relationships play out for them. The outreach festival's understanding and approach came across as realistic and constructive in a way that the ICF's at times did not.[32]

II. Can the Success that India has had be Repeated in Other Countries? – Or the Lesson of "Consequence"

To date, the Republic of India has defied manifold predictions of the imminent failure of its secular, federal democracy. The attempt to build on and accommodate diversity, rather than to impose uniformity, has not fragmented and destabilized the country and its people, contrary to warnings of foreign experts.

---

[30] One plenary speaker's assessment of the contemporary situation was more sceptical. Meghnad Desai, the Anglo-Indian economist, argued that since 1989, there has not been a single national purpose, such as the freedom struggle or secularism, that all Indians agree upon. Bollywood and cricket have facilitated national cohesion instead. "A whole new story needs to be created as to why India is a nation with a true and organic unity in diversity and not one presumed". Meghnad Desai, *Unity in Diversity* (revised), INDIAN EXPRESS (29 November 2007).

[31] Specifically, the festival provided a platform for public hearings, youth parliaments, and children's workshops as well as opportunities for selected groups from different parts of India to learn about each other's customs through exhibitions, performances, and food and handicraft stands.

[32] As a report on the outreach festival argued, "[a]ny conceptual learning needs to be complemented through the actual ground based knowledge of challenges

(The Constitution, for example, was deemed by an eminent British constitutional historian at its enactment to be "too long, too detailed and too rigid".[33]) It is more difficult, however, to explain how exactly the country has been able to maintain its unity than it is to document and detail diversity.[34] At a minimum, it is agreed that India did not survive by copying the West. The founders – particularly M.K. Gandhi, Jawaharlal Nehru, B.R. Ambedkar, and Vallabhbhai Patel – had their own vision of the Republic, which they tenaciously sought to realize. The problems that faced their country, so the collective thinking went, were different from those of other countries and therefore called for different solutions. India's resultant constitutional structure diverged significantly from the then dominant tenets of federalism; it crafted its own political institutions; and it built on its own traditions. Since India's founding, its political system has evolved and adapted to changing situations, most notably through repeated constitutional amendments. This process has likewise been characterized by departures from existing templates and experiences elsewhere.

In short, the country poses an incomparable fact pattern, which has been addressed largely by unconventional means and with widely unexpected success. The Republic of India is "an ungainly, unlikely, inelegant concatenation of differences" that, decades after its foundation, still exists as a single political unity.[35] Some novelties of its political system may be cited:

- The scale, context, and functioning of democracy in India are without compare, especially among decolonized states. India has held 14 general elections under universal suffrage, with some 400 million casting votes in the latest in May 2004. The number of elected representatives in the Indian system is also the largest ever anywhere. This is in a country where the GDP is less than US $500 per capita, and fewer

---

to development". Briefing the Volunteers at Sanjah Safar, *Conference Newsletter* 3 (8 November 2007).

[33] Ivor Jennings *in* Nariman, *supra* note 13, at 1.

[34] Arora, *supra* note 18, at § 11.

[35] SUNIL KHILNANI, THE IDEA OF INDIA 179 (2nd ed. 2003). For a review of the 1st edition *see* Amartya Sen, *The Vision That Worked,* TIMES LITERARY SUPPLEMENT 3 (8 August 1997).

than two adults in three are literate. Indian democracy is vibrant, characterized by popular participation in politics and elections, innumerable political parties, a vital and free press, as well as a dynamic pluralist culture.

- Not only does India as a whole display astounding diversity, but so do its parts. Both the Union and the States must constantly mediate disputes between different identities and seek to reduce disparities in the population. The federation has had to be reorganized severally to prove its inclusiveness, that it is able to meet the aspirations (linguistic in particular) of its people.[36] Taken too far, state reorganization (especially the creation of new sub-national units) can bring 'balkanization'. The history of Nigeria offers proof. Nigeria, which once had three sub-national units, has been divided into 36 in an attempt to appease different ethnic groups. Extreme fragmentation is now a serious concern there.[37] In India, however, the attempt to achieve unity in diversity via state reorganization has so far proven successful. Many of yesterday's separatists and insurgents have changed into today's leaders and lawmakers with "remarkable ease",[38] and the Republic has remained intact.

- As befits an attempt to accommodate the world's most politically diverse population, the Constitution of India is the world's longest. Nonetheless, the word "federation", or any variant thereof, is not mentioned once.[39] The near chaos in 1947 led the founders to refuse to be bound by theory and to

---

[36] Nonetheless, the federation remains under pressure to safeguard the interests of all types of minorities. The youngest State of the Union, Jharkhand, which was created seven years ago to fulfil regional aspirations, has a comparatively small population of 28 million, but its citizens display deep differences in language, religion, caste, and economic status. Akhtar Majeed, *India's Extreme Diversity Makes Pluralism Imperative,* 7(1) FEDERATIONS MAGAZINE 10 (October/November 2007).

[37] Strengthen the Institutional Arrangements at the Grassroots Level, *Conference Newsletter* 4 (7 November 2007).

[38] Arora, *supra* note 18, at § 9. Here the example of the Gorkhas is typically cited to demonstrate that deep differences can be accommodated. In the 1980s, Gorkha nationalists in West Bengal sought to gain independence through violence; an offer of broad autonomy short of full-fledged statehood enticed advocates of the rights of Nepali-speakers to campaign non-violently as political parties in the state.

take a non-dogmatic approach to federalism. They modified established ideas about the federal government and its relations with sub-national units and created "a new kind of Federation to meet India's new kind of needs".[40] Notable here are the characteristics associated with unitary and non-unitary forms of state organization that Indian federalism combines. The country's hybrid Constitution has been (in-)famously described as "quasi-federal" or "a Unitary Constitution with federal features".[41]

- Another peculiarity of the Indian Republic is its local government, which was chosen as a theme of the Conference programme. The Constitution had always provided for three levels of government, namely Union, States, and local bodies. (The founders felt that a country of India's size and diversity would only be governable if local initiative were accorded a role.) The Constitution was, however, dramatically amended in 1993 to establish self-rule at the local level. The 73rd and 74th amendments have had a great impact on decision-making, enhancing grassroots democracy and participatory governance and furthering Gandhi's vision of India as a unity of many self-sustaining and autonomous "village republics". Specifically, bodies like *Panchayats* and *Nagar Palikas* (village and city councils) have brought over three million citizens into elected office[42] and have enabled communities to plan and implement their economic development.

Indians at the ICF, and their political representatives in particular, were keen to share their country's experience with the wider world. India, they felt, has much to contribute to other countries. (For example, its innovation in local government led to calls for

---

[39] The word "Union" was chosen in art. 1 to describe the coming together of the States.

[40] Nariman, *supra* note 13, at 3.

[41] K.C. Wheare *in Id.* at 16. Read also "India is not a federal set up in its truest form". Chatterjee, *supra* note 8, at 4. Lastly, read "Indian federalism has moved beyond textbook formulations; it bristles with many paradoxes". Ash Narain Roy, *Cajoling and compromise drive India's multi-party system*, 7(1) FEDERATIONS MAGAZINE 7 (October/November 2007).

[42] Women in particular have been empowered through an accompanying system of reservation.

power to be devolved to the grassroots elsewhere in order to strengthen unity in diversity.[43]) Attempting to repeat the success that India has had in other contexts is certainly tempting. The Indian experience seems to offer tried and true approaches to resolving difficulties of difference. It has been argued that the Indian experience is relevant for Europe, providing "interesting parallels and contrasts" to the European project of "creating a united community in an environment of huge diversity and historic tensions".[44]

Repeating the Indian experience elsewhere is, however, made problematic by the very singularity of the challenge of diversity facing India and of the political system chosen in response. The founders would have agreed with the Indian academic at the ICF who admonished participants that "[w]hile benchmarking and flagging best practices, we need also to guard against losing sight of cultural sensitivities".[45] The system that they designed corresponds to the country's situation and is a deliberate experiment in "building on and accommodating diversity".

Indeed, the novelties of the Indian political system put into question the conventional framework of discussion on governance. As a contemporary historian put it, "[i]f India didn't exist, no one would have the imagination to invent it".[46] The exercise of democracy in India is, for example, impossible to understand in terms of Athenian, and maybe any other historical or modern, democracy. These novelties have liberated political concepts from cultural contexts: "[i]n the absence of India, the prejudices about the non-West [...] would pass for wisdom".[47] Arguably,

[43] Chatterjee, *supra* note 8, at 3. Further outcome and potential for further improvements, *Conference Newsletter* 5 (8 November 2007).

[44] Anderson, *supra* note 10. Read also Haselbach, *supra* note 14, who described the European Union as another endeavour to develop unity in diversity. Lastly, read Arora, who argued that Europe will have to decide whether it wants to be the type of integrated union that India is. If it decides to be so, it will have to solve the problems that India has solved, such as multilingualism and cooperation between levels of government. Interview with Balveer Arora, *Conference Newsletter* 7 (6 November 2007).

[45] Arora, *supra* note 18, at § 12.

[46] Kesavan *in Id.* at § 10.

India's experience is so significant that the nature of diversity, democracy, and federalism themselves should be rethought.[48] It seems, for example, that if India is to remain stable and united, the competences of the Union and the States cannot be defined at the expense of each other. Paradoxically, both levels of government must be strong for the federation to be strong. (The increasingly assertive village and city councils must also be allowed sufficient space in the political system.) Taken to the extreme, the lesson to be drawn elsewhere from the Indian experience may be that there are different means to the end of unity in diversity. While federations may have the same goal and face common challenges, the public institutions, processes, and policies devised to accommodate and manage diversity must be adapted to the context and history of each country. Put otherwise, just as India's many religions remind us that there are many paths to attaining the ultimate, the novelties of its political system suggest that there are "no models, only variations on a theme".[49]

III. What Does the Indian Case Study Suggest about the Nature of Federal Systems and the Insights to be Gained in Comparing Them? – Or the Lesson of "Disillusionment"

Following on the answer to the preceding question, the influence of 'ground realities' upon the design of a political system should be examined more closely and given more weight in the analysis than they typically are. For example, the statement of the Indian External Affairs Minister that State reorganization and other peaceful changes in India's federation have been facilitated by "the core value of the unity and integrity of the nation in the constitutional scheme"[50] is wanting in its explanatory power. Legal support is undoubtedly needed to achieve a pluralistic political system, and more precisely, "a sound institutional architecture for federalism remains key to the accommodation of diversity".[51] Alone such provisions are, however, not enough.

---

[47] *Id.*

[48] Similarly "[t]he..." future of Western political theory will be decided outside the West. And in deciding that future, the experience of India will loom large." (KHILNANI, *supra* note 35, at 198.)

[49] Arora, *supra* note 18, at § 3.

[50] Pranab Mukherjee, *Keynote Address of the Minister for External Affairs of India* 8 (5 November 2007).

Lawmakers' ability to engineer particular outcomes in areas of public life that are deeply rooted in history, human beliefs, and geography should not be overestimated. Likewise, Friedman's solution for the contemporary crisis in Pakistan, namely that "Pakistan, which has as much human talent as India, could use an Akbar",[52] is facile. Friedman should be reminded that there is in Pakistan, "the Land of the Pure", an active will to dominate, to assert a national identity over distinct identities (e.g. ethnic and geographic), that has led from the founding of the state onwards to the official attempts to impose uniformity. If a country's leaders and political system are expressions of its society, Akbar could not be reincarnated as the leader of Pakistan.

Seen from the ground up, India's achievement looks quite different. Its success in reconciling unity and diversity is likely due not so much to its political 'superstructure' as to its social 'substructure'. Although it is a relatively new state, the country has a 5,000 year-old civilization. Unlike Pakistan, a country created to meet a political need, India did not have to invent its own 'story'. The Republic's founders may well have been visionaries, but what was decisive to its political history is that India enjoyed a certain sense of unity. It was not unity at a governmental level; an independent modern nation-state was not lying in waiting. It was unity at a subliminal level, a "unity based on shared values, on co-existence of diversity and on respect for alternate thoughts and ideas".[53] More specifically, the roots of federalism can be traced deep in Indian society. Through millennia, "the history of its small, self-sustaining rural communities has been primarily republican and federal".[54] The significance of federation was realized and federal republics flourished; "federation in ancient India was synonymous with unity and strength".[55]

Extensive potential for unity was, in other words, extant at independence. The challenge then, as now, was to realize this potential, to give adequate institutional expression to unity. The

[51] Neerja Gopal Jayal *in* Outcome, *supra* note 43.
[52] Friedman, *supra* note 16.
[53] Singh, *supra* note 29, at 1.
[54] Pande, *supra* note 12, at 2. Read also KHILNANI, *supra* note 35, at 17.
[55] Mukherjee, *supra* note 50, at 2.

Republic's founders sought to transform the struggle for freedom into a common project of nationhood by building upon this basis. For example, Gandhi, who feared that India might become a 'Hindu Pakistan', founded on one faith alone, sought to suppress the latent will to dominate by calling on the native traditions of peace and tolerance.[56] Enjoying a basis for political unity is, of course, not the same as realizing that unity. The task of striking the fine balance between manifold identities, of reconciling competing national and sub-national interests, and of managing contradictions between unity and diversity is not an easy one. It is, however, easier when there is a narrative of cultural heritage to be drawn upon, and much easier when that heritage is one of acceptance of heterodoxy, ongoing dialogue, and pluralism.[57]

The claim that public respect for diversity has to emerge from within the polity is for its part not one of cultural determinism. It is not meant to suggest that some traditions are more hospitable to federalism than others. (In contrast, see the overly exuberant statement of an ICF organizer that "federalism is part of the DNA of the Indian people".)[58] Instead, this claim recognizes that a functioning federal system requires "a common political will of citizens and groups of citizens to live together in harmony. Mechanisms of negotiation, conciliation and compromise [then] have to be created".[59] The success of a federation in meeting the expectations of the polity is, in other words, determined ultimately by its social embeddedness and not by its institutional framework.

If the preceding is correct, managing diversity within unity is not merely a matter of technique or of finding 'the right tools' to solve particular problems. It is also a matter of developing a common political will. Unfortunately, the treatment of the latter at the ICF was not commensurate with its importance. Some academics and

---

[56] Appropriately, the Constitution of India emphasizes not only the common future but also the common past of the Indian nation.

[57] Further AMARTYA SEN, THE ARGUMENTATIVE INDIAN: WRITINGS ON INDIAN HISTORY, CULTURE AND IDENTITY Part I (2005).

[58] Pande *in* Arnold Koller, *Welcome Address* 3 (5 November 2007).

[59] Daniel Thürer, *Analytical Written Summary for Subtheme 1.3 – 'Managing Conflict and Diversity'* § 11 (emphasis in original; on file with author).

community activists did address this matter at the dialogue tables and work sessions of theme 1. They emphasized the importance of dialogue, trust-building, and tolerance in developing the requisite will, processes that were in turn to be encouraged through civic education and civil society organizations.[60] Such contributions were, however, the exception at the ICF; elected officials and civil servants dominated the Conference, and they showed themselves to be limited in their treatment of its overall theme. Again, the alternative event about diversity and governance held near the Conference venue proved more realistic in its understanding and more constructive in its approach. The organizers of *Sanjha Safar* criticized the practice of federalism in India today as short-sighted and self-serving. This practice has, they argued, adversely affected identity and inter-connectedness: "[w]e have not been able to make our federation a federation for the people". They offered the festival as an opportunity for citizens to talk about their experiences and for youngsters to learn "to build bridges between cultures".[61]

The consequences of this claim for the significance of substructure in the design of a political system are wide reaching, both for comparative federalism as a practical and scientific undertaking and for federalism as a solution to problems of diversity. The 4th ICF, like its predecessors, was intended by its organizers to assist practitioners in meeting challenges in governance. It was based on two major premises, namely that comparing specific federal systems can provide general insights into federalism and that federalism can help promote democratic polities amid social diversity. In keeping with the organizers' intention, the Forum chairman and former Swiss President, Arnold Koller, urged participants to develop "'Principles of Federalism', in the sense of best federal practices that each federation should for its own benefit consider as a guideline that ought to be followed, and only set aside when compelling reasons so require".[62]

---

[60] Outcome, *supra* note 43.

[61] People can talk for themselves, *Conference Newsletter* 8 (7 November 2007).

[62] Koller, *supra* note 58, at 7.

If, however, substructure is so significant to the design of a political system, the rationale for gathering elected officials, civil servants, academics, and community activists from around the world to discuss federalism is cast into doubt. Specifically, it challenges the organizers' confidence in the potential of comparative federalism to enhance understanding as well as their confidence in the potential of federal governance to deal with conflicts arising out of diversity.

This first home truth was made all too plain in presentations and discussions at the ICF. Many practitioners showed themselves to be unaware, tentative, or both about studying other countries. The expert papers that had been sent to them beforehand had not had the effect intended. More discouragingly, those practitioners who were able and willing to compare systems found it difficult to move beyond platitudes about federalism. How insightful or useful are the following all-too-typical statements regarding reconciling unity and diversity from work session 1?[63] "Diversity and pluralism should be welcomed as strengths of a polity rather than as weaknesses"; "Where there is a will, there is a way"; "*globalisation* demands [...] weaving our dreams together to make this world a better place to live in"; "The world is one [...]. Every thing, living or non-living, appears to be different, but from inside they are the same. And herein lies the very understanding of 'Unity in Diversity' [...]. It is applicable to individuals, groups and units making up the federal structure".[64]

This is not to argue that due to its different history and context each federation is unique and can learn nothing from other federations.[65] That would be excessively relativistic and a self-

---

[63] These remarks unfortunately cannot be attributed to specific participants, since the Chatham House Rule was in effect at the dialogue tables and the work sessions.

[64] Most leniently, one was inclined to agree with the participant who said of the presentations, all of which answered the question posed, 'can unity and diversity be reconciled?', in the affirmative: "I remain unconvinced; I prefer the Scottish verdict 'not proven'."

[65] Similarly "[i]l existe aujourd'hui presque autant de systèmes fédéraux que de fédérations. Nous savons tous qu'un 'modèle unique' n'existe pas et que chaque pays doit trouver la formule qui lui convient." Micheline Calmy-Rey, L'unité dans la diversité: le défi et l'opportunité du fédéralisme, *Statement of the President of the Swiss Confederation* 5 (5 November 2007).

fulfilling prophecy. Practitioners should exchange experiences with and be open to learning from their foreign counterparts. Nor is it to argue that federalism as an idea has no fixed content. Such an understanding would run the risk of this form of state organization being abused by leaders for their own ends. Knowledge and technical advice regarding federalism should be disseminated to existing federations, to transitional federations, and to countries in conflict that are considering federalizing. Instead, the preceding is to argue against placing too much hope in such efforts at intergovernmental learning. There are various political strategies (*qua* institutions, policies, and practices) for the sustainable accommodation of diversity, federal or otherwise. The configurations of differences among groups can also vary between countries (by difference type, distribution, degree of mobilization, etc.). As some strategies are likely more effective in some circumstances than others, the form of state organization adopted to respond should also vary. Lastly, it may be advisable to target different strategies at the same contending group at different times or at different groups at the same time. In short, the variability of the challenges presented and of the strategies available limits the potential of comparative federalism.

Although the truth regarding the inherent capacity of federal governance may be no more welcome than that regarding comparative federalism, it is as basic. This second home truth should underlie analysis of the possibilities that federalism could offer the likes of Nepal, Sri Lanka, or Iraq (*infra*). Federalism is gaining adherents around the world today.[66] It is attractive, as it appears to enable people to deal effectively with governance concerns (e.g., realizing one's distinct identity through the political system).[67] This form of state organization should, however, be considered comprehensively and dispassionately before advocating its widespread adoption. When it is, federalism is revealed to be no panacea for all ills arising out of diversity.

[66] The federal concept is, it was often said at the ICF, a 'global movement': two-fifths of the world's population is already governed under a form of federalism, and many countries are moving towards it. Interview with Mark Tully, *Conference Newsletter* 6 (8 November 2007).

[67] Federal political systems have provided the closest institutional approximation to the complex multicultural and multi-dimensional economic, social and political reality of the contemporary world." Ronald Watts, An Introduction to the

Federalism and a federal system have not always proven viable or successful everywhere. The death of existing federations [68] should not be overlooked in celebrating the birth of new. Federalism in North Africa and the Middle East has signally proven "an idea whose time is yet to come".[69] Similarly, weaknesses inherent in a federal form of state organization should not be overlooked in favour of their strengths. Facilitating the aspirations of groups in society can, for example, lead to the reification of differences, to sub-national units turning in on themselves, to atomization of the nation, and finally to separation from the federation. Respecting diversity through federalism may work against the achievement of a legitimate and stable political order. In short, there may be difficulties of difference that a federal system, however cleverly designed and adroitly implemented, cannot manage alone. Differences relating to identity and collective self-perception are especially difficult, if not impossible, to bargain over.[70] They may prove themselves immune to resolution through the dialogue, discussion, and democratic debate among groups that federalism is to make possible.

A presentation on accommodating deep differences by an advisor for regions and governance affairs to the Iraqi Prime Minister served as a test case for this proposition. Hanan Alfatlawi shared

---

themes of the 4th International Conference, *Conference Reader – 4th International Conference on Federalism* 19. President Patil called for federalism, as a "strategic tool", to be put to service in building not only individual nations but also "an equitable global order." P. Patil, *supra* note 18. Lastly "[the concept of federalism] can evolve into a stage from where help to develop inter planetary activities by bringing all countries of the world together can be rendered". Shivraj Patil, *Keynote Address of the Home Minister of India* 6 (5 November 2007).

[68] As a participant from South Africa noted, her country is centralizing: the number of provinces and the status of implementers of national policies are being reduced.

[69] Xan Smiley, *Arab federalism, anyone?*, ECONOMIST – THE WORLD IN 2008 92 (2007). Past experiments with this form of state organization in the United Arab Republic, United Arab Emirates, and Yemen have failed. In the region today, difficulty in defining territory (in Algeria), a minority group holding out for independence (Morocco), inability to agree to division of power on the national level (Lebanon), etc., have defeated attempts at national reconciliation between contending groups by means of federalism.

[70] The contrast here is between the politics of linguistic, religious, ethnic, and cultural differentiation and that of socio-economic differentiation.

her fear that federalism in her country is "facing abortion". Its successful introduction faces innumerable challenges, the most immediate being that federalism (like democracy and rule of law) is a new term and concept in Iraq, which for three decades endured the tyranny of a minority. Today, she continued, Iraqis desire something other than a strong central government. Accommodating the contemporary divisions in Iraqi society between ethnic, linguistic, and religious groups will require mutual comprehension, common persuasion, and joint effort. Any 'solution' imposed from outside by the international community is certain not to succeed. What will ultimately determine the fate of federalism in Iraq, Ms. Alfatlawi concluded, will be the "attitude and thinking of the people".[71]

With this conclusion, we find ourselves in effect back where we started. The analysis of the Iraqi PM's advisor confirms the prior claim of substructure's significance in the design of a political system. When the two are considered together, the prospects for the success of federalism in Iraq are not promising. Indeed, a vicious circle seems to be at work. It is argued that Iraq will not survive as a single political unity unless it federalizes, federalism being the most effective strategy for managing differences. In order to realize self- and shared rule simultaneously, a federation requires respect, consideration, and support between governments on the same or different levels. More fundamentally, it requires understanding and trust among contending groups. These values must already be widespread in the society in question for federalism to be able to build upon them. Iraqi society is, however, characterized not by pluralism but by profound divisions among its various groups that are expressed in communal violence. These divisions will have to be overcome before federalism can facilitate peaceful and productive co-existence. To succeed in Iraq, federalism will have to create its own preconditions. Federalism is, however, a form of state organization for the accommodation of diversity, i.e. a strategy for conflict management and not for conflict resolution.

[71] Enroute to Federalism, *Conference Newsletter* 7 (8 November 2007).

E. OUTLOOK

In his message to the 4th ICF, the chairman of the organisation committee wrote that participants were "all coming together, for no other purpose, than to learn from one another, inspire one another and through this Conference [to] establish a truly vibrant community of federal practices". Elsewhere in the message, he stated that his country's hosting of the ICF "sends a very powerful signal to the rest of the world of India's commitment to federal values and philosophies".[72] These statements about the Conference's goal stand at cross-purposes to one another. The divergent explanations might be excused as a 'slip of the pen' but for the fact that they reveal a larger, serious flaw in the ICF's conception. This flaw, namely the event's tendency to politicization, threatens to detract from the contribution that the ICFs might make to the cause of federalism and better governance.

The Conference organizers stressed that theirs was no ordinary intergovernmental affair, nor for that matter an academic symposium or a business fair. There was to be no political grandstanding, no statements of official positions, and no negotiation of international agreements. While the principal actors were practitioners of federal democracy holding various offices at various levels, all participants were to share ideas and experiences with one another: "participants are treated equal [sic], as learners who have been provided an environment conducive to a free and frank dialogue".[73] Similarly, the Conference was structured so as to stimulate learning. Thematic dialogue tables and work sessions rather than political speeches were to constitute its core. Practitioners were expected to engage themselves fully in the discussions, to contribute to and profit from the diverse experiences and the new insights.

Unfortunately, the Conference proved unable to realize this aim due to a pervasive politicization. First, the programme worked against the organizers' stated goal. For example, the ICF was

---

[72] Pande, *supra* note 12, at 2.

[73] *Factsheet, 4th ICF.*

addressed by many local 'VVIPs', including the Indian President and former President, the Prime Minister, four Union ministers, four chief ministers, and twelve governors.[74] In addition, the content of individual presentations and discussions was politically charged. The most obvious instance of how the Conference in New Delhi was instrumentalized by the host government (foremost among other governments) came during the opening speech of the Indian Prime Minister. Though facing an international audience, Singh chose to reflect in part on a current concern of the Indian federation, namely party models and the management of Union-State relations.[75] As he presumably hoped, Singh's reflections made front-page headlines in next day's Indian newspapers. Finally, the choice itself of the country to host the event was intended to make a public statement. India's hosting of the 4th ICF was timed to coincide with the 60th anniversary of its federation. To quote the chairman of the organisation committee again, the Conference "is a celebration of human diversity, of democracy, of devolution and decentralization [...]. That the world's largest democracy plays host to this celebration in the diamond jubilee year of our independence is fitting and apt".[76]

The risk of the ICF being hijacked for political purposes is not new. The 1st ICF was used by the Canadian Prime Minister to promote federalism domestically. Deliberately held in the separatist heartland, Jean Chrétien ensured that the Conference emphasized the benefits for Quebec of remaining in the Canadian federation. The Conference reached its climax in the panegyric of U.S. President Bill Clinton on federalism in Canada and around the world.[77] This sort of instrumentalization looks to be perpetuated at the next ICF, which is to be held in Addis Ababa in 2010. Ethiopia is then to be "the centre of attention", and the country is expected "to lead the federal movement in the

[74] Sonia Gandhi, President of the Congress Party, the largest party in the coalition government of India, cancelled her attendance at the last moment.

[75] Singh, *supra* note 29, at 4.

[76] Pande, *supra* note 12, at 2.

[77] "[Canada] has shown the world how people of different cultures and laguages can live in peace, prosperity and mutual respect. In the United States, [...we] look to you; we learn from you". Bill Clinton, *Closing Address to the International Conference on Federalism of the President of the United States of America*, Mont Tremblant 1 (8 October 1999).

neighbourhood and the continent".[78] Ethiopia, which is home to over 85 different ethno-linguistic groups, has a history of federalism (and democracy) that dates only from the 1990s.[79] The Central Government would like to gain international approval for its conflict-ridden federation. As one of only three federations in Africa, Ethiopia would also like to showcase how federalism might facilitate unity in diversity.

Whatever particular form it takes, politicization detracts from the free and fair exchange of ideas and understandings at the ICFs. The Indians at the Conference generally preferred to celebrate the 60th anniversary of their Republic's founding rather than to attempt to learn from their foreign counterparts. Despite any "habitual interest in lessons from others"[80] that Indians may have, the locals seemed to view the 4th ICF as an opportunity for the wider world to focus on India's success and to learn something from its experience - and not vice versa.[81] Politicization also detracts from the intellectual rigour of the ICFs. The fundamental claim of this Conference was that India's political system should be considered a model for other countries. This claim was, as explained, inadequately grounded, theoretically and empirically. The end result is that the intergovernmental learning about the theme of unity in diversity was diminished and that those lessons learned by participants were not necessarily those that had been intended.

[78] The road ahead...Ethiopia, *Conference Newsletter* 2 (8 November 2007).

[79] Further Federation in a Federation, *Conference Newsletter* 6 (8 November 2007); Mehari Taddele Maru, *Ethiopian Constitution Protects Diversity*, 7(1) FEDERATIONS MAGAZINE 15 (October / November 2007).

[80] Anderson, *supra* note 10.

[81] The Indian organizers of a related conference also held in New Delhi in 2007 showed a similar attitude. The promise in the conference's title of mutual learning ("India and the Worldwide Movement for Democracy: What India Can Learn from Others' Experiences and What It Has to Give") turned out in the conference's description to be rather one-way: "[t]he past two decades or so have seen global consolidation of democracy though institutions are still weak in many nascent democracies. The Indian experience has been quite instructive, particularly its institutional innovations. There is obviously a lot that India can share with the wider world".

7

The Uniform Civil Code Debate in Indian Law: New Developments and Changing Agenda

WERNER MENSKI

A. INTRODUCTION: WHAT HAPPENS IF ONE ASKS FOR THE MOON?

Post-colonial India's modernist ambition to have a Uniform Civil Code, written into Art. 44 of the Indian Constitution of 1950 as a non-justiciable Directive Principle of State Policy, concerns not just an Indian problem but a universal predicament for lawyers and legal systems. What is the relationship between personal status laws and general state-made laws? To what extent should the formal law allow for, or seek to restrain, the legal implications of religious and socio-cultural diversity? To what extent does a state, whether secular or not, actually have the power and legitimacy to decree and enforce legal uniformity? There are many more agendas at play here than simply the central issue of legal authority, focused on the power of the law, or simply "religion" vs. "law", or "culture" vs. "law", as we are often still led to believe.

The recent developments in India's law relating to the much-debated Uniform Civil Code agenda illustrate that Indian law is turning its back on supposedly European or "Western" models and has been developing its own country-specific and situation-sensitive methods of handling complex socio-legal issues. There may be some important lessons here for European lawyers, in terms of managing cultural diversity through plurality-conscious legal intervention rather than the traditional insistence on state-centric legal uniformity.

The key lesson from this evidence is that personal status laws may well survive the much-desired uniformity of legal reforms all over Asia and Africa and probably elsewhere too. The future of the world lies not in simplistic legal uniformity but in considered, carefully weighed respect for diversity. Globalisation, we are told, comes out prominently as localisation,[1] creating new hybrid entities of ever-growing plurality. We must therefore learn to handle and understand more deeply how plural legal arrangements operate and what their potential is for making progressive improvements to human lives and sustainable development.

At first, India's persuasively official post-colonial programme for introduction of a Uniform Civil Code seemed to follow the West, embodying a newly invigorated civilising mission, a clarion call for consolidated nation-building and the achievement of legal modernity through top-down, state-driven secularising reforms. This national vision for development was fervently embraced by Eurocentric and Europhilic modernists everywhere and India was much praised for this agenda item. Many Indians, including some Supreme Court judges, fired this supposedly "progressive" ambition with authoritative and seemingly persuasive calls for fundamental reforms, demanding less confusion in the jungle of personal laws, sometimes even claiming to be able to rid India of "culture" and "tradition", "customs" and "religion", all those contaminating and supposedly "extra-legal" elements that allegedly impede proper functioning of a state-led legal framework.

Roughly half a century later, it is clear that India's socio-legal reality has taken a trajectory different from that expected by modernists. The jungle of legal plurality is still there. We find more state law but no Uniform Civil Code. The perennial calls for legal uniformity have become quieter and certainly much less convincing if one considers the new, incompletely studied events

---

[1] WERNER MENSKI, COMPARATIVE LAW IN A GLOBAL CONTEXT: THE LEGAL SYSTEMS OF ASIA AND AFRICA 4 (2nd ed. 2006).

in the meantime. These illustrate the hybrid nature of all law and thus teach us about the central relevance and urgent necessity of understanding legal pluralism as a living reality. By 2001, and not coincidentally - as we shall see - two weeks after 9/11, it became clearer that post-colonial India did not in fact aim for the kind of Uniform Civil Code that so many modernist observers and stakeholders had been calling for. Instead, as the author has shown elsewhere,[2] India relearnt an ancient lesson about demanding the impossible, culturally envisaged as asking for the moon. In the ancient Indian story, the child god Krishna asks his mother Yashoda to give him the moon as a toy and the clever doting mother hands him a mirror with a reflection of the moon.

In post-modern India, nimble thinking of this kind has resulted in well-considered production of a mirror image of the desired object of the Uniform Civil Code in the form of a harmonised personal law system. A motherly central state and its core institutions, an activist and very powerful Supreme Court and a Parliament not incapable of speedy action (in that order), have taken well-choreographed steps to achieve this particular outcome. India has quite consciously over decades developed a fascinating reflection of the original ideal of the Uniform Civil Code. It takes the form of a sophisticated, harmonised system of legal regulation that maintains and skilfully uses the input of personal status laws and yet achieves a measure of legal uniformity. While the boundaries of Indian general law and personal laws have thereby become ever fuzzier, neither Hindu law nor Muslim law, nor indeed any of the various other, partly seriously outdated minority personal laws, have been abolished. The legal jungle has, as indicated, become thicker. Yet, contrary to what secular modernists allege and fear, this development is extremely progressive, apart from being quite instructive for global legal theory.

In India, a new civil code was earlier, quite simplistically deemed to be able to pick the best elements from various legal systems.[3] This convenient mix-and-match image reflects a blind belief in

[2] Werner Menski, *Asking for the Moon: Legal Uniformity in India from a Kerala Perspective*, (2) KERALA LAW TIMES 52 (2006).

[3] Further NARMADA KHODIE, READINGS IN UNIFORM CIVIL CODE (1975); TAHIR MAHMOOD, AN INDIAN CIVIL CODE AND ISLAMIC LAW

legal positivism that borders on dictatorial illusions and feeds on oversimplified Austinian and Napoleonic images of law making. Instead, Indian family laws have been skilfully reformed and harmonised in such a way that the newly configured Indian legal system of the post 9/11 era has extremely sensitively built the various traditional legal systems and new social welfare concerns into a gradually consolidated form of post-modern social welfare law. The conceptual roots of this go back to ancient Indic concepts of macrocosmic and microcosmic duty, and thus to indigenous natural laws and related socio-legal concepts. More tangible legal foundations of this plurality-conscious legal regime have been developing almost imperceptibly through positivist legal interventions, at least since the mid-1970s under Indira Gandhi's much-debated Emergency rule. These foundations emerged more clearly in September 2001, and since then they have been embellished by new statutes and case law almost yearly.

Since 2001, the contours of India's new welfare-conscious legal structures have been particularly plain to see in India's radical post-1985 regime of post-marital maintenance entitlement for all ex-wives until death or remarriage, which builds on the world-famous *Shah Bano* decision of 1985.[4] This was followed by the Hindu Succession (Amendment) Act of 2005, the Prohibition of Child Marriage Act of 2006 and most recently, the remarkable Maintenance and Welfare of Parents and Senior Citizens Act of 2007. These purposeful innovations are in essence a deliberately covert transformation of social welfare laws in India, a country that may now be economically booming, but that still teems with hundreds of millions of people living below the poverty line. There are powerful constitutional agendas here requiring the Indian state to intervene in gendered imbalances and to construct a more effective social welfare net that does not require money from the state, but relies on social and moral normative orders to provide remedies.

The present chapter highlights these interconnected developments and crucial changes of agenda in the Indian legal system, which

---

(1976); VASUDHA DHAGAMWAR, TOWARDS THE UNIFORM CIVIL CODE (1989).

[4] *Mohd Ahmed Khan* v. *Shah Bano Begum*, A.I.R. 1985 S.C. 945.

still displays and operates an intricate combination of general laws and personal laws. These recent ultra-modern (or rather post-modern) developments have not been openly debated. Too many stakeholders and academics seem to oppose, mostly for ideological reasons, what has been happening on the ground. As a result, knowledge and scholarship on Indian laws continue to be seriously misled and misguided about crucial aspects of the deeply contested nature of current Indian legal developments. Much is becoming certain, however: India does not and cannot follow the West's positivist legal trajectory, because it would not survive as a viable nation if its legal system ignored persistent internal diversities and the socio-legal predicaments of hundreds of millions of disadvantaged people. Indian law, maybe even more so than in the past, must remain diversity-conscious today. It has to carefully manage this diversity in ways that many observers find not only incredibly complex but plainly incredible. Nonetheless, the slow train of Indian democracy moves on through history, while neighbouring Pakistan, Sri Lanka and Bangladesh have suffered repeated derailments due to a lack of democratic management skills and a deficient respect for plurality. The outcome for India is not "the moon" of a Uniform Civil Code but an amazingly close mirror image of this ideal that seems to work in practice.

Thus, beyond the partly ideological struggles obstructing our views of current Indian legal developments, these innovations contain important lessons for the wider world on how to manage cultural diversity through legal interventions. The central argument is that post-9/11 India acts like a management *guru* to the globalising world about how to handle cultural diversity through a sophisticated system of legal pluralism, relying on concepts and experiences of the past, but also looking to the future, not afraid to experiment with new, potentially explosive mixes of ingredients in the legal laboratory.

B. THE "PROBLEM" OF MANAGING DIFFERENCE AND LEGAL PLURALISM

Today, no country in the world has only one type of people within its borders, since migration is not only an ancient human phenomenon, but has become ever more ubiquitous.[5] A much underrated legal consequence has been that personal status laws everywhere continue to migrate with people and then impact on the application of family laws, making them ever more international.[6] In socio-legal reality, such personal status laws of recent migrants, "ethnic implants" rather than formal transplants,[7] raise important new questions, especially in the global North, about how we should manage cultural diversity in law.[8] Such questions are awkward and may still be brushed aside by formally trained lawyers in many jurisdictions by insistence on legal dogma, national cohesion and a predilection for legal uniformity. This preference is conceptually and emotionally reinforced where a country's legal history suggests a movement from earlier customary laws and local diffuseness towards national uniformity, as embodied in the common law tradition of England or in the legal histories of many continental European countries. However, across Asia and Africa, in Latin America and elsewhere, historically grown personal status laws have not simply gone away because states wish them to. Different legal histories co-exist and continue to operate, often unofficially. This fact is increasingly recognised in these regions and in global jurisprudence as valuable, giving rise to post-modern reconfigurations of what common-sensical sustainable laws should take account of.[9] Foreign transplants may be officially powerful,[10] but may not reach every village and certainly not every citizen's heart or mind. Often banished to the realm of unofficial laws,[11] innumerable personal status

---

[5] SATVINDER JUSS, INTERNATIONAL MIGRATION AND GLOBAL JUSTICE 1 (2006).

[6] Compare JOHN MURPHY, ETHNIC MINORITIES, THEIR FAMILIES AND THE LAW (2000) and JOHN MURPHY, INTERNATIONAL DIMENSIONS IN FAMILY LAW (2005) *with* PRAKASH SHAH, LAW AND ETHNIC PLURALITY: SOCIO-LEGAL PERSPECTIVES (2007).

[7] MENSKI, *supra* note 1, at 58.

[8] Werner Menski, *Rethinking Legal Theory in Light of South-North Migration, in* MIGRATION, DIASPORAS AND LEGAL SYSTEMS IN EUROPE 13-28 (Prakash Shah & Werner Menski eds., 2006).

[9] Further BUOAVENTURA DE SOUZA SANTOS, TOWARD A NEW LEGAL COMMON SENSE (2nd ed. 2002); MASAJI CHIBA, ASIAN INDIGENOUS LAW IN INTERACTION WITH RECEIVED LAW (1986).

[10] ALAN WATSON, LEGAL TRANSPLANTS: AN APPROACH TO COMPARATIVE LAW (2nd ed. 1993).

laws survive particularly strongly in the global South, continue to prosper below the formal legal surface, and often form part of the second type of what Chiba calls "official law".[12] Since all countries appear to have their own culture-specific legal histories and have constructed their legal systems over time as best suited to their people or leaders, there is not one "law of the world", no one model that every state could just follow. Much work remains to be done by scholars to understand this fully, and lawyers are often not at the forefront of thinking in this field.[13] It seems that legal minds have often been numbed by positivist temptations of asking for the moon, even decreeing that the moon should appear.

This means that legal pluralism in a globally interconnected world that has yet to develop one world law despite many strenuous efforts has become an ever more important topic. Globalisation has actually increased the local and regional diversity of religions, customs and laws, and thus impacts almost everywhere directly on formal legal structures. While the desire for equality-conscious and nationally uniform legal regulation is of course strong and justice, we are still often told, means equality rather than equity, legal pluralism is a fact and indeed remains the norm.[14]

C. THE CHALLENGE OF LEGAL PLURALISM FOR INDEPENDENT INDIA

Explicit recognition of the reality of legal pluralism, of course, challenges long-dominant, clearly Eurocentric, positivist presumptions about the desirability of legal uniformity and its link with "rule of law". While India as a former colony has not been immune from such influences and presumptions, it has a

---

[11] These laws are not officially recognised by a state but exist in social reality. *Compare* CHIBA, *supra* note 9 (discussing the interaction of official law, unofficial law and "legal postulates") *with* MENSKI, *supra* note 1 (elaborating on the notion).

[12] CHIBA, *supra* note 9, at 5–6; MENSKI, *supra* note 1, at 124.

[13] Historians and other social scientists often have a far too limited and restrained, positivist understanding of "law" and its possibilities of skilful intervention. Further: SUFIA UDDIN, CONSTRUCTING BANGLADESH: RELIGION, ETHNICITY AND LANGUAGE IN AN ISLAMIC NATION (2006) (presenting an excellent recent discussion of such academic struggles).

[14] John Griffiths, *What is Legal Pluralism?*, 24 JOURNAL OF LEGAL PLURALISM AND UNOFFICIAL LAW 1–56 (1986).

richly documented ancient experience of operating in complex systems of legal pluralism[15] that centuries of Muslim rule and British colonial domination could not erase. The post-colonial Indian state, divorced from Islamic Pakistan, was tempted to follow Western-dominated legal and political thinking, but was also pulled by M.K. Gandhi towards ancient Hindu concepts of governance and law. Fortunately, the leaders at the time perceived that India as a composite whole would have to make sense of its own plurality-conscious heritage in the light of new socio-legal realities and would have to live with legal pluralism, even if this was not always going to be easy.

Today, one may observe that this often tortuous experience has actually turned out to be for the benefit of the country as a growing nation and that it contrasts favourably with that of India's neighbours. When British India was carved up at midnight on 14/15 August 1947 between India and Pakistan, Pakistan fooled itself into believing that it could become a country for Muslims, with disastrous results, as we know now, even for Muslim minorities, let alone others. India, however, was aware that post-colonial Bharat, the sovereign Republic of India, would need to be the home to many different kinds of people with many different kinds of laws.

So after long and ferocious debates in the Constituent Assembly, the Indians put into their Constitution of 1950 a compromise programme for the future, which seemed to privilege legal

---

[15] Recent studies by Sanskrit-based scholars have brought this out well. For example:

> [t]he expert tradition of Dharma during the centuries immediately preceding the common era appears to have been vibrant and dynamic as shown by the numerous contradictory opinions of experts recorded in the extant Dharmasūtras. Such diversity of opinion belies the common assumption that ancient Indian society was uniform and stifling under an orthodoxy imposed by Brahmins. If even the experts recorded in these normative texts disagree so vehemently, the reality on the ground must have been even more chaotic and exhilarating.

PATRICK OLIVELLE, DHARMASUTRAS 18 (2000).

uniformity and raised an expectation that there should eventually be a Uniform Civil Code. This overarching policy aim, as an ambition for the future, was laid down in art. 44 of the Indian Constitution of 1950, a Directive Principle of State Policy:

> The state shall endeavour to secure for the citizens a uniform civil code throughout the territory of India.

The original aim and ambition of a Uniform Civil Code as a common code shared by all citizens has simply not materialised. We have today a mirror image of the legal uniformity envisaged by the Constitution makers. Complete legal uniformity will never materialise in India or anywhere in the world. Indeed, we see, almost 60 years after the first post-colonial agenda for legal uniformity was set, how Indian family law has skilfully used a different model of uniformity of laws, namely harmonisation, which the original law makers may not have perceived as a viable option, but which has turned out to be the dominant and official legal reality in contemporary India.

This Indian method of operating a uniform law without having a codified Uniform Civil Code has gradually developed under our very noses over several decades. Most Indians and most academic observers have not noticed this, however, and the Indian state has had its own agenda for not making clear to people what it was doing. Still, these are not haphazard developments. The Indian state has acted purposefully, albeit silently and surreptitiously, cautiously and gradually harmonising the various Indian personal laws along similar lines without challenging their status as separate personal laws. The Indian experience shows that this does not require the admittedly dangerous radical step of a newly implemented uniform enactment in family law for all citizens.[16] Instead, India has devised a strategy of carefully planned minor

---

[16] DHAGAMWAR, *supra* note 3, at 76 (highlighting the danger of widespread public unrest). Some more recent Indian legal writing, inspired from Canada, appears to dismiss such risks and pushes ahead with reformist human rights agenda even if it means suffering for some people. JAYA SAGADE, CHILD MARRIAGE IN INDIA: SOCIO-LEGAL AND HUMAN RIGHTS DIMENSIONS (2005).

changes over a long time-span, actually an intricate interplay between judicial activism and parliamentary intervention,[17] which has left the various bodies of personal law as separate entities. Post-modern India, therefore, seems to have found a rather exciting solution to the conundrum of legal uniformity that may well be suitable for many other countries.

As a result of this strategy, the various Indian personal laws now look more like each other than ever, but they are still identifiable in terms of "ethnic" and "religious" identity as Hindu, Muslim, Parsi, and Christian law, not only by their titles but also in substance. This observation also holds true for Muslim law in India, despite being largely uncodified and the apparent reluctance of Muslim leaders and spokespersons to contemplate statutory legal reform. The fact that Indian Muslim law was not subjected to codification (as many Hindu nationalists have continued to demand) pleased and reassured the Muslims, but it did not save Indian Muslim personal law from being affected by the post-modern reconstruction process. Rather incautiously, in fact, Indian Muslims themselves demanded a separate personal law after the *Shah Bano* decision.[18] We know today that they speedily got from Rajiv Gandhi's government what they wanted, namely a separate Muslim law enactment that appeared to exempt Muslims from the general law regulations of the Criminal Procedure Code, 1973.[19] But the substance of that law, as we should have understood from many High Court decisions since at least 1988,[20] was not really different in material respects from the secular provisions of the 1973 Code that Muslims wanted to evade.
In effect, Indian Muslims fell out of the frying pan into the fire by

[17] India's new Prohibition of Child Marriage Act of 2006 illustrates this interplay. It renders Indian child marriages voidable, not void *ab initio* after judges had warned that it would be "absolutely brutal" to render all child marriages void. WERNER MENSKI, HINDU LAW: BEYOND TRADITION AND MODERNITY 368 (2003) (discussing *V. Mallikarjunaiah* v. H.C. *Gowramma*, A.I.R. 1997 Kant. 77, at 81).

[18] *Shah Bano, supra* note 4.

[19] The Muslim Women (Protection of Rights on Divorce) Act, 1986 No. 25, Acts of Parliament, 1986.

[20] *Ali* v. *Sufaira*, (1988) 2 K.L.T. 94; further WERNER MENSKI, MODERN INDIAN FAMILY LAW 246–294 (2001).

demanding a new separate law: under S. 3(1)(a) of the 1986 Act, a divorcing Muslim husband now became liable to potentially much higher maintenance payments to his ex-wife than under S. 125 of the Criminal Procedure Code with its then upper limit of 500 Rupees (equivalent to a few British pounds or Euros) per month. The full extent of this clever legal engineering was buried rather than openly admitted in the many words of the Indian Supreme Court in the *Danial Latifi* decision of 2001.[21] After 15 years of sitting on this initially hotly-debated constitutional petition, the Court rendered its decision at a strategic moment, a fortnight after 9/11. The Court held that the *Shah Bano* decision had been good law, thus reinforcing the general social welfare principle that Indian ex-husbands have to maintain their ex-wives until they die or remarry. Further, it held that Indian law could still legitimately make reasonable classifications between citizens by promulgating a separate Act for Muslims only. Thirdly - and this could have caused Muslim riots, but did not do so two weeks after 9/11 - the Court firmly held that Indian Muslim husbands remained under an obligation to maintain their ex-wives, as laid down in S. 3 of the 1986 Act[22] and confirmed by many High Court decisions.[23]

Careful reading of these decisions teaches that the Indian Constitution with its wider social welfare agenda would not, and could not, tolerate principled total exemption from social welfare agenda when matters of Muslim personal law were at stake. Thus, it only *appears* as though Muslim personal law in India has remained largely uncodified *shari'a* law. In reality, it has been equally subject to the skilful combined efforts of India's judiciary and Parliament to harmonise all Indian personal laws without abolishing the personal law system. So the Indian state tiptoed slowly and carefully around the issue of legal reforms, cleverly manipulative like an ancient Indian ruler inspired by the Indian science of governance (*arthaśāstra*). Ancient lessons about outwitting one's adversaries, here a potential internal enemy, had to be most adroitly applied. Indian Muslim law could not

---

[21] *Danial Latifi* v. *Union of India,* (2001) 7 S.C.C. 740.

[22] *Supra* note 19.

[23] MENSKI, *supra* note 20.

be allowed to remain outside the constitutional umbrella, but equally it could not be abolished. So it actually helped the post-modern Indian state that Muslims, in an incautious moment, had demanded a separate statutory law for themselves. They promptly got it - though not on their terms, as we now know.

Hence Indian law has not been static over the last 50 to 60 years. But the various subtle movements - often highly politicised and perceived as dangerous for communal harmony in a pluralistic state dominated by Hindus and Hindu concepts - have had several deeper silent agendas that have not been abandoned despite communal riots, accusations of fundamentalism and now terrorism. Led by the almost invisible hand of senior "secular" bureaucrats, India has by now virtually reached its aim of constructing a uniform personal law for all Indians through engineering much greater harmonisation of personal laws and thus achieving substantial equality of all citizens. Admittedly, this is difficult to understand, and it seems hard for communal politicians and modernist scholars to swallow.

The continuing challenges of legal pluralism in a nation marked by unity in diversity, combined with the historically grounded resilience of the personal law system in India, mean that most Indians today, common citizens and academics alike, as well as most foreign observers, look with some puzzlement at a mirror image of the originally anticipated phenomenon of India's Uniform Civil Code. Indians, it seems, are still almost as confused as Western legocentric scholars about the practical applications of plurality-conscious navigation. Somehow post-modern India managed to navigate this. The next section considers briefly the extent to which such acute plurality-consciousness may be rooted in Indian history.

D. THE RELEVANCE OF HISTORY

India entered what its first Prime Minister, Jawaharlal Nehru, called a "tryst with history" upon independence at midnight on 14/15 August 1947. A major task for the new government was setting the agenda for much-needed change to achieve a better future. However, setting the agenda is one thing and achieving development another: past and future need to be combined, as lawyers focusing on developmental issues have had to acknowledge again and again. History contains fruitful lessons as well as fetters on ambitions for radical legal reform.

Evolution rather than revolution was the envisaged path of post-colonial Indian legal development; India could not simply abolish the personal law system overnight. Hence, as part of an intricate compromise, art. 44 in the Indian Constitution, as a Directive Principle of State Policy, laid down the original policy aim of secular nation building. It aimed to achieve, gradually rather than at once, more far-reaching equality for all citizens. Justice was not served on a silver platter, but it began to move more within reach of the common citizen.[24] The somewhat pompously guaranteed right to equality in Art. 14 of the Indian Constitution became a new *Grundnorm*, but was not thereby automatically turned into socio-legal reality. Within the Fundamental Rights of the same Constitution, the qualified equality under Art. 14 was matched by further important basic equality guarantees under Art. 15 and 16, which permit the Indian state to make several special protective provisions for certain classes of people, particularly women, children and members of historically disadvantaged communities. All of this reflects deep awareness that new laws do not create facts overnight and that the ideal of equality remained at best a long-term goal, certainly not socio-legal reality effected by the stroke of a pen. Awareness of the limits of law also meant that various forms of protective discrimination would probably need to remain part of Indian law for a long time to come, however much fought over. For India, these are lessons well learnt from history.

However, other ambitious Indian agendas for law reform were partly built on the legocentric claim that legal reform can happen fast, predominantly through secular codification; the lawmaker's pen was to offer potent remedies in India today. This legislative ambition has remained powerful in many Indian minds. Tempted

---

[24] Werner Menski, *Introduction: The Democratisation of Justice in* India, in GURJEET SINGH, LAW OF CONSUMER PROTECTION IN INDIA: JUSTICE WITHIN REACH xxv-liv (1996).

to be legal positivists at heart, with ambitions to reach modernity by jumping in leaps and bounds, many of India's citizens supported reformist agendas and expected further reforms. Excessive optimism was quickly cooled by Nehru's realisation that in order for law reform to be effective in society, people themselves would have to change their ways of doing things.[25]

India's colonial rulers, after assuming sovereignty in 1858, had engaged in massive law making by statute, creating Anglo-Indian law, a new official law composed of many statutes and cases. Similarly, post-colonial Indian law makers undertook vigorous codification through statute and judicial precedent as part of nation building. This led almost directly to the rapid and dramatic failure of the Hindu Code Bill project of the early 1950s.[26]

By the 1980s though, emerging post-modern legal scholars began to view this propensity towards codification critically as dominant Western "model jurisprudence".[27] By then, Western-style positivism had managed to portray itself as advanced, modern, and thus superior. It still occupies the moral high ground, albeit with increasingly severe criticism.[28] It was not, however, part of earlier Indian legal history that law reforms occur predominantly through top-down legislation. India has other powerful memories of legal history, and it could, and can, creatively rely on different methods of setting agendas and implementing socially beneficial reforms.

It seems, however, that these historical lessons had gradually been overshadowed by colonial intervention. The idea that a developed legal system should take codified form was firmly implanted in the minds of scholars and lawyers, as well as historians and

---

[25] This is cited with approval (but apparently insufficient impact on that scholar's subsequent thinking) in Jaya Sagade, *Law and Social Reforms in Rural India with Special Reference to Child Marriages*, 1 SUP. CT. J. 27 (1981), and SAGADE, *supra* note 16.

[26] Further M.P. JAIN, OUTLINES OF INDIAN LEGAL HISTORY ("4th ed" 1981); J. D. M. DERRETT, HINDU LAW PAST AND PRESENT (1957); J. D. M. DERRETT, RELIGION, LAW AND THE STATE IN INDIA, Ch. 10 (1968).

[27] CHIBA, *supra* note 9.

[28] WILLIAM TWINING, GLOBALISATION AND LEGAL THEORY (2006).

other social scientists, by the mid-nineteenth century. This kind of evolutionist thinking, traceable to Sir Henry Maine, influenced not only the trajectory of English Common Law, but soon became a dominant global image. Even though it is much criticised today,[29] many people, not only lawyers, still reflexively think of law as a fixed set of rules made by the state in the form of codes. We are tempted to essentialise law into a tool of codification, even a static body of codified rules. The image of the Code Napoleon as an embodiment of law remains powerful[30] outside France or Continental Europe, even in the so-called common law world in Asia and Africa, though people are aware that socio-legal reality tends to be quite different. Somehow, there are mental blocks when it comes to identifying the internal plurality of law and making clear distinctions between different types of law. History has not taught us enough about the crucial messages contained in legal pluralism, a supposedly new theory that is actually an ancient theme, sidelined and ignored in the Enlightenment and the rush towards modernity.

From his armchair perspective, Sir Henry Maine had perceived the ancient Hindu texts as codes.[31] Maine was therefore at least willing to accept that Hindus were somewhat civilised people. Although they did many repugnant things, it was accepted, to the chagrin of the then ruling Muslims, that Hindus had their own laws. This acceptance was important, because the colonial history of India might otherwise have developed quite differently, more like in parts of Africa, where the British assumed that the locals had no laws at all and that civilisation needed to be brought to them, including in the form of socio-legal norms. Images of a virtual *tabula rasa* or *terra nullius* justified massive appropriation of property as well as prominent impositions in specific territories of English common law as it stood at a particular point of time.

---

[29] PETER SACK & JONATHAN ALECK, LAW AND ANTHROPOLOGY (1992).

[30] Pierre Legrand, *How to Compare Now,* 16(2) LEGAL STUDIES 236 (1996) (discussing the particular mentalité of French law).

[31] GEOFFREY A. ODDIE, IMAGINED HINDUISM (2006) (discussing various historical constructions of the image of Hinduism and Hindu law).

Lawyers should have been aware that this particular process never occurred in India on a large scale.[32] The British themselves did not really introduce English law into India, as they could have done. English law was only imported for colonial staff in the major cities, not in the *mufassil*, the hinterland. On one hand, the British themselves did not want to be governed by local Muslim laws, the "official law" at the time of the British East India Company. On the other, they did not really wish to go as far as imposing English law on their colonial subjects. From 1765 onwards, most clearly in Warren Hastings' scheme of 1772, the British recognised that there were different laws for different groups of people in India, based primarily on religious affiliation. Hence they divided the whole legal field into "general law", matters like criminal law, contract and commercial law, and "personal laws", basically matters of the family and of religion.

Much writing claims that the British invented and introduced the personal law system into India.[33] The personal law system is, if anything, an earlier Hindu institution actually. It reflects the recognition of different forms of belief and practice among a large population that mostly gave crucial importance to local customs, as the early *smriti* texts state. Early Christians, Jews, Parsis and then Muslims could live under Hindu domination and follow their own personal law systems. Local Muslim rulers and the Moghuls in turn accepted the same system with some modifications, seeing the advantages of cosmopolitan plurality.[34] The British colonial structures were merely a kind of superstructure fitted into the pre-existing Indian framework. Apart from adding some laws for themselves, the new rulers merely assimilated to the Indian legal environment and increased its legal diversity by their presence.

The British did eventually introduce significant changes to the legal framework as a whole when they codified what came to

---

[32] We should also remember that much of "colonial India" was not under direct British rule, but under what in Africa and elsewhere was called "indirect rule", largely retaining local legal and political structures, not to speak of social norms and value systems.

[33] M.B. HOOKER, LEGAL PLURALISM (1975).

[34] Raziuddin Aquil, *Hazrat-i-Dehli: The Making of the Chishti Sufi Centre and the Stronghold of Islam*, 28(1) SOUTH ASIA RESEARCH 23–48 (2008).

be called the general law, as planned by Hastings in 1772, such that India acquired the Indian Penal Code of 1860, the Indian Evidence Act of 1872 and the Indian Contract Act of 1872 among many enactments. In the realm of personal laws, however, the legislative interventions were very few and none took the form of comprehensive codification. Even the British-inspired codifications of the general Indian law after 1860 were not simple transplants of existing English law. They were carefully crafted complex new constructs, designed for use in a colonial territory rather than in England itself. The best example is the Indian Penal Code of 1860, which remains in force all over the subcontinent, while England remains without codified criminal law.

The deeply flawed assumption that ancient Hindu law had earlier been codified through the *śāstric* texts and was further codified through British colonial interventions is accordingly based on a series of incorrect lessons from Indian legal history. This confusion certainly misled colonial and later law reformers in India into believing that ancient Hindu codes could be simply replaced with new secular rules. It also prevents many scholars and common citizens from understanding the complex nature and structure of current Indian laws as well as the present place of Hindu law within this complex structure.[35] The prominent predilection for the ambitious agenda of secularisation through codifying law reform has its roots in such confusion and remains evidently as powerful as ever, not only in India. Uniform visions seem to cloud the mind when it comes to understanding the trajectory of India's post-modern uniform civil code agenda. While history remains relevant, its lessons about legal pluralism have manifestly not been fully learnt.

E. HINDU LAW AND RELIGION AS INDIA'S DOMINANT SYSTEMS IN A PLURAL CONTEXT

The mental image of legal codification is obviously also closely related to global debates about religion and its relationship with law. The idea that Moses came down from Mount Sinai with

---

[35] MENSKI, *supra* note 17.

God's commandments is familiar in most of the world. The claim made centuries later that a man called Mohammad received God's law to pass on to the world, and especially to all those who were willing to accept this message, became an equally powerful symbol of the innate strength of religious law and the foundation for a new world religion. The worldwide spread of Christianity and Islam confirms that such images of how humans are linked to the Universe constitute not only religious messages, but also contain powerful political, social and legal guidance, creating holistic systems of Truth and knowledge on which later man-made legal systems could be built.

Through contact with divine authority, the Pope came to be perceived as God's representative on earth and the Prophet of Islam became much more than a mere messenger: they gained personal authority and power, also in political, social and legal terms. Such a person then tends to become a leader, the first ruler, the man who effectively controls the law, because he alone had direct contact with the religious source. But as long as God remains the supervening force, such a human figure does not, indeed must not, become the dominant maker of law.[36] The later secularisation of law, also of Islamic law, could occur - though not without much agonising - once natural law and positivism had become linked, making *siyasa shar'iyya* as Islamic "good governance" human and partly secular, while still religiously legitimised as a tool to implement and maintain the Law of God. Today, all legal systems, whether religious or state-centric, are under global pressure to secularise (if not to internationalise), while there is also considerable countervailing pressure to localise and, indeed, often to Islamise.[37] Historically, Islamic law is therefore certainly not alone in resisting uniformity and modernising pressures; medieval Christian law once also resisted claims of the superiority of state law and various forms of resistance are also reported from Africa and elsewhere.[38]

---

[36] MENSKI, *supra* note 1, at 294–298.

[37] PATRICK GLENN, LEGAL TRADITIONS OF THE WORLD: SUSTAINABLE DIVERSITY IN LAW 51 (2004) (speaking of "a number of globalizations going on").

[38] MENSKI, *supra* note 1, at 13.

As an internally plural entity India is dominated by complex Indic forms of values, ethics and religions, with no agreement over what to call such religious phenomena as "Hinduism",[39] and where and how to draw boundaries. "Hinduism" is manifestly not a religion based on direct divine revelation through human agents. Its sources are largely chthonic[40] but no less sophisticated than the ancient Greek models that underpin "Western" civilisation and "our" traditional concepts of natural law. While there is no centralised belief system focused on one Hindu God, there is the concept of a unifying linking force. It is, however, overshadowed in daily life by polytheistic practices and beliefs and a plethora of local and sectarian manifestations of religion.

This reality dominates the various Hindu cultures and societies, and thus the whole of India's socio-religious arena. There is no central figure of a Hindu Prophet as a special person, instead there were many Vedic sages (*rishis*) who have "heard" the Vedic hymns in a process of revelation (*shruti*). Later generations passed on this ancient knowledge through chains of human memory or remembrance (*smriti*), which is also the technical term for a huge class of ancient texts. Consequently, it is not possible in Hinduism and Hindu law, as it would be in Judaism, Christianity or Islam, to make a strong claim that there must be uniformity of belief and shared basic concepts of the religion. Very early on, Hindus agreed to disagree and cultivated respect for internal diversity. They refused to claim that humans could know precisely who God was and instead admitted (as Christians and Muslims actually also do in their own ways) that it is beyond human capacity to fully comprehend ultimate Truths. Thus, Hinduism as India's majoritarian belief system allowed and developed a plurality-focused body of theory and of practice that has led directly to the present confusing and messy picture of Hinduism as a collection of sects rather than one stratified religion. This also explains continued reliance on Hindu customary law, even in modern statutes, such as S. 7 and 29(2) of the Hindu Marriage Act of 1995 in relation to customary solemnisation of marriages

[39] Julius J. Lipner, *The Rise of "Hinduism"*; or, *How to Invent a World Religion with only Moderate Success*, 10(1) INTERNATIONAL JOURNAL OF HINDU STUDIES 91-104 (2006).

[40] GLENN, *supra* note 37.

and customary divorces. On top of this, the inability to neatly define a "Hindu" creates many fuzzy boundaries for determining allegiance to any particular personal law. The temptation to argue for one law for all Indians arises to some extent out of frustration about such pluralism.

The fact is, however, often overlooked that Muslims and Christians do not have internally uniform legal systems either. Muslims have been arguing forever over the meaning and implications of certain Arabic words and expressions.[41] The Muslim concept of legal pluralism, *ikhtilaf* or "tolerated diversity of opinion", indicates that Islamic law can also be perceived as a holistically interlinked and internally plural system, so that there is no uniform Islamic law, just as there is no such thing as uniform Hindu law. The innate diversities of Hindu belief and practice meant that Hindus have often been treated as primitive, especially by those who rely on divine revelation. While Muslims accepted Christians, Jews and Parsis as people of the book (*kitabiyya*) and allowed themselves to marry women from those communities, they shunned so-called idol worshippers.[42] In response, many Hindus developed defensive strategies, some would say inferiority complexes, and have claimed that "Hinduism" has long had all the paraphernalia of other world religions. It appears that prominent thinkers of neo-Hinduism and later Hindu fundamentalism were partly incited by Muslim aggression,[43] an observation that remains true of Hindu nationalist tendencies among overseas Indians today.

In colonial times, Hindus tried to convince the British and others that their religion had a holy book too, foremost the Veda.[44] Hindus

---

[41] While this has had some relevance for legal development in modern India, it cannot be explored further here.

[42] Some old reported cases from India, however, show that Muslims sometimes defined Hindus as *kitabiyya* to justify marriage to a Hindu woman. After all, many Hindus also have religious texts and may treat such a text as a kind of holy book, especially the epic Ramayana.

[43] JYOTIRMAYA SHARMA, HINDUTVA: EXPLORING THE IDEA OF HINDU NATIONALISM (2003).

[44] The predicament of comparability is hardly new: the seven volumes of the *History of Dharmashastra*, originally written towards the end of the colonial period, were partly designed to prove to the colonial powers that Hindus had "proper" law, even if it meant that Kane often overstated his case. Read PANDURANG VAMAN KANE, HISTORY OF DHARMASHASTRA (1968) (1930–1962).

today like to claim (apparently with considerable justification) that their system of religion and law is older than that of "the others", and by no means inferior. Many Hindus also claim there is one God, whether the more impersonal Brahma or *bhagwan*, or Krishna or Rama, an ideal ruler figure, who became a still more prominent Hindu deity partly through Ayodhya-inspired Hindu nationalism (*hindutva*).[45] In fact, the argument is now frequently made that Hindu concepts should prevail in India because they constitute the intellectual property of the demographic majority. One can see how easily this line of reasoning turns arguments for a Uniform Civil Code into attempts to Hinduise the nation and to simply get rid of Muslim and Christian personal laws. The "fundamentalist" reasoning that India's future should be determined mainly or even exclusively by Hindu majoritarian concepts (more so while India had a Hindu nationalist government for several years) added some sobering realism and important reservations about the Uniform Civil Code debates towards the end of the twentieth century. But few Indian writers are discussing this openly, leaving Europeans and North Americans to fussy debates over the crisis of secularism in India.[46]

F. LEARNING TO RESPECT DIFFERENCES IN INDEPENDENT INDIA

Since Independence, it has become crystal-clear that India would have to be the home of all kinds of people and not just a Hindu state. This is exactly where the shoe pinches for many nervous observers. With only a slowly decreasing demographic majority of 85% to 80% Hindus according to the 2001 Census, independent India will remain Hindu-dominated for a very long time. Minorities would probably face more difficulties if minority protection were not so securely anchored in the Indian Constitution.[47] The majoritarian Hindu law is not allowed by a

[45] The storming and destruction of an old mosque in Ayodhya in December 1992 provoked huge debates, outrage and communal riots across India.

[46] ANURADHA DINGWANEY NEEDHAM & RAJESWARI SUNDER RAJAN, THE CRISIS OF SECULARISM IN INDIA (2007).

[47] INDIA CONST. art. 14 (protecting equality before law); INDIA CONST. Art. 15 (prohibiting discrimination on the grounds of religion, race, caste, sex or place

plurality-conscious Constitution to become the law of the land. The post-colonial construction of diversity-conscious Indian identity has undoubtedly been difficult, but it has also brought some unexpected results, as the present chapter illustrates.

Scholars who argued vigorously for a Uniform Civil Code have expressed frustration about long "sterile debates" while voicing doubts about the possibility of its implementation.[48] Some prominent Indian legal scholars now privilege recourse to international values,[49] but local "identity postulates" appear necessary in plural entities infused with local notions.[50] The problem with writing that favours legal uniformity is that it seeks to minimise the influence of Hindu law, really of all personal laws, as a basis for Indian law making, while privileging state-made secular laws and even international law over the culturally-anchored laws of the people of India.[51]

How to deal legally with cultural differences is, of course, a conundrum observed all over the world today, not just in India. On the level of ideology, uniformity is emphasised to achieve conformity to some kind of dominant model, formally to the exclusion of other voices. Earlier, that formal model, often through colonialism, became "the West's", and for India more specifically that of the British. Both coloniser and colonised assumed that there was a desirable advanced method by which a vast country could be run and administered coherently, a precursor to current global trends. We can easily see how, on a global level today, such kinds of tensions become even more inextricable.

---

of birth). Further INDIA CONST. Art. 25–28 (concerning the right to freedom of religion); INDIA CONST. art. 29–30 (concerning cultural and educational rights).

[48] DHAGAMWAR, *supra* note 3, at 76.

[49] SAGADE, *supra* note 16.

[50] "Identity postulate" is explained by Chiba as a term focused on construction of identity of a particular people, a set of values and ethics rather than a body of rules. MASAJI CHIBA, LEGAL PLURALISM: TOWARDS A GENERAL THEORY THROUGH JAPANESE LEGAL CULTURE 180 (1989).

[51] Notably J.D.M. Derrett still saw reservations in 1968 about the ability to make law through statutory intervention as an "apparently unpractical point of view". DERRETT, *supra* note 26, at 76.

During post-colonial reconstruction, with its reformist euphoria from the 1950s onwards, India was in danger of losing sight of its traditional respect for local and cultural difference. At Independence, India had several options, in particular the traditional decentralised, Hindu-centric Gandhian approach and the ebulliently modernist state-centric, secular approach of Ambedkar. Nehru found himself torn between the two approaches. Gandhi wanted to emphasise the village, local cultures, customary norms, and thus legal plurality, focused on the self-controlled ordering systems of traditional Hindu *dharma*.[52] He thought that justice would be better served by taking account of the facts and circumstances of every case rather than following codified precedent. Modernists around Ambedkar preferred a strong central state with codified laws and as much legal uniformity as possible. While Gandhi was perceived as wanting a "return" to ancient religious and cultural models, the modernists wanted to "advance" and to follow "the West" as much as possible, abandoning the shackles of the past. Ambedkar himself wanted to see a secular modern India with the same laws for all, a Western-style model like France or Germany, though others were bitterly opposed to this.[53] While the temptation to make India a Hindu-dominated state was present and to some extent embodied by Gandhi, those in control, above all Nehru and his coterie, won out and set India upon the road to a peculiar kind of secularism, unique to India and widely misunderstood or, rather, inadequately understood. In essence, Indian secularism means equidistance of the state from all religions. It is not based on a separation of law and religion, but recognises their holistic interconnections and seeks to guarantee minorities equal treatment in a Hindu-dominated new state.

Thus diversity-conscious realism prevailed over uniform ideology and the Indian Constituent Assembly soon got down to formulating India's new Constitution of 1950. Law reform was

---

[52] MENSKI, *supra* note 17, at 94–107.

[53] On Ambedkar's contribution, there is a huge literature. Read S.K. DHAWAN, DR. B.R. AMBEDKAR: A SELECT PROFILE (1891–1956) (1991); 1 & 2 K.L. CHANCHREEK, DR. B.R. AMBEDKAR: PATRIOT, PHILOSOPHER, STATESMAN: ECONOMIC WRITINGS (1991); NAZEER H. KHAN, B.R. AMBEDKAR ON FEDERALISM, ETHNICITY AND GENDER JUSTICE (2001).

written into the national programme of development; the existing plurality of laws with the personal law system as a central element was now simply re-anchored within the overarching framework of the Constitution. This presents an intricate compromise between uniformity and diversity, centrality and localism. Although the Constitution seems to Americans and others to be similar to the U.S. Constitution, it is actually typically Indian, full of recognition of differences between various groups of people and respectful of diversity at many levels.[54] There is reluctant admiration worldwide for the fact that this Constitution has been so successful in guiding India's massive democracy.[55] Much of that success must be attributed to this explicit basic structure of a compromise between uniformity and diversity.

Uniformity became a big issue in the constitutional debates. Ambedkar vigorously argued for a Uniform Civil Code as a secularising device, designed to get rid of Hindu law and of "tradition" altogether.[56] He was apparently less concerned about Muslim law. His project of uniformity and modernity failed, however, for good reason: the Indian leadership under Nehru had already realized that uniformity could not be decreed by the stroke of a pen. In the same way, more recent Hindu nationalist attempts to get rid of Muslim law through pushing the agenda of the Uniform Civil Code have also failed miserably, and respect for diversity has come out triumphant. As indicated, the Uniform Civil Code was put on hold in 1950 and instead, it was put into the Constitution as a future agenda item, one of the many Directive Principles of State Policy. Art. 44 states that "[t]he state shall endeavor to secure for the citizens a uniform civil code throughout the territory of India".[57]

What did and do such words mean? A phrase like "shall endeavour to secure" reads like an admission that uniformisation would be

---

[54] Marc Galanter & Jayanth Krishnan, *Personal Law Systems and Religious Conflict, in* RELIGION AND PERSONAL LAW IN SECULAR INDIA: A CALL TO JUDGMENT 270–300 (G.J. Larson ed., 2001)

[55] E.g., GRANVILLE AUSTIN, THE INDIAN CONSTITUTION: CORNERSTONE OF A NATION ix (1999).

[56] *Supra* note 53.

[57] INDIA CONST. Art. 44.

a very difficult process, with no timetable given and no clear agenda beyond the eventual aim of greater uniformity. Purposely left vague, this provision has been seen by various authors as having no hope of ever being implemented, that is as "no more than a distant mirage".[58] But significantly, these same words of Art. 44 are still interpreted today by leading secularity-focused legal scholars of India as a binding programme for action.[59]

During the ferocious debates about Hindu law codification in India in the 1950s, it became quite clear that even Hindu law as a whole was far too diverse internally to be subjected to rigid uniformisation and codification. The various local and customary rules of Hindu law could not be fitted into a uniform Hindu law code, so the ambitious project of codifying Hindu law was abandoned early on. Instead, four Acts were passed in 1955 and 1956 to regulate selected aspects of Hindu law, most notably the Hindu Marriage Act in 1955. So in legal reality, India ended up with a complex regime of Hindu law regulation that gave rise to most interesting litigation in years to come, but that was by no means uniform. Buddhists, Jainas and Sikhs were also subsumed under Hindu law during this reform process.[60]

In addition, the personal laws of Muslims, Christians, Parsis and Jews, the option of using a secular legal regime (as provided under the Special Marriage Act of 1954), and many regional laws and amendments were largely left intact. Indian law, therefore, followed the familiar South Asian strategy of focusing primarily on reforming the majority law and leaving the various minority laws alone. The jungle of Indian family laws remained a dense forest.[61]

---

[58] ANTONY ALLOTT, THE LIMITS OF LAW 216 (1980).

[59] Virendra Kumar, *Uniform Civil Code Revisited: A Juridical Analysis of John Vallamattom*, 45 JOURNAL OF THE INDIAN LAW INSTITUTE 315-334 (2003).

[60] Werner Menski, *Jaina Law as an Unofficial Legal System, in* PETER FLUEGEL, DISPUTES AND DIALOGUES: STUDIES IN JAINA HISTORY AND CULTURE 417-435 (2006).

[61] In their own way, Pakistan and later Bangladesh did exactly the same for Muslim law, again without complete success in terms of legal unification and reform.

G. THE PERSISTENCE OF LEGAL DIFFERENCES IN MODERN INDIA

After the initial decade of modernising Hindu law reforms in the 1950s, India remained a country, like almost all others in Asia and Africa, in which different personal laws for different groups of people were applied. This "backward" situation is frequently critiqued with reference to the possibility afforded an Indian Muslim man, even today, to marry up to four wives at the same time, while other Indian men can have only one wife.[62] That at least is the impression from the outside, looking only at the statutory law and noting the absence of statutory regulation or control of polygamy in Indian Muslim law. Few people have had the time to study what happened and happens in socio-legal reality.[63] The issue in Indian law inevitably became whether it was constitutional to maintain such distinctions between Indian citizens on the basis of religion. Should citizens have vastly different rights and duties merely because they belonged to a particular religious community? Since the law cannot abolish these communities, could, and should, Indian law at least remove the discriminatory legal consequences of social and religious differences? This issue has remained deeply controversial and has been most interestingly litigated as regards post-divorce maintenance for women under Indian law.

Following the much-cited and heavily misused *Shah Bano* decision of 1985,[64] which even many people in the West claim to know about (though they may know nothing else about Indian law), the decision of the Indian Supreme Court in *Danial Latifi* in 2001 merely restated the existing legal position, namely that making reasonable distinctions between citizens on the basis of criteria such as religion would not be unconstitutional in itself.[65]

[62] Under the Muslim personal law (*shari'a*), based on Quran'ic verses, up to four wives are allowed to Muslim husbands. In contrast, S. 5(i) of the Hindu Marriage Act of 1955 prohibits polygamous marriage for Hindus and makes it a crime under S. 17. The Hindu Marriage Act, 1955 (No. 25, Acts of Parliament, 1955).

[63] MENSKI, *supra* note 20, at 139–230; MENSKI, *supra* note 17, at ch. 10.

[64] *Shah Bano, supra* note 4.

[65] *Danial Latifi, supra* note 21.

Not surprisingly, however, between the 1950s and 2001, the debates about the Uniform Civil Code in India, and about legal uniformity in general, have continued to be lively. While the old Gandhian/Nehruvian dichotomy has never gone away, the discourse took various forms at different times, depending on the politics of the day and new developments in the law. At first, the demands of modernisation, leading to globalisation, led to a belief that modern India needed to follow the West, particularly Britain. The author's predecessor in London, Professor Derrett, argued vigorously until the early 1970s[66] that when it came to family law reforms, India could do no better than to copy English family law and follow the steps of modernisation taken in London. This advice was less geared towards uniformity than somewhat culture-blind modernisation, despite Derrett's deep insights into Hindu law and Indian legal traditions. Derrett's views began to change after reading Indian cases about the effects of the new regime of Hindu divorce law after a 1964 amendment.[67] This new Act assumed gender equality, but made it easier for Hindu men to throw their wives out of the marriage and out of the house, thereby engineering a unilateral divorce that led to what Derrett called the "own wrong problem".[68] Prevented from entering the house every time they tried to come back, frequently beaten with polluting leather sandals (*chappals*), wives were simply expelled from the matrimonial home when the husband stated that, as far as he was concerned, the marriage had broken down. Derrett's acute realisation that failure to take account of cultural factors in the application of family laws could cause unforeseen social disasters in a patriarchal legal system is documented in his last book on Hindu family law.[69] After noting that the Marriage Laws (Amendment) Act of 1976 had resulted in still more amazingly gender-insensitive case law, the grand master retired. Thereafter, when the Indian state sought to introduce further divorce law reforms in 1981, including the principle of "irretrievable breakdown" borrowed from English law, even Indian women's groups rose in opposition and the Bill was defeated.

---

[66] *Supra* note 26.

[67] The Hindu Marriage (Amendment) Act, 1964, No. 44, Acts of Parliament, 1964 (adding two new grounds for divorce among Hindus).

[68] J. D. M. DERRETT, A CRITIQUE OF MODERN HINDU LAW (1970).

[69] J. D. M. DERRETT, THE DEATH OF A MARRIAGE LAW (1978).

Although India stopped copying English legal developments in matrimonial law around 1981, havoc had been caused in Indian society by these modernising and uniformising Indian family law reforms. It had become possible for an Indian husband to enjoy the "first night" after a traditional wedding, to claim the next morning that something was wrong with his wife, and to demand virtually instant nullity. Any excuse or minor blemish would become a legal ground to terminate the marriage.[70] It was frightening; women were given no chance to plead their side of the story. North Indian judges, in particular, would simply decree divorce even though irretrievable breakdown did not exist on the statute book.

Such grave social and legal consequences of unthinking modernisation in the realm of Hindu family law gradually made many Indian judges rethink their strategies of dealing with family conflicts. Blind modernisation came to be seen as undesirable from about 1988 onwards.[71] A more careful approach was gradually, but by no means systematically, taken. Considering the facts and circumstances of each case more closely, courts now sought to ensure that women and children should not be disadvantaged by liberal divorce laws, since it was obvious that men could often afford better lawyers and exploit unfair advantages.

Accordingly, Indian judges in several High Courts and the Supreme Court, but not Parliament, became the main motor for important gradual, almost imperceptible, legal developments that also impacted on the question of the Uniform Civil Code. The shift to the judicial arena and expansion of the judicial domain are not unique to family law, falling in line with scholars' observations of a general judicialisation, if not emerging juristocracy, in Indian law.[72] It is highly significant in the present context that it was not primarily problems of gender difference but the economic consequences of their decisions that made Indian judges rethink

---

[70] *Bikkar Singh* v. *Mohinder Kaur*, A.I.R. 1981 P&H 391; *Balbir Kaur* v. *Maghar Singh*, A.I.R. 1984 P&H 417.

[71] MENSKI, *supra* note 20, at 72–138 (examining the relevant case law).

[72] RAN HIRSCHL, TOWARDS JURISTOCRACY: THE ORIGINS AND CONSEQUENCES OF THE NEW CONSTITUTIONALISM (2004).

the implications of judicial interventions in family law.[73] Since India does not have, and will most likely not develop, a Western-style welfare state, it became necessary to embark on a major restructuring of family law policies, especially as regards access to divorce and maintenance provisions after divorce.

During this period, one can observe a subtle gradual shift away from dogged demands for a Uniform Civil Code and uniform legal regulation for all Indians towards a system in which justice as a relative matter (*nyāya*) reasserted itself. Of course, there were still quite prominent cases in which courts criticised the absence of a Uniform Civil Code.[74] Surprisingly, this kind of argument could still be heard, if less frequently, even after 2001 in Indian courtrooms[75] and some older Indian academics continue to push legal uniformity as a desirable aim for India.[76]

There are many signs that most Indian judges have by now become post-modern realists the hard way. It has been held that where a litigating couple is desperately poor, the husband or wife could not be expected by the law to maintain the other; both parties would have to suffer this misfortune together.[77] Where, in contrast, one spouse is significantly better placed than the other, that spouse, normally the man, has a legal obligation to share his wealth.[78] While modern Hindu law, in its enthusiasm for modernity, also introduced the gender-equal rule that a wife

---

[73] *Soundarammal* v. *Sundara Mahalinga Nadar*, A.I.R. 1980 Mad. 294.

[74] *Shah Bano, supra note 4. See also Jorden Diengdeh* v. *S.S. Chopra,* A.I.R. 1985 S.C. 935, at 935–936, 940.

[75] A recent example is *John Vallamattom* v. *Union of India,* where V.N. Khare, then Chief Justice of India, stated that "[i]t is a matter of regret that Art. 44 of the Constitution has not been given effect to. Parliament is still to step in for framing a common civil code in the coxuntry. A common civil code will help the cause of national integration by removing the contradictions based on ideologies". Notably, this was two years after the uniformising legal developments analysed in the present chapter. *John Vallamattom v. Union of India,* 2003(3) KLT 66 (SC), at 80.

[76] *Kumar, supra* note 59.

[77] *Sivankutty* v. *S. Komalakumari,* A.I.R. 1989 Ker. 124 (holding that poverty is "a misfortune that has to be shared by the wife also").

[78] *Gladstone* v. *Geetha Gladstone,* 2002(2) KLT SN 126 (Case No. 155) (holding that "[e]very Indian citizen is bound to maintain his wife and children. That is a tradition of the society").

might have to maintain the husband if she is better placed,[79] Hindu men who have tried to argue that they should be maintained by their wife have been told to exert themselves and work for their family. Such men are virtually ridiculed by the courts,[80] unless they are disabled and reliant on the support of others.

The main new message of uniformity, then, is that all Indian men, as controllers of most of the property and resources in India, are primarily liable for the welfare of any wives and children in need of support. Full gender equality in Western garb is not quite what India has been seeking to achieve, nor would it be sensible to do so. A culture-specific reappraisal of moral responsibility was increasingly turned into emphasis on the legal obligation of males to maintain family members by the quiet activism or occasional deliberate passivity of the Indian judiciary.

H. CONTRIBUTION OF THE LEGISLATURE IN INTERACTION WITH COURTS

The Indian legislature has followed suit, most recently with the promulgation of the Maintenance and Welfare of Parents and Senior Citizens Act, 2007, another uniform social welfare law applying to all Indians. The new prevalent concern for social welfare principles in India strongly relies on ancient principles of responsibility within the family context. It had been reimported into the Criminal Procedure Code of 1973, which ominously defined a "wife" as including a divorced wife, but had had no immediate impact.[81] But because that Code applies to all Indians, it became possible for Muslim wives to ask for maintenance beyond the traditional iddat period of three months, in effect for lifelong maintenance. This is what set the ball of Indian post-modern legal developments rolling and contributed critically to the new pattern of harmonised personal laws.

---

[79] *Supra* note 62.

[80] *Kanchan* v. *Kamalendra*, A.I.R. 1992 Bom. 493.

[81] Explanation (b) of S. 125 of the Criminal Procedure Code of 1973 provides under that "'wife' includes a woman who has been divorced by, or has obtained a divorce from, her husband and has not remarried".

The famous *Shah Bano* case eventually surfaced from this legal issue.[82] After almost 40 years of marriage and several children, an elderly Muslim woman was thrown out by her lawyer husband so that he could enjoy life with a younger woman. He claimed that giving his old former wife the stipulated *iddat* money and the dower (*haq mahr*), together just a few hundred Indian Rupees, fulfilled his legal obligations towards her, relying on traditional Muslim law to exempt himself from any further liability. Long before the *Shah Bano* case, however, the increasingly activist Indian Supreme Court had established that a Muslim ex-husband would only be exempt from further payments to his ex-wife if the payments were sufficient for her "to keep body and soul together".[83] The legislature had evidently laid sound foundations for such judicial activism in the Criminal Procedure Code of 1973.

Thus, India's important social welfare considerations were introduced by a combination of judicial activism and legislative alertness to assist divorced Muslim wives against vagrancy and destitution. When Shah Bano's husband attempted to evade the social welfare argument of the Supreme Court, the judges (incidentally five Hindus) retorted, quite rightly, that even under certain Qur'anic provisions, there was an obligation on a divorcing Muslim husband to be considerate and generous to his former wife.[84]

In this manner, *Shah Bano* catalysed post-modern Indian legal developments in more recent statute law that scholars and other observers have found immensely difficult to unravel. Of course, this case and the 1986 Act protecting the rights of divorced Muslim wives created an enormous political outcry, at first among Muslims, later also among secularists. Initial concern about maintenance for divorced Muslim wives was soon overshadowed by the politicised football of the Uniform Civil Code, on which the judges had pronounced towards the end of the *Shah Bano* decision, which caused widespread riots and protests. Even *India Today*, a leading news magazine and apparently a major

---

[82] *Shah Bano, supra* note 4.

[83] *Bai Tahira* v. *Ali Hussain Chothia*, A.I.R. 1979 S.C. 362 and (1979) 2 S.C.C. 316.

[84] *Shah Bano, supra* note 4, at 952.

source of knowledge among overseas and other middle class Indians about Indian law, has not yet understood the intricacies of this saga. Relying on political gossip rather than legal analysis, journalists and even serious academics continue to engineer curious misunderstandings and serious misinformation about legal facts.[85]

Such problems of perception and insight are central to the present discussion. As just noted, we still frequently read of how Rajiv Gandhi quickly gave in to the rioting Muslims after the *Shah Bano* decision and in record time passed the Muslim Women (Protection of Rights on Divorce) Act of 1986, which took away all rights of divorced Muslim wives to maintenance from their former husbands.[86] Thus, suiting the more strongly emerging Hindu nationalist argument, the dominant allegation became that Muslim men were once more given exceptional privileges (in addition to permission to be polygamous) by the modern Indian state on the basis of religious exemption. Fortunately for India, this has turned out to be politicised gossip, cleverly engineered misinformation. Not only are such convenient fictions loved by the press, but many scholars and other people around the world uncritically continue to cite them as proof that the Indian state (or to be more precise in this political cauldron, the Congress Party) is still favouring Muslims excessively. Closely linked to this is the argument that it would be much better to implement a Uniform Civil Code, so that such communal politicking would become impossible. Clearly, the agenda of many commentators had become the abolition of Indian Muslim personal law through merging it into the Uniform Civil Code. Many modernist scholars unwittingly supported the agenda of Hindu nationalists, which explains some of the embarrassed silence around the present topic.

---

[85] For example, Ashutosh Varshney, *The Great Indian Political Churning,* INDIA TODAY INTERNATIONAL, 2 July 2007, at 12–13 (claiming that "[c]aught in a Muslim furore and understanding it little, Rajiv Gandhi used his three-fourths majority in the Lok Sabha to overturn the court's judgment").

[86] S.P. SATHE, JUDICIAL ACTIVISM IN INDIA: TRANSGRESSING BORDERS AND ENFORCING LIMITS 19 (2002).

As we are gradually realizing, legal reality was quite different, but many observers still find the truth incredible, because the myths of the *Shah Bano* saga remain so powerful. As a matter of hard fact, no upper limit on post-divorce maintenance payments was laid down by the Indian legislature in the 1986 Act.[87] This clearly meant that Muslim husbands were not only principally liable for the future welfare of their ex-wives, but also faced a potentially much higher and hence clearly discriminatory burden, since all other Indian ex-husbands might have to pay only up to 500 Rupees per month to an ex-wife. But nobody noticed this in the heat of the arguments. Everybody, including for some time myself, believed that Rajiv Gandhi had caved in to Muslim demands. So despite murmurs of disapproval about the 1986 Act, there were no Muslim riots on the street after its passage. The legislative ploy had worked, in that everyone was told (and was happy to believe) that divorcing Muslim men had no further legal responsibility for their ex-wives after the *iddat* period. The result was, of course, that modernists and secularists were now vigorously complaining that the Indian state had violated art. 44 of the Constitution by making a new personal status law specifically for Muslims. Loud claims were made (and curiously continue to be made in the global literature) that the Indian state allegedly let down all divorced Muslim wives.[88]

All of this has turned out to be a textbook case of scholarly fiction and confused politicised gossip. As we now know from the Indian Supreme Court's verdict in *Danial Latifi* in 2001, Indian Muslim wives have been protected all along by the *Shah Bano* precedent (which was confirmed as good law in 2001) and by the provisions of the 1986 Act itself, which were firmly defended as constitutionally valid.

In fact, we had quite subtly been told all of this much earlier by the Indian Supreme Court, carefully testing the waters through skilful *obiter dicta* in other decisions,[89] but nobody wanted to

[87] *Supra* note 19.

[88] Varshney, *supra* note 85; SATHE, *supra* note 86.

[89] *Secretary, Tamil Nadu Waqf Board* v. *Syed Fatima Nachi,* A.I.R. 1996 S.C. 2423; *Noor Saba Khatoon v. Mohd. Quasim* (1997) 6 S.C.C. 233.

believe this. It also seems now that nobody was supposed to understand this fully until the right moment came, two weeks after 9/11, to present these facts to the nation in the authoritative Supreme Court decision in *Danial Latifi*. All along it had been the law that Muslim ex-husbands under the 1986 Act, like all Indian ex-husbands under the provisions of S. 125 of the Criminal Procedure Code of 1973, were liable for the welfare of their ex-wife until they made adequate provisions for the woman's survival at a level appropriate to the parties.

While this was certainly not the officially distributed version nor what the press and "activist" human rights watchers picked up from the controversy, this politically difficult and potentially dangerous (in terms of another Muslim backlash of riots or worse) conclusion had earlier been gradually documented by an increasing number of High Court decisions. These have existed in reported form since about 1988, with particular strength and elaborate arguments in the Kerala High Court.[90] But who reads Indian High Court decisions? The law of India – gradually and unnoticed – had begun to be that all Indian ex-husbands, including Muslim men, would have to pay maintenance to their ex-wives until they die or remarry. There was no escape route. Under the special provisions of the new 1986 Act, as noted, Muslim husbands actually found with few exceptions that they were now subject to a tougher regime of responsibility, since there were no upper financial limits. Also the courts began to watch more closely that actions should be more strictly time-bound.

Under S. 3 of the 1986 Act, as interpreted progressively by the High Courts in dozens of reported decisions, not only did a Muslim ex-husband have to maintain the ex-wife during the *iddat* period (which any decent Muslim should do anyway, but many fail to do), but within that period he also had to "make and pay" provisions for the time thereafter. In other words, if a Muslim divorced wife reached the end of her *iddat* period and the husband had not maintained her and had not made reasonable provisions for her future welfare (which might include arranging

[90] *Ali* v. *Sufaira, supra* note 20; read also Menski, *supra* note 20, at 231–94 (discussing many subsequent cases in that and other Indian High Courts).

a remarriage for her), the ex-wife could claim both entitlements in court once the *iddat* had finished. The author has seen for himself in South India how effectively this may assist women in bargaining for their rights within the family.

At the same time, the author is aware of the rightful criticism that going to court to enforce one's entitlements remains a major problem for most women in India, perhaps especially for lower middle class Muslim ex-wives claiming their rights under the 1986 Act.[91] Justice, indeed, is not delivered on a silver platter. Nonetheless, the new laws have contributed enormously to women's empowerment in this regard. Meanwhile, there are more recently reported cases that raise questions about Muslim women who claim potentially unfair benefits, so that some men, again in Kerala, have quite rightly begun to ask the courts to reassess gender justice.[92]

I. TOWARDS LEGAL UNIFORMITY DESPITE PERSONAL LAWS

Worse for India's Muslim husbands, as noted in passing, was that while the Criminal Procedure Code of 1973 had fixed an upper limit of 500 Rupees, there were no financial limits on the ex-wife's entitlements under the 1986 Act for Muslims. Everything depended now on the financial circumstances of the spouses. Indeed there is a decision, again from Kerala, where a Muslim woman who had a million Rupees successfully claimed more money from her millionaire husband.[93] No riots followed this decision either. It appears that this further reassured the lawmakers, faraway in Delhi but watching carefully, that the time was nearly right for more steps to secure better financial protection for all Indian women.

---

[91] Sylvia Vatuk, *Where Will She Go? What Will She Do? Paternalism Toward Women in the Administration of Muslim Personal Law in Contemporary India, in* RELIGION AND PERSONAL LAW IN SECULAR INDIA: A CALL TO JUDGMENT 226 248 (G.J. Larson ed., 2001); Galanter, *supra* note 54.

[92] Werner Menski, *Double Benefits and Muslim Women's Postnuptial Rights,* (2) KERALA LAW TIMES 21–34 (2007).

[93] *Ahammed* v. *Aysha*, 1990 (1) KLT 172.

Unnoticed by virtually all legal scholars and other observers, legal uniformity in this particular area of Indian law has come in through the backdoor, or as a reflection of the moon in a mirror held up to an obviously patriarchal society. While Indian Muslims had earlier used so-called religious arguments to escape from the official Indian social welfare regime with its basic rule that in a patriarchal society, men should be primarily responsible for the welfare of women and children, this argument has backfired badly. India's judges as gatekeepers of the Indian welfare system firmly cajoled such Muslim sharks back into the post-modern Indian net of social welfare arrangements. That system is not built on direct state-made support as in Western countries, but was cleverly designed to ensure that families look after attached individuals and more specifically, that men remain responsible for the welfare of their ex-wives and children.

As the judicial interpretations of the 1986 Act (foremost *Danial Latifi* in 2001[94]) show, the Indian state bureaucracy seems to have realised that it should sacrifice, or rather de-prioritise, the principle of formal legal uniformity if the higher object of securing equitable legal entitlements can be achieved otherwise – all the more if to do so is fiscally prudent. Thus, it was apparently decided that Indian Muslims can have or keep their specific personal laws if they want them and insist on them, but they cannot claim exemption from social welfare obligations that apply uniformly to all Indians. The uniformised post-modern Indian law has therefore begun to incorporate some benign elements of traditional *shari'a* law, which contemporary patriarchal South Asian Muslims and their jurists (guided to some extent by leading Muslim scholars like Tahir Mahmood) may not fully wish to accept. In fact, this would not be the first time that a principle of Muslim law has been adopted elsewhere in Indian law.[95]

The *Danial Latifi* decision and its manifestly pro-women approach in forcing Muslim men to make appropriate arrangements for the

---

[94] *Danial Latifi, supra* note 21.

[95] In 1976, the Marriage Laws (Amendment) Act inserted S. 13(2)(iv) into the original Hindu Marriage Act, permitting a Hindu wife exit through divorce from a marriage into which she had been virtually forced, a rule taken from Muslim law. The Marriage Laws (Amendment) Act, 1976, No. 68, Acts of Parliament, 1976.

future maintenance of their ex-wives did not, as noted, lead to riots on the streets of India at the time. However, it has not been debated fully, as a leading commentator on current developments in Indian gender justice observed.[96] A deeper reason for this studied silence appears to be that the decision in *Danial Latifi* represents an embarrassing defeat for legal modernism and most positivist legal scholars as much as for traditional Muslims. The almost stunned reception of the decision enabled an alert government to swiftly make two further significant piecemeal enactments in related areas to pave the way for greater legal uniformity in Indian family law.

Hardly noticed so far, a further decisive legal development in Indian family laws occurred only two days after the *Danial Latifi* decision, on 24 September 2001, with the passage of the Code of Criminal Procedure (Amendment) Act. This small but highly significant piece of legislation is now making itself felt, as more women and other disadvantaged family members realize that they have legal rights against men who control the family property.[97] Since the legislative intent was not made clear,[98] the question remains whether this is purposeful silence, legislation by stealth, or a planned new strategy to reinstate a higher level of legal uniformity.

It is evident, though, that this particular Act cannot be an accident and that it does three important things at once. Firstly, the Act simply removed the earlier ceiling for maintenance of 500 Rupees in S. 125(1) of the Criminal Procedure Code of 1973 for all Indians. This reinstates legal uniformity in the level of liability to maintain ex-wives for all Indian ex-husbands. This has resulted in litigation by wives and relatives of the middle class and not just at the lowest levels of society as before, where vagrancy and homelessness were central issues. Secondly, the 2001 Act strengthens rights to

---

[96] Flavia Agnes, *Interview with Tanu Thomas K.*, THE TIMES OF INDIA, 29 August 2003 (stressing that "the press has chosen to ignore it and the general public is unaware of it").

[97] Menski, *supra* note 92.

[98] Werner Menski, *Reluctant Legislative Activism*, (1) KERALA LAW TIMES 35–41 (2004).

maintenance pendente lite or interim maintenance in recognition of the fact that so many claimants suffer from tardy implementation of the laws.[99] Thirdly, and closely linked, the Act promises in another proviso speedy disposal of such cases, as far as possible, within sixty days from the date of the service of notice.

We must take these new provisions seriously, even if their implementation will take time and will probably never be perfect. After all, this is India, where state law is only one type of law that people may use. The Indian state, however, appears to mean business here, though people will need time to learn to use (and as always, to abuse) this new law. There will also be much resistance. For example, some more Indian women may be killed in "dowry-related" murders if they make claims to financial support that are seen as unacceptable. Above all, judicial alertness will be needed to implement the undoubtedly beneficial Indian legal provisions on post-divorce maintenance, which may well be some kind of symbolic legislation. This is bound to impact on deeply gendered relations in Indian society today and in the future. This significant legal reform shows the way for a gender-sensitive realignment of responsibilities of Indian family members to each other, remaining within a patriarchal context, which no amount of state law can abolish. While this type of law seems based on quite different assumptions than other recent laws made by the Indian Parliament (such as the Hindu Succession (Amendment) Act, 2005, which seems to privilege individual property rights), other recent enactments have reinforced individuals' liability for close family members.[100]

Most relevant for the present discussion on Indian legal uniformity is thus that the protective legal framework first created for Muslim ex-wives under the 1986 Act has now been extended to all Indian ex-wives. Virtual legal uniformity has been successfully reinstated after the 1986 Muslim personal law detour, though formally the relevant law is found in the amended 1973 Code and in the 1986 Act. In substance, there is no difference any more, but the identity of the personal law structure has been preserved.

---

[99] Vatuk, *supra* note 91.

[100] The Maintenance and Welfare of Parents and Senior Citizens Act of 2007.

The story of the gradual extension of such protection to all Indian citizens in need is thus a textbook example of the continuing power of activist and progressive personal law enactment in Indian law, ultimately designed to strengthen protection of individual rights, national cohesion and legal uniformity (in that order of importance). Indian men might well feel that they are all, irrespective of religion and personal laws, in the same perilous boat. Getting married under Indian law now clearly means (as of course it did before) that men take on serious responsibilities for women and children, potentially for life, whether the marriage lasts or not. Thus, in an unexpected way the agendas of uniform nation building and support for traditional marriage arrangements have been conflated, leading to what some commentators have long seen as oppression of Indian men,[101] a topic about which much more may soon need to be said.

J. SUPPORTING EVIDENCE FROM GROWING UNIFORMITY OF INDIAN DIVORCE LAWS

An equally telling example of the gradual move towards a uniform Indian family law system that retains the personal law structure while implementing legal equality across the personal law spectrum comes from recent developments in Indian divorce law, specifically concerning Indian Christian law. This personal law, earlier codified in the Indian Divorce Act of 1869 and the Indian Christian Marriage Act of 1872, was hopelessly outdated and in need of reform. The Christian divorce law was originally promulgated at a time when divorce was granted with utmost reluctance and only in the most exceptional circumstances, mainly due to "religious" opposition from the Churches. After the liberalising reforms of Hindu divorce law in 1976, similar secularising reforms were introduced into Parsi divorce law in 1988. Muslim *shari'a* law permits fairly easy divorce of either spouse, while favouring the husband's *talaq*, the traditional Muslim unilateral divorce formula of 'I divorce you'.[102] Christian divorce law, therefore, came to stick out as discriminatory and

[101] TAHIR MAHMOOD, PERSONAL LAWS IN CRISIS (1986) (discussing the early warnings).

[102] Indian Muslim women can, and apparently do, use the quite liberal provisions of the Dissolution of Muslim Marriages Act, 1939.

thus unconstitutional. Virtually imprisoning Christian spouses in unhappy marriages while allowing everyone else easier exit routes, this law cried out for modernisation, but Parliament did not act for decades. Until recently, a Christian wife was virtually chained into a marriage forever, while her fellow citizens of other religions could seek divorce when required.

Under the Constitution of India and its equality provisions, this was clearly a case demonstrating the need for a Uniform Civil Code. Instead of asking Parliament to produce a Uniform Civil Code and thus offering Christian women the mixed blessings of an easy divorce regime, India's judges had already given up on Parliament, which was seen as too busy with its own politicking. By 1995, after several unsuccessful attempts, the High Court of Kerala finally experimented with an alternative form of bringing about legal uniformity, removing certain restrictive words from S. 10 of the old Indian Divorce Act of 1869, so that an Indian Christian wife could now seek divorce on the grounds of cruelty, like any other Indian citizen.[103] This daring step of judicial lawmaking never ceases to surprise the author's students in London, until they learn about India's public interest litigation and the various forms of judicial activism on the subcontinent. Through this skilful, simple process of legal intervention, again in Kerala and restricted to that state until 2001, greater legal uniformity was achieved while keeping the personal law system intact.

Parliament eventually got the message that legislative action for the whole of India was overdue, but waited for the right time to reclaim the initiative. It is perhaps no coincidence again that, only two days after the *Danial Latifi* decision, on 24 September 2001, the Indian Parliament passed the Indian Divorce (Amendment) Act, 2001 (Act No. 51 of 2001). This Act finally addressed the long-standing complaint that Christian spouses, particularly Christian women, were disadvantaged in access to divorce. The 2001 amendment has brought Indian Christian divorce law broadly into line with the other divorce laws of India under the various personal laws and the largely optional provisions of the

[103] *Mary Sonia Zachariah* v. *Union of India*, 1995(1) KLT 644 (FB).

secular Special Marriage Act of 1954. Once more we see how legal harmonisation was achieved while retaining the personal law structure.

In S. 10, the new Act provides ten grounds for dissolution of marriage among Christians, plus an additional ground for the wife if she can prove that "the husband has, since the solemnization of the marriage, been guilty of rape, sodomy or bestiality".[104] Some lawyers and activists in India, especially in the South, had fought long and hard for these amendments, which clearly represent another piece of the jigsaw puzzle of Indian legal uniformity that is now in place after prolonged lobbying and repeated setbacks.

K. CONCLUSIONS

In the West, we struggle with handling the various old and new challenges of cultural diversity, particularly now concerning "ethnic implants" introduced into our legal systems by massive migrations from Asia and Africa.[105] Interestingly, India seems to have found a harmonious way to handle such age-old cultural diversities and the resulting pluralism of personal laws, namely leaving various strategic spaces for diversity when it matters, while controlling other spaces more strictly. In light of the evidence presented here, there can be no doubt that the post-modern Indian state has been systematically restructuring the country's social welfare laws, related to securing at least minimal strategic support for those citizens who are dependent on others. The state has done so at the intersection of criminal law and family law, killing two birds with one stone as it were. While making the various personal laws more uniform and holding men across the board more explicitly accountable for the welfare of women, children, and now senior citizens, post-modern Indian law uses criminal law techniques to enforce social obligations. These agendas are apparently more important to the Indian state than the politics of personal law.

---

[104] The Indian Divorce (Amendment) Act, 2001, No. 51, Acts of Parliament, 2001, § 10(2).

[105] MENSKI, *supra* note 1.

The newly activated social welfare orientation of the modern Indian state has relegated the political football of the Uniform Civil Code to a minor place on the league table of agendas. Notably, Indian law has not demanded full state control of marriages and does not require the formal registration of most marriages. With few exceptions (in particular marriages involving foreigners) the solemnisation of marriages remains a matter for society and customs, for clans, families and the concerned individuals, and not for an inefficient state bureaucracy. At the same time, matters of financial security for wives and children appear to have become more important to the Indian state than the more explicitly political and high-profile issue of legal uniformity or the formal detail of marriage registration. Europeans naturally tend to find this unsystematic and baffling, to say the least, and are tempted to view lack of formal state control as inefficient and proof of India's backwardness.

More deeply analysed, the Indian welfare state is shown here to be highly sophisticated in regulating this messy field through a plethora of informal devices like applying presumptions of marriage rather than insisting on formal documentation and empowering women by granting them statutory rights to maintenance. Of course, as regards maintenance law, the Indian state is now simply saving itself from welfare claims of its own disadvantaged citizens, throwing the burden back to the claimant's family in order to save its own coffers, promising access to justice to people who need the support of the courts. A post-modern state can only use such strategies, however, if it has not totally abandoned and legislated away traditional legal systems and their socio-cultural frameworks of values. It can only reinvent and reuse *dharma, sadacara* (good behaviour), *izzat* (honour and status in society) and related concepts to rescue the desperately poor, abandoned, or divorced wives and other citizens if it is willing to co-opt "tradition". This seems exactly what has happened in India, and it explains why there is so much embarrassed and partly annoyed silence about these new legal developments in post-modern India. Many modernist and secular observers are simply miffed about India's refusal to become "modern", and they may also be baffled by these new developments. At any rate, their silence is quite remarkable.

The integrated social welfare reforms in India that were analysed here raised important gender-related concerns. Existing dependencies on overwhelmingly male agents of control over resources will probably continue to prevail worldwide whatever gender-sensitive, equalising reforms are contemplated, since even modern Western laws have not fully removed and curtailed patriarchy and gender discrimination. Western laws have only managed to remove some glaring discrepancies and the most direct forms of discrimination. The Indian state, it seems, does not believe in aggressive gender revolution, preferring subtle strategies of diversity-sensitive evolution. That this movement towards a better future is considered too slow by many activists is clear, but the post-modern Indian state is concerned with remaining realistic and nervous about provoking riots and upheaval. Accordingly, the Indian state does not officially promise its citizens the moon, knowing that it would only be able to deliver a somewhat modified reflection of the desired object. There are also signs (from many judgments in particular) that government agencies in India realize that the social welfare promises of Western states have not been fully implemented and are now, to some extent, regretted, not the least due to spiraling costs and mounting bills. It would be worth examining those cases in detail.

Thus, realistically accepting patriarchy and informality as a fact, which is hardly a difficult task for Indian lawmakers - though it goes against the ideals of many activists - seems to have become a newly invigorated *Grundnorm* for Indian law today. Before male chauvinists rejoice too loudly, let us note that the flipside of this post-modern coin is that domineering men are now increasingly legally and not just morally obligated to use their discretionary control over wealth and resources within families for the benefit of all family members, so that no welfare burden is placed on society and/or on the state. Post-modern constitutional *dharma* in India, hardly a new item in the tool box, relies again on self-controlled ordering within the traditional joint family network. This means that men who hold the position of manager (*karta*) and control the family purse strings have to be actively involved in social welfare for those who depend on their financial support.

The Indian state has, certainly since 2001, become much clearer about the ultimate aim of the developmental agenda: Constitutional directives seek to avoid millions of destitute women, children and now the elderly, living on the road or the pavement of major cities, hungry, thirsty, and desperate for survival. This overriding agenda item has been clearly confirmed by the promulgation of India's amazing Maintenance and Welfare of Parents and Senior Citizens Act of 2007.

The post-modern Indian state has learnt that welfare obligations are most definitely not a matter for direct control by the Indian state. They are not tasks that state agencies could reasonably and realistically fulfill. The state has thus again learnt to delegate obligations to society, a historical lesson that was never really forgotten. Since the number of welfare claimants under any category would in India be enormous, fiscal prudence, as much as a desire to protect women, children and the elderly, demands that a delegated approach to social welfare be taken. It took post-colonial India several decades to implement this approach in a complex interplay of eventually post-modern statutes and case law, learning useful lessons along the way about sustainability of social welfare schemes that rich European nations are painfully tackling at the moment. German pensioners, for example, are faced with reduced commitments by the welfare state to pay for their medicines, complex operations, and many other entitlements that they are used to. They are often deeply disappointed with such developments, even though they may be well off. India quite rightly wants to avoid getting into these kinds of problems in the first place by promising citizens too much as part of the social contract.

While such critical matters of social welfare have moved centre-stage, the case for the introduction of a Uniform Civil Code has steadily become less prominent and less urgent. In fact, the agenda of uniform legislation is now far less convincing, more so since the continuing personal law system demonstrates that it can take care of the pressures of potential inequality through the intricate process of gradual harmonisation of all Indian personal laws and supervision by criminal and constitutional laws. The Indian post-modern state is also helped by the fact that the various personal law systems act as ethnic identifiers of India's celebrated unity in diversity. Thus India, more noticeably since those fateful weeks in September 2001, has achieved the equivalent of a Uniform Civil Code, though not as the lawmakers of the 1940s envisaged. The agendas have been reshuffled, but not totally changed, priorities have been readjusted, but the nation prospers, and vulnerable individuals are better protected than before.

Legal and scholarly debates, however, still lag seriously behind the actual development of the law, both in statutory and case law form. These new laws with their fine-tuned recognition of plurality are deeply sensible. The author has always had problems with the political and legal ideology of total uniformity of laws, as he finds the suggestion that a new uniform family law should, or could, be created by Parliament for all Indians totally impracticable. Formally enforced legal uniformity can hardly lead to the situation-specific justice that the systems of *dharma, nyāya and shariat* in their idealistic ambitions all sought and seek to achieve. India can operate a formally uniform national legal system, like the Constitution and much of the general law, but the "living law" itself, and particularly family law, will always be largely culture-specific and marked by differentiations. Asking for a Uniform Civil Code in the simplistically uniform style desired by the law makers of the 1950s was therefore like asking for the moon. Today, India can show those who still expect to see a uniform family law the mirror image of harmonised personal laws, as Mother Yashoda did for little Krishna. That is all that can be achieved by a diversity-conscious state through the agenda of uniform statutory law reform, even if it formally omits Indian Muslim personal law almost entirely.

The challenge now is to make the existing personal laws work better for as many Indians as possible in socio-legal reality, within the protective framework of the Indian Constitution. This is a huge challenge in every respect, but it is by no means unique to Indian law. The lessons that India can draw from its scenario of continued plurality will be of much relevance to legal scholarship and governments worldwide. If legal systems in Europe can now increasingly accept non-traditional forms of marriage as legally recognised unions, for example, there is no good reason why further diversity-conscious arrangements could not be made.

It seems however, that the key agenda item in all of this is not really or mainly cultural or ethnic diversity, but the extent and firmness of state control. In other words, the critical element is positivism and its voracious appetite for demanding control of our lives. In the mainly legocentric Western legal systems, there is normally a dominant expectation of ultimate state control. States feel entitled to demand formal marriage registration and refuse to recognise any other marital arrangements and authorities as legitimising agents. Indian law shows, however, that such a demand continues to be perceived as unrealistic. The author suggests that this is not evidence of lack of development but confirmation of India's sophistication in handling cultural diversity and legal pluralism.

The best illustration is the well-considered refusal of India to introduce compulsory marriage registration. After high-profile calls in its favour by some Supreme Court judges, the Compulsory Registration of Marriages Bill of 2006 was put before Parliament as a Private Member Bill by a female *Rajya Sabha* (Upper House) member, Mrs. Vanga Geetha. The Bill portrays itself as a panacea for child marriages, polygamy, and women's legal insecurity regarding marital status. However, it has been sitting on the shelf of Parliament for many, many months now, while other significant pieces of legislation, like the Prohibition of Child Marriage Act of 2006, have become law.

If we check a little more carefully, we find the following dramatic legocentric flaw in this demand for the moon: S. 5 of the 2006 Bill suggests that "the marriage performed after the commencement of this Act shall be null and void if not registered within sixty days of solemnization of marriage". This wording alone explains why this Bill will not be passed. It would cause havoc in Indian society to have such a law on the statute book.

Particularly as regards the family law of any legal system, the systemic interplay of uniformity and plurality reflects the multiple realities of human life. A good law should be about "the good life", about which we do not all have the same visions. For example, not everyone wants to get married. How then do we draw the precise boundaries between various forms of relationship and a legally recognised marriage? Indian law appears to be deeply aware that total state control in this regard is not only unrealistic, but ultimately wrong and immoral, because abusers of law and of people will seek to rely on formal rules to claim advantage over weaker persons. Diversity-conscious respect for difference and its legal recognition is perhaps a better strategy for achieving justice than the blindfolded Eurocentric and simply modernist desire to get rid of difference and diversity altogether through legal reform.

8

Level Playing Fields: The Post-Colonial State, Democracy, Courts and Citizenship in India

SUBRATA K. MITRA

A. THE PUZZLE: CITIZENS AND THE STATE IN THE TIME OF GLOBALIZATION

This chapter analyses the legal, political and moral basis of citizenship in the contemporary world. India is analyzed here as a case in point of a general category of 'changing societies' emerging from colonial or communist rule. Citizenship, once considered a part of the general problem of nation-building, has increasingly acquired the character of a salient problem in its own right. This change in perspective is the result of globalization and the world-wide diffusion of basic norms of human rights. When today minorities' lives, dignity and welfare are at risk - be it in Kashmir or Kosovo, the world at large considers itself morally bound to intervene, if not militarily, at least in terms of the invocation of law and good conduct. As such, both the national sovereignty and legitimacy of the post-colonial state seem contingent on its success in turning its whole population into citizens. Success in this regard, the chapter argues, depends in turn upon the ability of the post-colonial state to gear its laws, courts and administration towards effective management of identity and the constitutional incorporation of core social values (see Figure 2). The Indian 'experiment' in 'making citizens out of subjects' holds important lessons for other states ensconced in multicultural societies.

B. THE CONTEXT OF RESEARCH

The problem of citizenship in post-colonial states refers to two different issues. First, as free-standing actors in international law, these 'new states' share the imperative of national security, identity and welfare on equal terms with stable, post-industrial states, though their material and political conditions are vastly different. Second, in contrast to stable, industrial democracies of the West, these new states need to transform *subjects and immigrants* – marginal social groups – into citizens entitled to all political and social rights. The difference arises from the fact that unlike in Western countries, the state in non-Western countries preceded rather than followed the successful formation of the nation. As exemplified in contemporary Iraq, international organizations and Western military alliances, acting in the name of peaceful intervention, have increasingly cut into the national sovereignty of these countries. Changing societies, whose sovereignty and political stability are generally less established than older, (mostly) Western states', are particularly vulnerable to threats of intervention. Making subjects into citizens by attending to their security, welfare and identity – endogenous variables over which the nation-state can exercise its control – is therefore an issue of great importance for these societies.

Citizenship, as a subject of political analysis, has seen a remarkable renaissance in the 1990s.[1] This revival of interest is partly related to the end of the Cold War and the re-emergence of nationalism in the successor states issuing out of Soviet rule. Separatist movements advance claims to independence or self-government. Another factor contributing to the interest in citizenship, as mentioned, is the increase in transnational migration, leading to the creation of minority communities in the host societies. Nation-states must work out how to deal with claims of separatist and immigrant minorities – which to accept and which to reject. Social scientists have tried to determine whether claims of minorities can be addressed in the framework of citizenship, challenging thereby

[1] E.F. Isin and B.S. Turner, *Citizenship Studies: An Introduction, in* HANDBOOK OF CITIZENSHIP 9 (B.S. Turner and E.F. Isin eds., 2002).

the idea of territorial citizenship.[2] Citizenship has been challenged in other ways too. Some argue that it has been 'devalued' and is in decline, postulating the advent of human rights codes and post-national membership in its place.[3] Others advance the slightly different argument that transnational realities, where migrants maintain ties to multiple societies, transform the nation-state and with it the very basis of national citizenship.[4]

India, as the world's largest liberal democracy, shares some characteristics crucial to citizenship with Western liberal democracies. This sets it apart from most post-colonial states. Further, India is extremely diverse, where different categories of minorities often coexist in a conflict-ridden relationship. These minorities include religious communities, castes, and indigenous communities known as 'tribals'. The first aspect of India as a case study is a new innovation in citizenship laws – the introduction of 'Overseas Citizenship of India' in 2003. This form of membership is clearly different from traditional citizenship, but it cannot be easily categorized as another common form of membership. This innovation makes citizenship in India a 'layered' concept: within the same territory, different categories of citizenship, with different levels of rights and entitlements, co-exist. The second aspect of India as a case study is the gradual shift in the notion of citizenship from a liberal, secular and inclusive basis to a more exclusive, ethnic conception of citizenship that is defined in terms of descent rather than territory. The third aspect of India as a case study is its status as a multicultural state. India's Constitution

---

[2] I.M. Young, *Polity and Group Difference: A Critique of the Ideal of Universal Citizenship*, 99 ETHICS 250 (1989); W. KYMLICKA, MULTICULTURAL CITIZENSHIP (1995); G. MAHAJAN, THE MULTICULTURAL PATH: ISSUES OF DIVERSITY AND DISCRIMINATION IN DEMOCRACY (2002).

[3] T. SOYSAL, LIMITS OF CITIZENSHIP: MIGRANTS AND POSTNATIONAL MEMBERSHIP IN EUROPE (1994); D. JACOBSON, RIGHTS ACROSS BORDER: IMMIGRATION AND THE DECLINE OF CITIZENSHIP (1996).

[4] N. Glick Schiller, L. Bash and C. Szanton Blanc, *From Immigrant to Transmigrant: Theorizing Transnational Migration,* in TRANSNATIONAL MIGRATION 121 (Ludgar Pries ed., 1997); A. ONG, FLEXIBLE CITIZENSHIP: THE CULTURAL LOGICS OF TRANSNATIONALITY (1999); A. Appadurai, *Grassroots Globalization and the Research Imagination,* 12 PUBLIC CULTURE 1 (2000); U. Hannerz, *Transnational Research, in* HANDBOOK OF METHODS IN ANTHROPOLOGY (H. Russell Bernard ed., 1998).

recognizes both individual and group rights. Various public institutions like the judiciary and the national commission for minorities and the competitive political process provide the institutional arrangement necessary to produce a level playing field for competing claims to citizenship.

India, as a site of research, offers both the challenges of industrial and globally connected states as well as those of poor states, ensconced in transitional societies. Since the liberalization of the economy in 1991, India has been pursuing the interests of Indians resident in foreign countries through world organizations like the WTO or through the mechanisms of the United Nations. At the same time, internationally visible issues of human rights violations in Kashmir, communal violence against minorities, and the welfare of women, former untouchables or forest dwellers (tribals), have impacted on Indian legislation regarding the rights of citizens. The sections that follow will analyze India's responses in terms of the consequent institutional arrangement, legislation, and social, economic and political reform.

C. NATIONALITY *vs* CITIZENSHIP

In his famous oration "Freedom at Midnight", Jawaharlal Nehru announced the birth of India as the soul of a 'nation, long suppressed' finding 'utterance' in the institutional arrangements of the post-colonial state.[5] While his intention to find a rightful place for India in the comity of nations was both explicit and firm, a similar clarity was not to be found in his understanding of the actual stakeholders of this new nation. The legal vision of the architects of the new republic saw citizenship in terms of territoriality, a definition that went back to the Treaty of Westphalia (1648). The hiatus between the moral definition of Indians in terms of community and the legal definition in terms of territory was first challenged in the language of riots of the 1950s that led to the redrawing of India's internal boundaries. The definition was revised once more due to the demand of Indians living abroad for succession to property in India. This

[5] SUBRATA K. MITRA AND V. B. SINGH, DEMOCRACY AND SOCIAL CHANGE (1999).

led eventually to the Persons of Indian Origin Card (PIO), which explicitly recognizes the rights of citizenship, not as binary, but as incrementally gradual. The ultimate prize of double nationality is in the offing, bringing the discourse full circle, away from the exclusive reliance on territory.

The experience of transitional societies regarding the relationship of nationality and citizenship differs sharply from that of industrial societies. In the latter, the nation, speaking in the name of the collective body of citizens, appeared before the state, whereas in the former, the states, issuing out of colonial or communist rule, had to create nations, with citizens as stakeholder. The chapter suggests that turning subjects into citizens is possible only if the institutional arrangement that governs the concept is *co-authored* by the state and society, standing, respectively, in the case of post-colonial states, for imported norms of equality and embedded values. Globalization, which has seen an Indian 'Diaspora' of twenty million people, has provided additional incentives for developing the legislative basis of a 'layered citizenship'.

Permeable – or at least semi-permeable – borders are "undermining the traditional territorial basis of democracy and creating new political spaces which need democratizing."[6] While nationality or "national communities" used to provide the framework of democratic decision making in the past, the new 'global forces' remain beyond democratic control and undermine the territorial organization of state and community. This phenomenon also affects the nexus between democracy and citizenship. Liberal models of democratic sovereignty, largely confined and "over-identified" with the territory of nation-state,[7] are not only eroded by the theoretical challenges and the practical problems arising from minority rights and "multicultural citizenship",[8] but also have to cope with a transnational arena of world politics and more localized cross-border contexts.[9]

---

6 JAMES ANDERSON, TRANSNATIONAL DEMOCRACY: POLITICAL SPACES AND BORDER CROSSINGS (2002).

7 *Id.* at 6.

8 KYMLICKA, *supra* note 2.

9 ANDERSON, *supra* note 6, at 6.

These new political "spaces" have led to changes in the concept of citizenship. "Border-crossing trans-nationalism could be an escape from the confining rigidity of national frameworks and state territoriality: it might provide new opportunities for more participatory forms of democracy and augment the limited democracy traditionally on offer."[10] There are indeed widely differing opinions about how national territorial citizenship is – or should be – changing and about what should be done within and beyond states. There are disagreements about the feasibility of defending and strengthening nationality. As new institutional arrangements govern political processes, the nation is being supplemented or even displaced by other territorial frameworks (such as the European Union), by non-governmental organizations (NGOs) and transnational social movements, or indeed by Diasporas. The active exercise of citizenship is no longer linked to some common 'identity' and 'community'; citizenship has become a moving target that shifts back and forth between territorially defined national communities within state borders and non-territorial (often transnational) communities defined in ethnic and functional terms.[11]

Nationality and citizenship may depend on each other, but they are not necessarily congruent.[12] Within the bounds of comparative constitutional theory, nationality conveys either a status or legal relationship that establishes a state's jurisdiction over an individual. The effects are double edged, cutting into international and constitutional law. The International Court of Justice, in its famous *Nottebohm* judgment concerning the exercise of diplomatic protection on behalf of a naturalized citizen, held that

> the legal bond of nationality had to correspond to social reality. Nationality had to be supported by a genuine, existential and emotionally rooted commitment to the state; otherwise, it would be ineffective and

[10] *Id.*
[11] *Id.* at 7.
[12] STEFAN KADELBACH, UNION CITIZENSHIP (2003).

> not give rise to any obligations vis-à-vis the claimant state. This restriction is primarily significant for individuals who possess more than one nationality. It accords with the conflict of laws and statutes of many states to choose the effective nationality as a reference point in such cases. Under international law, nationality therefore serves to resolve collisions of jurisdiction. [13]

D. TURNING SUBJECTS INTO CITIZENS: A NEO-INSTITUTIONAL MODEL AND A TOOL KIT

Just as the legal right to citizenship is accorded by the state, identity, and following from it the moral right to belong, is what people give to their claims to citizenship. When both converge in the same group, the result is a sense of legitimate citizenship where the individual feels both legally entitled and morally engaged. If not, the consequences are either legal citizenship devoid of a sense of identification with the soil or a primordial identification with the land but no legal sanction of this. These situations can lead to violent disorder, inter-community rioting and civil war. In a post-colonial context, citizens are a liminal category, a 'hinge group'[14] that connects the state and society (see Figure 1 on next page). Orderly, legitimate citizenship is possible only if the concept is co-authored by the modern state and the traditional society. India, this chapter asserts, has achieved something along these lines through 'layered citizenship.' The Indian strategy has consisted of making rebels into stakeholders. The Constitution, innovating institutions and citizenship, has acted as a backdrop to a set of institutions, political processes and policies.

The Indian record of successfully turning subjects into citizens has cross-national signific ance. Rather than being a unique attribute of Indian culture, it is based on an institutional arrangement

---

[13] *Id.* at 11.

[14] 'Hinge groups' are politically bi-lingual, encompassing both modern and traditional idioms of politics. They act as political interpreters and intermediaries between the modern state and the traditional society.

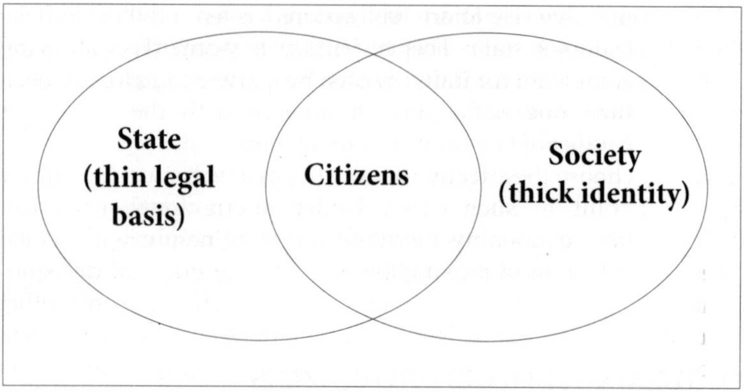

Fig.1: The Modern 'Post-colonial' State, Traditional Society and Citizenship: Overlapping Legal and Moral Categories.

containing several important parameters. First are the legal sources of citizenship as formulated in the Indian Constitution (articles 5–11), the Constituent Assembly Debates (or CAD, which provide insights into the controversy surrounding specific articles), and the enabling and amending legislation of the national parliament. 'Judicialisation' of citizenship is another method of synchronizing the provisions of the law and the new demands emerging from society.[15] The assertion of identity and linkage to India has emerged as a basis of Indian citizenship, supplementary to birth and residence. Property and citizenship have constantly been interwoven: the questions as to who can own property and how much have had fluid answers. In the case of Kashmir, the laws have always had a slightly different tinge due to the special agreement that the Indian Acts would not be normally applicable in Kashmir.[16] In the last decade, case law has tended towards a more flexible and all encompassing understanding of Indian stipulations regarding property and, of course, the onset

[15] *Izhar Ahmad Khan* v. *Union of India* (UOI), AIR 1962, SC 1052. The case dealt in detail with the following questions: the rights to and of citizenship, partition related citizenship, the value of a passport in determining citizenship, and domicile versus citizenship. At issue was the constitutional validity of section 9(2) of the Citizenship Act, 1955, which provision dealt with the termination of citizenship. This judgement exemplified the policies that discouraged multiple or even dual citizenships, holding that upon acquiring in any manner the citizenship of another country, an Indian citizen automatically loses Indian citizenship.

[16] *Bachan Lal Kalgotra* v. *State of Jammu and Kashmir*, AIR 1987, SC 1169.

of economic liberalization has spurred even further judicial liberalization of these concepts. Similarly, recent laws allowing NRIs (Non-Resident Indians) to own property have already been registered in case law.

Drawing on his previous work on governance,[17] the author asserts that India's relative success on the issue of citizenship can be attributed to the unusual vigor and imagination with which these tools of citizen-making are used by the political decision-makers in India. Typically a three prong attack is made on conflict issuing out of the hiatus between general legal norms of the state and the assertion of political identity contesting the state. India makes stakeholders out of rebels by adroitly combining reform, repression and selective recruitment of rebels into the privileged circle of new elites (see Figure 2).

Fig.2: Culture, Context and Strategy in Turning Subjects into Citizens: A Dynamic Neo-Institutional Model.

E. SOME EMPIRICAL ATTRIBUTES OF THE INDIAN MODEL

Why has India been more successful than many post-colonial states in turning subjects into citizens? The explanatory model specified in Figure 2 rests on five empirical arguments relating to (a) India's institutional arrangement (the Constitution), (b) laws linked to India's social visions, (c) the double role of the state – as neutral enforcer and as a partisan, supporting vulnerable social

[17] SUBRATA K. MITRA, THE PUZZLE OF INDIA'S GOVERNANCE: CULTURE, CONTEXT AND COMPARATIVE THEORY (2005).

groups – in producing a level playing field, (d) the incorporation of elements of bargaining theory into Indian law and political practice and finally, (e) judicialisation – evidence of the courts at work in turning subjects into citizens.

I. The Constitution

The Indian Constitution (like most constitutions) avoids the terminology of nation and nationality. Citizenship is the constitutional key word for dividing the world between 'us and them'.[18] Citizenship thus is a form of adherence to a body politic that identifies a person as a full member thereof. In India too, *citoyens* – those creatures of the enlightenment – are united by freedom, equality and brotherliness. The Preamble to the Constitution of India announces this intention with boldness and clarity.

> WE, THE PEOPLE OF INDIA, having solemnly resolved to constitute India into a SOVEREIGN SOCIALIST SECULAR DEMOCRATIC REPUBLIC and to secure to all its citizens: JUSTICE, social, economic and political; LIBERTY of thought, expression, belief, faith and worship; EQUALITY of status and of opportunity; and to promote among them all Fraternity assuring the dignity of the individual and the unity and integrity of the Nation; IN OUR CONSTITUENT ASSEMBLY this twenty-sixth day of November, 1949, do HEREBY ADOPT, ENACT AND GIVE TO OURSELVES THIS CONSTITUTION.[19]

---

[18] "The question of citizenship became particularly important at the time of the making of our Constitution because the Constitution sought to confer certain rights and privileges upon those who were entitled to Indian citizenship while they were to be denied to 'aliens'. The latter were even placed under certain disabilities." DURGA DAS BASU, INTRODUCTION TO THE CONSTITUTION OF INDIA 74 (2001).

[19] Preamble, Constitution of India.

The Constitution includes citizens' rights, which are intended to protect the individual from arbitrary interference by state authority. Almost all of these rights are, however, not limited to the state's own nationals. What is constitutive for an Indian citizen's status are positive rights (especially social rights) and political rights (primarily the right to vote and to stand for election). In historical comparison and political theory, they constitute the criterion of exclusion that distinguishes the fully effective status of a citizen from other forms of membership, especially from that of mere subjects.[20]

The status of a citizen also incorporates social rights (e.g., the directive principles jurisprudence and now the entire jurisprudence that evolved with the judicial activism of the Indian Supreme Court).[21] In this context, social class also plays an important role in the citizenship debates. The view that citizenship can be understood as a status that gives one the rights to a certain bundle of entitlements, benefits and obligations derives from T.H. Marshall (1950). Marshall's catalogue of civil, political, and social rights is based on the cumulative logic of struggles for expanding democracy in the nineteenth and early twentieth centuries. Civil rights arise with the birth of the absolutist state, and in their earliest and most basic form they entail the rights to the protection of life, liberty, and property; the right to freedom of conscience; and certain associational rights, like those of contract and marriage. Political rights in the narrow sense refer to the rights of self- determination, to hold and run for office, to enjoy freedom of speech and opinion, and to establish political and non-political associations, including a free press and free institutions of science and culture. Social rights come last in Marshall's catalogue, because they have been achieved historically through the struggles of workers', women's, and other social movements of the last two centuries. Social rights involve the right to form trade unions as well as other professional and trade associations; health care rights; unemployment compensation; old age pensions; as well

---

[20] KADELBACH, *supra* note 12, at 12.

[21] T.H. MARSHALL AND T. BOTTOMORE, CITIZENSHIP AND SOCIAL CLASS (1992); R. Dahrendorf, *The Changing Quality of Citizenship*, *in* THE CONDITION OF CITIZENSHIP (B. van Steenbergen ed., 1994).

as child care, housing, and educational subsidies. These social rights vary widely across countries and depend on the social class composition prevalent in any given welfare state democracy.[22]

II. *Legal Sources of Citizenship and the Constituent Assembly Debates*

Citizenship may have had its origin in political struggles and political philosophy, but the constitution treats it essentially as a legal concept. The Indian Constitution employs it in Part II (articles 5–11). While drafting this section, the Constituent Assembly sought to figure out who would, as of 1950, have a right to Indian nationality and citizenship. The absence of racial distinctiveness as a prerequisite for citizenship was explained by a crucial exchange in the CAD.[23] Citizenship proved to be among the most disputed issues during the Constituent Assembly: it was debated for almost two years and was subject to more than 120 proposed amendments. This trend continued both in further policy initiatives and in their interpretation.

The CAD were restricted to ensuring that the articles dealt with the situation as it existed at that particular time; all other rules were left to Parliament to decide. These articles were mainly intended to clean up the concept of who could be Indian. All acknowledged it as a privilege, and the attempt was made to delineate with a clear conscience those who had opted out of the newly formed Indian territory. Thus, though the international community was present in the minds of the drafters, their main concern was the result of Partition and how it translated into the identity of an Indian. The attempt was more to figure out how to de-link the cultural concept of nationality with the political right.

---

[22] SEYLA BENHABIB, POLITICAL THEORY AND POLITICAL MEMBERSHIP IN A CHANGING WORLD 410–11 (2002).

[23] "I thought that an Indian is a very easily recognizable person. When combined with domicile, it is easier to define it, But if the Professor thinks that an Indian cannot be recognized and that it is necessary to lay down who is an Indian, what is his colour and complexion and so on, I would leave it to him to suggest a suitable definition. I think the existing definition is capable of being understood without any difficulty." P.S. Deshmukh's optimism for an"easy" solution was misplaced. While the results look fairly effortless and straightforward, drafting the citizenship articles was one of the most contentious issues of the Constitution Assembly, with almost 120 amendments moved. P.S. Deshmukh, constituent Assembly Debates, Volume IX, 11 August 1949

At the outset, article 5 clearly reflects Dr. Ambedkar's and other members' sustained demand for granting all those born on Indian soil the right to Indian citizenship by setting out the purpose of the articles and the desire to curtail this purpose to the question of citizenship at the commencement of the Constitution.

> Article 5. Citizenship at the commencement of the Constitution. At the commencement of this Constitution, every person who has his domicile in the territory of India and-
> (a) who was born in the territory of India; or
> (b) either of whose parents was born in the territory of India; or
> (c) who has been ordinarily resident in the territory of India for not less than five years immediately preceding such commencement, shall be a citizen of India.[24]

The logical sequence is maintained by article 6, the next article concerning citizenship, which deals with migrants from territory of the undivided India, now Pakistan.

> Article 6. Rights of citizenship of certain persons who have migrated to India from Pakistan. Notwithstanding anything in article 5, a person who has migrated to the territory of India from the territory now included in Pakistan shall be deemed to be a citizen of India at the commencement of this Constitution if-
> (a) he or either of his parents or any of his grand-parents was born in India as defined in the Government of India Act, 1935 (as originally enacted); and
> (b)(i) in the case where such person has so migrated before the nineteenth day of July, 1948, he has been ordinarily resident in the territory of India since the date of his migration, or

[24] Art. 5, Constitution of India.

> (ii) in the case where such person has so migrated on or after the nineteenth day of July, 1948, he has been registered as a citizen of India by an officer appointed in that behalf by the Government of the Dominion of India on an application made by him therefore to such officer before the commencement of this Constitution in the form and manner prescribed by that Government;
> Provided that no person shall be so registered unless he has been resident in the territory of India for at least six months immediately preceding the date of his application.[25]

The problem of re-migration was tackled in article 7, which, while stating that no one who had migrated to Pakistan was a citizen of India, made provision for people who had re-migrated to India from these territories. These people were required to have a permit of resettlement or permanent return issued by the proper authorities.

> Article 7. Rights of citizenship of certain migrants to Pakistan. Notwithstanding anything in articles 5 and 6, a person who has after the first day of March, 1947, migrated from the territory of India to the territory now included in Pakistan shall not be deemed to be a citizen of India; Provided that nothing in this article shall apply to a person who, after having so migrated to the territory now included in Pakistan, has returned to the territory of India under a permit for resettlement or permanent return issued by or under the authority of any law and every such person shall for the purposes of clause (b) of article 6 be deemed to have migrated to the territory of India after the nineteenth day of July, 1948.[26]

---

[25] *Id.*, Art. 6.
[26] *Id.*, Art. 7.

The root of the idea of PIO can be glimpsed in article 8, which deals with people residing outside India at the time of independence. It gives them the right to apply for citizenship based on origin – again subject to the provision that the person has registered at an Indian mission in the country of residence.

> Article 8. Rights of citizenship of certain persons of Indian origin residing outside India. - Notwithstanding anything in article 5, any person who or either of whose parents or any of whose grand-parents was born in India as defined in the Government of India Act, 1935 (as originally enacted), and who is ordinarily residing in any country outside India as so defined shall be deemed to be a citizen of India if he has been registered as a citizen of India by the diplomatic or consular representative of India in the country where he is for the time being residing on an application made by him therefore to such diplomatic or consular representative, whether before or after the commencement of this Constitution, in the form and manner prescribed by the Government of the Dominion of India or the Government of India.[27]

The need to demarcate between the citizens of the newly partitioned territories is captured in article 9, which states that those who have voluntarily acquired foreign citizenship lose Indian citizenship claims.

> Article 9. Persons voluntarily acquiring citizenship of a foreign State not to be citizens. No person shall be a citizen of India by virtue of article 5, or be deemed to be a citizen of India by virtue of article 6 or

[27] *Id.*, art. 8.

> article 8, if he has voluntarily acquired the citizenship of any foreign State.[28]

Article 10 makes every effort to include everyone the CAD have not expressly disallowed to be or remain citizens of India. This article would probably have to be relied on by persons in India in the unenivable position of being stateless, often refugees with no proof of identity and expressly disowned by neighbouring countries.

> Article 10. Continuance of the rights of citizenship. Every person who is or is deemed to be a citizen of India under any of the foregoing provisions of this Part shall, subject to the provisions of any law that may be made by Parliament, continue to be such citizen.[29]

> Article 11. Parliament to regulate the right of citizenship by law. -Nothing in the foregoing provisions of this Part shall derogate from the power of Parliament to make any provision with respect to the acquisition and termination of citizenship and all other matters relating to citizenship.[30]

The Constituent Assembly thus made a distinction between five categories of persons:

(1) Persons domiciled in India and born in India (i.e., persons who formed the bulk of the population of India. The period of domicile was a minimum of five years. Although subsequent case law decided that mere domicile was not enough (*Abdul Sattar* v. *State of Gujarat, AIR* 1965 *SC* 810), the person had to fulfill one of the other conditions in the article.);

---

[28] *Id.*, Art. 9.
[29] *Id.*, Art. 10.
[30] *Id.*, Art. 11.

(2) Persons who are domiciled in India (i.e., persons not born in India but have resided in India. For instance, persons who were the subjects of the erstwhile Portuguese or the French Settlements in India, or persons, though not born in India, who have resided for a long time with the undoubted intention of becoming Indian citizens.);
(3) Persons who were residents in India but who migrated to Pakistan;
(4) Persons resident in Pakistan and who migrated to India; and
(5) Persons who or whose parents were born in India but were residing outside India, and those who migrated to Pakistan but who returned to India after going to Pakistan.

The articles referred to citizenship specifically on the date of the commencement of the Constitution. The intent was not to lay down a permanent law of citizenship for this country. Article 6 effectively allows Parliament to take away citizenship from those who are declared to be citizens on the date of the commencement of the Constitution by the provisions of article 5 and to grant citizenship to those originally disallowed this privilege by the Constitution.

Religion, as a marker of citizenship, was explicitly rejected by the CAD, though there were members, like P.S. Deshmukh, who wished to include provisions that consolidated the rights of Hindus and Sikhs. The emphasis was more on territorial loyalty than religion. This included the important financial aspect of evacuee property. One of the most forceful arguments was based on the fact that re-migrants were to be granted Indian citizenship. All the questions left unanswered by the Constituent Assembly were to be decided by India's Parliament and the courts, which responded in a similar way, but with the courts displaying a slightly more flexible approach at times.

III. State as Both Neutral and Partisan

The Indian state, which juxtaposes its neutral profile to that of a partisan, reinforces the capacity of weaker members of the political community to negotiate their way in favor of dignity, equality and citizenship. This dual attribute of the state has greatly helped India in achieving a generally peaceful and orderly transition.

Rudolph and Rudolph formulate this in terms of the multiple roles of the *post-colonial state* in India. The two scholars show how it has successfully incorporated some apparently contradictory values in order to create a space where different social groups can periodically negotiate the priorities for the politics of the day:

> Like Hindu conceptions of the divine, the state in India is polymorphous, a creature of manifold forms and orientations. One is the third actor whose scale and power contribute to the marginality of class politics. Another is a liberal or citizens' state, a judicial body whose legislative reach is limited by a written constitution, judicial review, and fundamental rights. Still another is a capitalist state that guards the boundaries of the mixed economy by protecting the rights and promoting the interest of property in agriculture, commerce, and industry. Finally a socialist state is concerned to use public power to eradicate poverty and privilege and tame private power. Which combination prevails in a particular historical setting is a matter for inquiry.[31]

The multiple roles of the post-colonial state as conceptualized by Rudolph and Rudolph is reinforced by the *dynamic neo-institutional model* of economy-society-state interaction (see Figure 2 on page 191), where the new social elites, themselves the outcome of fair and efficient political recruitment through democratic elections, play a two-track strategy and institute processes of law and order management, social and economic reform and accommodation of identity as a basis for inter- and intra-group negotiation. The key function of this model is to help establish an agenda for empirical research into the policy process by focusing on the key decision-making elite.[32]

---

[31] LLOYD I. RUDOLPH AND SUSANNE HOEBER RUDOLPH, IN PURSUIT OF LAKSHMI: THE POLITICAL ECONOMY OF THE INDIAN STATE (1987).

[32] Subrata K. Mitra, *Caste and the Politics of Identity: Beyond the Orientalist Discourse, in* CULTURE AND RATIONALITY: THE POLITICS OF SOCIAL

The Indian Constitution, thanks to the presence of many lawyers, politicians and members of the liberal professions inspired by Fabian socialism, rule of law and the values of consensus and accommodation championed by the Freedom Movement, accepted *social change* in its larger sense as the normative objective of the modern state and parliamentary democracy based on methodological individualism as the preferred method of achieving it. Therein lies a paradox: how can a state, based on a prior commitment to modernization and democracy generate a social program that would be seen by a society that, at least at the time of the promulgation of the Constitution, was still deeply committed to the Indian tradition? Not surprisingly, the paradoxical juxtaposition of the modern state and traditional society has been at the root of problems of governance and citizenship.

IV. *Enhancing the Bargaining Power of Weaker Sections*

Independence came to India not as a result of a revolutionary war but protracted negotiation – between the colonial ruler and the main actors in the freedom movement. The negotiation was complex because the discussions between the colonizer and the colonized intersected conflicts among the colonized themselves. This had one major consequence. The post-independence regime in India was based on power-sharing among adversaries, who in the process learned to use democratic institutions to constrain the struggle for power. Negotiation has therefore become an essential part of India's politics and indeed, of everyday life.[33] The constant

---

CHANGE IN POST-COLONIAL INDIA (1999); MITRA AND SINGH, *supra* note 5; MITRA, *supra note* 17.

[33] "Negotiation is a basic means of getting what you want from others. It is back-and-forth communication designed to reach an agreement when you and the other side have some interests that are shared and others that are opposed [...]. [P]eople negotiate even when they don't think of themselves as doing so. You negotiate with your spouse about where to go for dinner and with your child about when the lights go out." ROGER FISHER, WILLIAM URY AND BRUCE PATTON, GETTING TO YES: NEGOTIATING AN AGREEMENT WITHOUT GIVING IN XVII (2nd ed. 1991).

presence of conflict in the local arena is also indicative of the growing propensity of people from all backgrounds to assert their rights to dignity, basic needs and security.[34]

The political culture of bargaining that has developed in India in the course of the post-independence party competition can be best described in terms of 'principled negotiation', which underpins citizen-making in India.[35] The most crucial of these principles are the capacity of the negotiators to dissociate the profiles and personalities of actors from the interests being negotiated and the knowledge, particularly among the weaker partners, that there is an acceptable alternative to the agreement that has been or might be worked out during the negotiation, which makes it possible for them to be less obdurate and more confident in their negotiating style. Legislation like the 1955 Untouchability Offences Act, which criminalized the very use of the word untouchable to address someone, or reservation, which guarantees a minimum presence of the former untouchables in legislatures in proportion to their population, has raised these groups' BATNA (best alternative to a negotiation agreement). The sophisticated negotiations that one finds in the successful campaign of the Bahujan Samaj Party (or BSP, set up by Kanshi Ram and led by him and Mayawati, current Chief Minister of Uttar Pradesh) can be seen as the ultimate successors to the steadily growing profile and political clout of the former untouchables.

The sophisticated and sustained negotiation that one finds in the CAD gives an insight into the functioning of India's high politics at the crucial stage when power was transferred from the colonial

---

[34] The comments of Fisher *et al.* are perfectly appropriate for India's everyday life. "Everyone wants to participate in decisions that affect them; fewer and fewer people will accept decisions dictated by someone else. People differ, and they use negotiations to handle their differences. Whether in business, government, or the family, people reach most decisions through negotiations. Even when they go to court, they almost always negotiate a settlement before trial." *Id.*

[35] Fisher *et al.* describe the characteristics of principled negotiations as follows: [1] 'wise' and durable; [2] based on interests and not positions; [3] objective (inter-subjective) rather than subjective; [4] separate people from interests; [5] look beyond perceptions by putting themselves in other people's shoes; and [6] Principled negotiators know their BATNA (Best Alternative to a Negotiated Agreement). *Id.*

government to Indian hands. The question that can be raised by those unfamiliar with India is not so much about the requisite mental sophistication as it is the capacity to communicate across the differences of language, region, religion and the city-rural dichotomy. Does culture (shared norms) matter in negotiation (searching for mutually acceptable outcomes to a conflict over interests)? Does the question of cultural identity make sense in the face of the communications revolution, globalization and the search for a global society?

Those familiar with the bargaining that underpins Indian politics can also explain how, as these have evolved, bargaining across and not just within ethnic groups has become an integral part of India's politics. Further references to the negotiation literature help us understand the constant and continuous negotiation that goes on behind the formal outward agency. The literature shows us concrete examples of how negotiations work in terms of sequences.[36]

V. *Judicialisation of Citizenship*

As a result of consciousness of interests that are bargained over, the political process makes a veto player out of weak players. Their BATNA has been boosted thanks to legislation that has transformed the knowledge and self esteem of former untouchables. *Izhar Ahmad Khan* v. *Union of India* (*UOI*)[37] dealt in detail with the following questions: the rights to and of citizenship; the issues of partition related citizenship; the value of a passport in determining citizenship; and the question of domicile versus citizenship. The issue in the case was the constitutional validity of section 9(2) of the Citizenship Act, 1955, which dealt with the termination of citizenship. The decision exemplified the policies that discouraged multiple or even dual citizenship, as it held that upon acquiring in any manner the citizenship of another country, an Indian citizen automatically loses Indian citizenship. The amendment of the Act in 2003 has rendered the whole series of

[36] I.W. ZARTMAN AND M.R. BERMAN, THE PRACTICAL NEGOTIATOR 201-202 (1982).

[37] *Supra* note 15.

definitive judgments based on it obsolete while at the same time making it an important resource for judicial arguments.

The Supreme Court has interpreted the articles and the Citizenship Act in stricter and more generous ways, not giving any clear indication of the judicial attitude of and towards citizenship. It has reflected the policies as well as the emotions of the day. The task of carving out an identity that had been incompletely carried out by the legislature was taken up in the subsequent interpretations of these sections by the courts. Domicile and territorial links became important in this context. International conventions of domicile and ideas of political privilege were only accepted insofar as they reflected what the judges felt were in consonance with India's new, historical background. In this process, *Chakma refugees* from Bangladesh, who were said to be 'causing disturbances' in the areas they settled in, were denied the rights of domicile and citizenship by residence. Of course, the question of what constituted domicile was itself troublesome, and this debate had its roots in the Constitution drafting committee discussions where Alladi Krishnaswami's note on who should be a citizen and what precautions should be introduced in the Constitution succinctly indicates the subsequent thinking of policy makers and the judiciary. While the exigencies of the Indian political situation require to these conceptions to be qualified somewhat, we need not go to the other extreme. The merit of the present clause is that while retaining the birth-test, it emphasizes the connection with India and adds an additional, ethnic path to citizenship.

Even as late as in 1994 in *Mysore Wodeyar* (1994 Supp (1) SCC 191), the abolition of privy purses has also been linked to every Indian citizen feeling that India has one common citizenship and to the desire to inculcate in every citizen that he/she is an equal Indian first, irrespective of social particularities. This concept had also been applied to the questions of grants of land. Grants made by erstwhile rulers were subject to the recognition of the Indian state in consonance with the idea of the equal citizen. That the foreign resident is also being included in this family of the equal citizen is shown in cases where origins have been held to be valid grounds for wanting to have a house and buy property in India – formerly a right not granted to NRIs and by implication PIOs. In the 2003 case of *Atma S. Berar* ((2003) 2 SCC 3), Canadian citizenship was held to be no bar for a person who had links to his ancestral village wanting to buy or maintain property and live there. These cases also show the growing acceptance of the all important emotional factor, clearly reflecting the desire to include Diaspora communities in the emotional definition of an Indian. In the last decade, case law has adopted a more flexible and all encompassing understanding of an Indian with relation to property, which judicial liberalization has been accelerated by economic liberalization. Recent laws allowing NRIs to own property further emphasises the transformation of citizenship from territoriality to ethnicity in India. With global legal scenarios encompassing municipal laws, the question of identity in terms of psychological ties as opposed to physical ties to India has gained prominence. The courts have long held that citizenship is not necessary in order to have a home in the country.

F. *Conclusion: Negotiating Citizenship in Divided Societies*

Paradoxically, citizenship - the seventeenth century totem of exclusive political and economic rights, but confined to the bounded territory of a nation-state[38] - has once again emerged as a salient and complex problem amid globalization. The world-wide mobility of ideas and people - both legal and clandestine - has come to challenge political order in stable, liberal democracies where immigrants, often having a different religious background than the mainstream, demand both the legal right to citizenship on par with the natives and the recognition of their ethnic right to difference in the public sphere.[39] In changing societies, many of which adopted the norm of territorial citizenship at independence, transnational networks and cultural flows have emerged as challenges to the norm of territorial citizenship, sometimes with violent consequences.[40] In sum, terrorism, new communication technology, transnational movement of capital and labor, and

---

[38] This is attributed to the Treaty of Westphalia (1648) which led to the recognition of the territorial state as the ultimate, sovereign unit in national and international politics.

[39] Examples are the case of immigrants from North Africa in the suburbs of Paris and the controversy surrounding the headscarf in France and Germany.

[40] The reference here is to the rise of the language movement and the violent separation of Bangladesh from Pakistan as well as to the civil war in Sri Lanka.

global norms of human rights have brought the exclusive rights of the territorial state over its citizens into question.

We have seen some of the concrete and specific aspects of the global issue of citizenship in our analysis of India. The Indian Constitution accepts and recognizes citizenship by birth, descent and naturalization. The question of 'Who is an Indian?' nevertheless is complex. It is further complicated by the rapid internationalization of both territory and the individual. Affording citizenship one concise definition is accordingly difficult, if not impossible. Perhaps identity can be construed as private as well as public, namely, the identity one has of oneself with regard to countries and nations and the identity the public confers on the individual. Dual nationality was not discussed in much detail in the CAD probably because the nationality of the Subcontinent obfuscated nationality issues to the country. Loss of Indian citizenship as a result of acquiring that of another country is, however, mentioned in article nine.[41] The effects of Partition made it necessary to resolve citizenship issues first and foremost, and thus the CAD often and expressly state that the Constituent Assembly's area of concern was citizenship at the commencement of the Constitution.

Citizenship has evolved from meaning a political right by which a State identifies the people it governs to a benchmark of identity, and in today's global context, to one of the many identities the individual seeks to assert for him- / herself. The concept of a citizen has over the past decades become broader and less discriminatory. In addition to multiple citizenships, perhaps the most tolerant of citizenship ideologies, there are now concepts of different types of citizenships. For example, the European Union with its expanding and fluctuating notions of citizenship and India with its extension of citizenship to include single and dual citizenship explore the potential for transforming a dichotomous, territorial concept to one that is more nuanced, layered and straddles the separate worlds of home and abroad and defies ethnic categorization in the strict sense while being sensitive to ethnicity. These concepts more and more take into account present wisdom in making the

[41] Art. 9, Constitution of India.

acceptance or renunciation of citizenship as explicit acts based on individual will rather than on any state laws.

The CAD and subsequent debates on who is a citizen of India or who has the right to be a citizen were at no time linked to race. Gender played a part to the extent that the Indian Succession Act, which accepts international convention by stating that domicile of the wife is presumed to be that of the husband, was also not imposed blindly or literally. Recent arguments have taken into consideration the psychological link to the country and the understanding of the complexities in more practical terms of giving physical form to the Partition of the Subcontinent. PIOs were the subject of debate in discussions on some form of dual citizenship for persons belonging to this category as well as in a later attempt at simpler forms of registration for citizenship for those who wished to regain Indian citizenship. The legislature did not follow these up in the last sixty years, but efforts to do so are now being made.

It is possible in the political space of India today for communities to form and dissolve in order to re-emerge as part of other communities. Seen from a distance and over time, political transaction has taken manifold forms, ranging from voting and lobbying over protest movements to violent conflict. These in turn have produced knowledge of what leads to violence, instilling thereby greater understanding and accommodation of cultural and religious differences. Castes, religious communities and ethnic groups are all impregnated by the spirit of transaction and coalition building. The result is a significant empowerment of minorities.[42]

In India's multicultural society, the members of different communities, castes and language groups have risen to the highest levels, in public office as well as in sports, films or academia. The dark predictions of balkanization, periodically renewed, have

[42] When asked "Suppose there were no parties or assemblies and elections were not held - do you think that the government in this country can be run better?", 69% of Indians disagreed. But the number of Muslims, at 72%, making the same argument in favor of retaining the democratic structure, is even higher than the average.

not been borne out by events. The Indian model, a multicultural cooking pot, slowly melting away sectional differences on the

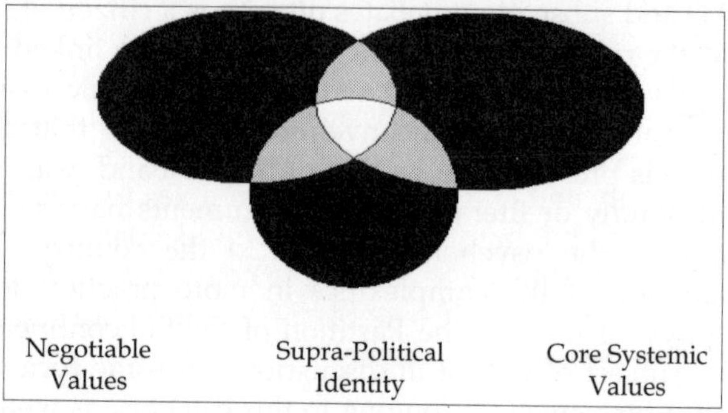

Fig.3: Negotiating Identity in Divided Societies.

steady fires of democracy, appears to be creating the prototype 'Indian' citizen, much like it happened in the United Sates – over the centuries since the founding of the state. The integration of nation, region and community is reminiscent of the Swiss solution, the accommodation of the cleavages of language and religion within the institutional space of a canton.

The long-standing controversy over India's personal law shows how different communities, who consider their laws on marriage, divorce, adoption and succession as essential to and constitutive of their identity, can still share a common territorial space. In Figure 3, one can see how separate and conflicting identities can still share a set of core values common to all the parties and open to judicialisation. Once this is achieved, like in the case of many personal laws co-existing within the same constitution, a private sphere, unique to individuals and groups, can be accepted as legitimate by all concerned. Under the sovereign presence of this core, different communities can negotiate the terms under which they can share the same territorial space (see shaded area in Figure 3), such as how, in a multi-religious village, the Hindu religious processions will take a specific route so as to avoid disturbing law and order, or how much space on the public roads can be occupied for Friday prayers.

Finally, in the contemporary world, globalization, which was supposed to make national boundaries less salient, has in fact revived their importance. The agenda of international politics is crowded with competing claims of the state and supra-stage agencies on the loyalty of individuals and ethnic groups. In the absence of global governance, states, acting in their capacity as the collective voice of their citizens, remain the primary agents of accountability and enforcement. The complex process through which subjects and immigrants become citizens, thus, pitches territoriality and ethnicity as competing norms for the entitlement to citizenship. Caught in this double bind, citizenship has become a contested category and a political problem of global importance.

Although this chapter is based on a country-specific study, the research design is comparative and cross-national in perspective. The Indian case opens up the analytical space for the comparative and general dimensions of the problem of citizenship. One learns from the Indian case that with regard to citizen-making in a post-colonial context, the constitution and law matter, but politics matters too, and most of all, history (path dependency) matters enormously. India's relative success at turning subjects into citizens, more successfully at least than neighbouring Pakistan or Sri Lanka, is a function of India's political structure, process and memory, woven together in an institutional arrangement that draws its inspiration from both the modern state and the traditional society. The chapter has focused on the general factors. A detailed discussion of the contextual features specific to India that also play an important role such as the uncertain nature of divinity in Hinduism are beyond the remit of this chapter, but need to be taken into account for a deeper inquiry into the role of religion, culture and context in providing space for citizenship in divided societies.[43]

---

[43] Subrata K. Mitra, Kashipur Revisited: Social Ritual, Electoral Politics and the State of India, in JAGANNATH REVISITED: STUDYING SOCIETY, RELIGION AND THE STATE IN ORISSA (Hermann Kulke and Burkhard Schepel eds., 2001).

Acknowledgements: I am grateful to Lionel Koenig and Anja Kluge for research assistance, to Julia Hegewald, Jivanta Schoettli, and Clemens Spiess for comments, and to the *German-Law Journal* for excellent editorial suggestions.

9

Review Essay – Dieter Conrad, "*Gandhi und der Begriff des Politischen: Staat, Religion und Gewalt*"

[Gandhi and the Concept of the Political: State, Religion and Violence], edited by Barbara Conrad-Luett with an introduction by Jan Assmann, Wilhelm Fink Verlag, Munich (2006).

MAHENDRA P. SINGH

A. INTRODUCTION

The invitation to review this posthumously-published work of a mentor and dear friend is a matter of immense pride and pleasure for the author. Its execution became, however, a serious challenge and took an enormously long time – without, in the end, the review doing justice to the work. The author had thought himself familiar with M.K. Gandhi's life and work as well as with some of Dieter Conrad's writings about Gandhi, but as the author started reading *Gandhi und der Begriff des Politischen: Staat, Religion und Gewalt* he realized that it was something quite different from what he had read about Gandhi in past. Apprehensive about his ability to write the review the author sought help. A longtime friend Professor Helmut Goerlich from Leipzig, who is well versed not only in German and comparative law but also in Western history, literature, political thought and philosophy, came to his rescue during a visit to his present university in January-February 2010. Helmut, with customary commitment and efficiency, read the whole book, discussed every aspect of it with the author and summarized it all in English. Helmut also explained why the book was so difficult to understand, namely due to its deep roots in Western (especially German) theology and political philosophy, which are critiqued in relation to the Gandhi's thoughts and practices, which themselves were not purely 'oriental' but Western influenced.

The author's familiarity with Conrad's writings started with constitutional law, Conrad's well-known contribution to the 'basic structure doctrine' in the Indian Constitution, and extended to a few of his writings on Gandhi. Much later the author read a collection of Conrad's writings, to which he also contributed a short introduction.[1] All that the author read by Conrad impressed the author by the quality and quantity of research and the thorough, but amicable critique of it. The author knew in particular of Conrad's engagement with Gandhi from late 1980, when he came into close contact with Conrad. Whenever the author asked after his research on Gandhi, Conrad told him reluctantly that it was about Gandhi's approach to human rights and that he wanted to finish it as soon as possible. Conrad grew increasingly frustrated with how the research dragged on, noting that he had invested so much time and effort researching a person with whom he differed in several ways. So strong was Conrad's perfectionism, however, that he would not finish research if he saw any gaps in it.[2] Well before Conrad's death but as his health was deteriorating, a common friend in Heidelberg was able to go through his manuscript on Gandhi. The friend told Conrad and the author that the manuscript could be submitted for publication as it was. Conrad's subsequent silence spoke loudly about his high expectations for his work. He remained engaged with this research until the end. It is sad that death prevented Conrad from seeing the work finally in print. His friends, family members, well-wishers and academic posterity must give due credit to his younger sister Barbara: she, with the tacit support of her husband Professor Luett, her sister-in-law Anna-Elisabeth Conrad and extended family members including Jan Assmann, edited it immaculately and ensured its publication. Having seen Conrad struggle with this work for well over twenty years and knowing his commitment to quality, the author was thrilled to find *Gandhi und der Begriff des Politischen* lying one day on his desk.

---

[1] DIETER CONRAD, ZWISCHEN DEN TRADITIONEN. PROBLEME DES VERFASSUNGSRECHTS UND DER RECHTSKULTUR IN INDIEN UND PAKISTAN. GESAMMELTE AUFSÄTZE AUS DEN JAHREN 1970–1990 (Jürgen Luett and Mahendra P. Singh eds., 1999).

[2] For this reason Conrad was also unhappy that he could not go to South Africa to check the contemporary literature and visit the places and people where and among whom Gandhi had spent his formative years of political struggle.

B. GANDHI AS POLITICAL THINKER

The book is divided into three main parts, each having two chapters. Part I examines Gandhi as a political thinker; Part II deals with religion and politics in Western perspective; and Part III deals with fundamental rights and duties.

Although the title of the book and of its first part (chosen by the editor) give the impression that the book is more about politics than law, Conrad and Gandhi were both lawyers by training and profession. Conrad headed the law department at the South Asia Institute of the University of Heidelberg until his retirement in 1997 and continued to engage himself in law until he died in early 2001. After his education and qualification as a barrister in England and a short stint in India as a lawyer (1891–1893), Gandhi practised law in South Africa for over two decades before his return to India (1914). Due to the fact that upon his return Gandhi renounced his legal practice and undertook fulltime struggle for Indian independence, he is known more as a political figure than a lawyer. His politics are, however, widely acknowledged to have been deeply influenced by his legal training and work. It could therefore be reasonably assumed that Conrad would select primarily legal issues from the life and philosophy of Gandhi. Conrad realised the difficulties in such an approach, noting in the book's opening sentence that legal issues in this context tended not to be discussed as such but were oriented toward general ideas kindness, fairness, truth and mercy and that reflection on the state, especially the modern European and American constitutional state, brings together material on two very different cultural settings.[3] Recognising these difficulties (but not entering into the methodological issues), Conrad concentrates on Gandhi's ideas relating to the state.

To begin with Conrad discusses Gandhi's mixing of religion (*dharma*) and politics.[4] Gandhi stressed the dependence of politics

---

[3] DIETER CONRAD, GANDHI UND DER BEGRIFF DES POLITISCHEN – STAAT, RELIGION UND GEWALT 25 (Barbara Conrad-Luett ed., 2006).

[4] Conrad is aware that the term *dharma* that Gandhi used cannot be completely captured in the term "*religion*", *Id.* at 29. For Gandhi's own clarification see quotation at 52.

on religion, arguing that "those who say that religion has nothing to do with politics do not know what religion means."[5] He justified his non-cooperation movement, civil disobedience and the struggle against British rule with his religious convictions, even if this led to animosity between Hindus and Muslims.[6] (To be more specific, Gandhi's mixing of religion with politics spurred criticism of his support the Khilafat movement, which intensified religious consciousness in the two major communities, and led to Indian Muslims branding him as a Hindu revivalist in a Hindu political party the All India Congress)

Religion had a double meaning for Gandhi. He was born a Hindu and therefore Hinduism was his religion. However, religion for him was not simply Hinduism as practised by orthodox Hindus or any other specific religious dogmas; it was about inner truth.[7] Gandhi often alternated between the terms religion and truth in his speeches and writings while at the same time supporting some practices of Hinduism such as cow protection.[8] Accordingly, politics also gained a double meaning for Gandhi. First, he emphasised the spiritualization of politics and second, he considered *ahimsa* (non-violence) as its essential element. Integrating *ahimsa* with his idea of religion, he conceded that *ahimsa* and truth were interchangeable. The core concept of politics for him was the demand that every political decision be morally sound. Conrad underlines this distinguishing feature of Gandhi's political thinking in comparison to the ideas dominant in the West. According to Conrad cunning and violence are considered by Max Weber among others[9] essential to Western politics.[10]

In contrast, Gandhi stressed the use of right means for achieving any ends, in line with his view of politics. He acknowledged that ends and means were interchangeable but argued that while ends could or could not be known, means are always known. Therefore

---

[5] *Id.* at 29.
[6] *Id.* at 48–50.
[7] *Id.* at 52 ff.
[8] *Id.* at 51.
[9] *Id.* at 71.
[10] *Id.* at 64.

right means must always be adopted and applied even if one does not exactly know the ends to be achieved.[11] In sum, Gandhi believed in the positive role of religion in politics, as it required politics to be conducted without the use of violence.[12]

Gandhi saw religion as a hidden feature of law. This should not lead to the assumption that law could not establish secularism or the secular state. Secularism made equal treatment of all religions possible and therefore did not exclude the role religion played in politics and law. Conrad looks at this role a little later, emphasising Gandhi's two-part understanding of religion, by which he could make out truth in all religions being the basis of politics and by which this truth could be viewed as different from the specific doctrines, traditions, cults, rites and myths of a specific religion. This type of truth one might also find in law. Law was perceived as an independent body of rules created by but different from politics, which it was constantly trying to enclose in conventions, principles, procedures and substantive laws. To the extent that the state supported law, it was invented and active at a considerable distance from cults, religions, conscientious beliefs or movements. Conrad finds this understanding of the state's nature also among the Indian freedom fighters who stood for the state's autonomy and independence. At the same time, these linked their indigenous traditions to their reform programs, as Conrad details. Gandhi joined the Indian freedom movement when it was already a decade old. Realising the multi-religious character of the Indian society, Gandhi looked for a common ground that integrated all religions and was suited for the creation of a nation based on a form of higher religion. He wanted to integrate, among others, Muslims and the downtrodden, especially the untouchables, within his concept of religion. Searching for such a basis of his politics, he rejected adherence to the colonial state and its policies and instruments of pacifying society. Gandhi preferred conflict and if necessary, bloodshed to achieve independence.

From the in depth and incisive examination of these complex and paradoxical notions of Gandhi Conrad draws Gandhi's perception

---

[11] *Id.* at 84.

[12] The book uses the German term "Gewalt", which contains the concept of violence as well as of force. Here, the author has translated it merely as violence.

of state and politics. To some extent this complexity in Gandhi and his religious practices supported his non-violent movement for freedom without defying the state, public authority and public order. It is on this basis that Conrad analogizes between Weber's idea of responsibility (*Verantwortungsethik*) and Gandhi's political action. This worldview of religion in Gandhi also lays down foundations for universal principles of political action applicable in any society.

C. RELIGION AND POLITICS IN WESTERN PERSPECTIVE

Part II deals with the evolving Western vision of religion and politics. It is this part of the book that incorporates Gandhi's unique contribution to politics highlighted in the introduction (see E. below)[13]

The two major divisions of this part comprise the theory of religious actions[14] and actual religious and political actions.[15] Conrad introduces the subject with the post-World War II claim of the German Catholic and Protestant churches about their role in public life, public opinion, governing institutions and the media. Two factors led to their claim: first, church doctrine that after the demise of Hitler's National Socialism, which had restricted religion to the private sphere, the churches should revive their pre-Nazi role of defining public policy and morality, and second, the support received from the Allies (especially USA and UK), who wanted the churches to be free from Nazi ideology so that they could be trusted partners. Conrad finds this development relevant for his comparison of the roles of great reformers like Gandhi and Martin Luther.

Conrad clarifies that the private public distinction is not so relevant for the churches because religion itself does not make such a distinction. The churches constitute an independent social actor in a system in which the state assumes the central role and

---

[13] The author found this part of the book especially difficult to follow due to his unfamiliarity with its subject matter. He had to depend extensively on the summary of and discussions with Helmut Goerlich.

[14] Conrad-Luett (ed.), *supra* note 3, at 95 ff.

[15] *Id.* at 114 ff.

in which the use of force becomes the main issue.[16] He analyses this issue with reference to 'political theology' concluding that theology is concerned with the use of force by individuals and not by the state. In a secular state, theology may therefore be little help in judging the use of force.[17]

Conrad proceeds to examine political ethics understood as the duty to use force. He relates Weber's idea of responsibility[18] back to Luther.[19] Princes' actions against sects ready to use force to defend territory in order that the Protestant church might survive and consolidate in their emerging states. Conrad links Luther's stand and strategy with Weber's *Veranwortungsethik* and supports it as the basis of political decision-making processes. He concludes that Luther's and Gandhi's actions were based on responsibility and as Luther preceded Gandhi, he implies that Luther had already set the example of political action on behalf of others. All the same, Gandhi bestowed uniqueness on responsible action by incorporating into it the concept of *ahimsa*.

Taking up discussion on *ahimsa* in a transcultural context, Conrad delves into the Indian traditions of Jainism and Buddhism as well as of Hinduism that taught *ahims*a as a fundamental principle of life to be observed. He traces the influence on Gandhi of Tolstoy, who also preached non-violence as a fundamental principle of life in society. While acknowledging some parallelism between Gandhi and the West regarding the practice of non-violence in politics, Conrad argues for the novelty of Gandhi's application of *ahimsa* to political action.

In sum, taking support from Part I and other writings of his on this aspect of Gandhi[20] and without renouncing his position that Western ideas substantially influenced Gandhi in his thinking and action, Conrad shows the uniqueness of Gandhi's application of

[16] *Id.* at 100–108.
[17] *Id.* at 108–113.
[18] *Id.* at 114 ff.
[19] *Id.* at 117 ff.
[20] Dieter Conrad, *Part III: Forming of Political Concepts,* in Luett and Singh (eds.) *supra* note 1, at 345 ff., 381 ff., 411 ff., 427 ff. and 447 ff.

*ahims*a to political action. He does so primarily with reference to Carl Schmitt as well as Weber and Luther. In the similarly-titled *Concept of the Political,* Schmitt expressed the political relationship in terms of friends and enemies. This relationship was inherently based on violence because one had to be prepared for armed struggle involving life and death between the enemies. The same idea is found in Weber, who defined political association ultimately in terms of its use of physical force and the state in terms of its monopoly over the legitimate use of force. Weber made his point clear by contradicting Tolstoy, who rejected the idea of violence in politics. Weber's writings are in turn derived from early theology legitimising state force or to violence in Luther's writings, especially his justification for obedience to the secular authority. Luther argued for participation of a Christian in the use of force by the state and distinguished between the use of force for oneself in order to meet one's worldly necessities and its use for others when it acquires representative and political colour as an action of a public figure. The latter type of action can also be traced and justified in Gandhi's writings and actions such as *satyagraha* or civil disobedience. What distinguishes Gandhi from these German thinkers, argues Conrad, is his rejection of physical violence in political action. To that extent Gandhi bequeathed a novel principle to politics that he established through his example of wresting Indian independence from the mighty British Empire through entirely non-violent movement.[21]

D. FUNDAMENTAL RIGHTS AND DUTIES

Part III deals with Gandhi's concept of rights and duties in terms of the right to subsistence and the rights to freedom and equality. Starting with the demand for fundamental rights during the British regime, Conrad reproduces Gandhi's famous letter to Julian Huxley at UNESCO. Gandhi wrote:

> I learnt from my illiterate but wise mother that all rights to be deserved and preserved came from duty well done. Thus the very right to live accrues to us only when we do

[21] Dieter Conrad, *Der Begriff des Politischen, die Gewalt and Gandhis gewaltlose politische Aktion, in* Luett and Singh (eds.), *supra* note 1, at 447 ff.

> the duty of citizenship of the world. From this one fundamental statement, perhaps it is easy enough to define the duties of Man and Woman and correlate every right to some corresponding duty to be first performed. Every other right can be shown to be usurpation hardly worth fighting for.[22]

Although the letter gives prominence to duties over rights, Gandhi's claim was associated with the freedom movement's radical call to reject rule that did not protect basic rights.[23]

Against the background of these preliminary remarks and their relevance to contemporary events, Conrad draws attention to two specific rights, relating to bearing arms and to abolishing the salt tax.[24] The rights were relevant in the context of the fight for freedom and existence. Gandhi considered salt as essential to human survival and its taxation as a crime against humanity. Gandhi used this argument for his Dandi March in 1930, which became the hallmark of the freedom struggle.

Conrad then discusses the rights to life and property. Tracing the evolution of these rights in the West, Conrad demonstrates that Gandhi believed in limited possessions but did not radically question inequality in wealth in terms of revolution. The link between life and property is based on self-respect and survival and on the idea that a person must be entitled to the fruits of his/her labour. These rights are discussed in the context of the right to basic necessities of life[25]. Conrad also discusses state socialism and the doctrine of trusteeship. Gandhi opposed the former and, supported the latter. State socialism as practiced in the USSR did not catch on with young Indian leaders of the time who were educated in England; most of them were instead influenced by

---

[22] Conrad-Luett (ed.), *supra* note 3, at 185.

[23] Remember that India was not yet independent when Gandhi wrote this letter on 25 May 1947.

[24] Conrad-Luett (ed.), *supra* note 3, at 191 ff.

[25] Dieter Conrad, *The Human Right to Basic Necessities of Life*, in Luett and Singh (eds.), *supra* note 1, at 289 ff., which Conrad also discussed in greater detail elsewhere.

Fabian Socialism. Gandhi added to it the doctrine of trusteeship, which he learnt from the principles of equity in English law. The doctrine of trusteeship was used to harness the large-scale modern modes of industrial production and supply of goods for the common interest of the society and people in need. The doctrine could not, however, take the form of a theory to be developed as an academic discipline or as a state practice. Gandhi adhered to it in the context of inter-generational obligations so as to ensure the basic needs of those who could not secure them otherwise. Finally, Conrad looks at the right to life in another light, namely in terms of self-abnegation or denial, which has been the part of Indian tradition and which Gandhi himself practiced. Nobody had any justification to take anybody's life, but everybody could minimise one's own wants and needs in order to ensure that everybody has enough to live on.[26]

The final chapter in the book deals with liberty and equality as two basic rights in the sphere of political action.[27] Under liberty Conrad discusses only the freedoms of speech and religion. While Gandhi argued for unrestricted freedom of speech, which he supported with *dharma* or the obligation to speak the truth, he restricted the freedom of religion to beliefs and conscience. Gandhi argued for the subjection of the freedom of religion to health and morality and the rights of other persons. As regards religious propagation and conversion, he left it to every individual to decide which religion he/she would like to practice. Religion should not bind anyone against his/her beliefs and conscience.

Equality is discussed in much more detail than liberty, as Conrad considers it the core of Gandhi's approach to rights and the foundation for his political action. This foundation was laid in early 20th-century South Africa when Gandhi himself experienced racial discrimination and humiliation at the hands of the British rulers. From then on, his formulation of equality was based on the idea of equality of all human beings as sons and daughters of God irrespective of their religion, race, sex, etc. The idea of equality was developed around the concept of self-

[26] Conrad-Luett (ed.), *supra* note 3, at 234 ff.

[27] *Id.* at 239 ff.

respect and not uniform treatment. Like his other doctrines and practices in life he preached for peace and harmony in society through equality. While he condemned the Hindu practice of untouchability, Gandhi remained equivocal on the caste system. His opposition to the practice of untouchability as well as his support for religious, racial, sexual and other forms of equality have immensely contributed to humanity, which has finally eradicated several degrading practices to the advantage of all and to the disadvantage of none.

E. STATE, VIOLENCE AND REVELATION

In addition to these three parts, *Gandhi und der Begriff des Politischen* includes a foreword by the editor on the book's background, a comprehensive glossary of Sanskrit and Hindi terms, a list of literary sources, a list of literature cited and referred to, an index of persons mentioned and an introduction.

This introduction by the historian and Egyptologist Jan Assmann is highly valuable, as it explains the book's core concept and its contribution to understanding Gandhi's idea of politics. Assmann addresses the argument that Gandhi's idea of politics will prevent the predicted 'clash of civilizations'. By contrasting Gandhi's and Western ideas of politics, Conrad draws attention to the fact that while violence is indispensable to politics in the Western theory, Gandhi believed and proved that politics could be conducted without violence and thus that non-violence could guide world politics. Assmann explains the novelty of this concept of politics, which is summed in Gandhi's statement that "to believe that what has not occurred in history will not occur at all is to argue disbelief in the dignity of man".[28] With references to different aspects of the book, Assmann argues that it is completely wrong to label Gandhi's principles as oriental as that denies them universal application. Assmann presents non-violence as visible symbolic suffering that disdains violence and provides an effective alternative for humanity. He highlights the contrast in Gandhi's theory by drawing attention to violence in the writings of Niklas Luhmann, Walter Benjamin, Jacques Derrida, Blaise

---

[28] *Id.* at 17.

Pascal, Michel de Montaigne and Schmitt. Gandhi's theory of politics, which is based on the ancient Indian perception of order in *dharma,* overrules the pessimistic anthropological concept of life and human nature in the West inherited from Thomas Hobbes. Conrad is critical of the most perverse manifestation of that anthropology in the 20th-century totalitarian state and draws support for Gandhian politics from Enlightenment thinkers such as Gotthold Ephraim Lessing and Moses Mendelssohn. Support is also found in ideas of the Freemasons in line with Gandhi's principles, especially ideas on religious practices based on truth rather than on revelation.[29]

With all these examples Assmann is highlighting and supporting a universal principle of tolerance in politics, law and religion. He argues from Conrad's depiction of Gandhi that, beyond religion there exists a higher faith in the realisation of responsibility toward others. It enables political leaders to act as representatives for their kin. Such a leadership does not claim to rule but introduces a politics of emancipation from the colonial powers and the idea of a new law-abiding spirit of truth, wisdom and tolerance. Truth rather than authority becomes the ultimate basis of legitimacy.

F. CONCLUSION

Due to the author's inadequate command of the German language and of the book's subject matter, this review cannot come close to the quality of the book. May it at least spur the desire of English readers to have *Gandhi und der Begriff des Politischen* translated into English. The enormous amount of knowledge and the extensive research on Gandhi in it would then be effectively accessible worldwide - certainly in those societies that he led and inspired. An English edition would be highly useful for further research on and understanding of Gandhi as well as for the guidance of humanity in practicing politics effectively without violence.

---

[29] *Id.* at 18.

About the Contributors

Soli J. Sorabjee

Soli Jehangir Sorabjee is a renowned Indian jurist. He holds or has held senior offices in the Indian government and in national and international organizations. He is the recipient of several awards for his human rights work.

In 1971, he was designated Senior Advocate by the Supreme Court of India. He served as Solicitor-General of India from 1977 to 1980 and as the Attorney-General of India from 1989 to 1990 and from 1998 to 2004.

Soli Sorabjee was appointed by the United Nations as a Special Rapporteur for Nigeria in 1997 to report on the human rights situation in that country. He was a Member and then Chair of the UN Sub-Commission on the Promotion and Protection of Human Rights from 1998 to 2006. He served as a Member of the Permanent Court of Arbitration at The Hague from 2000 to 2006.

Soli Sorabjee has defended the freedom of press in many landmark cases before the Supreme Court of India and has been instrumental in the revocation of censorship orders and publication bans. In 2002, he was honoured with the Padma Vibhushan award, the second-highest civilian award in India, for his defense of freedom of speech and the protection of human rights.

Soli Sorabjee has been a prolific writer in both academic and popular publications concerning protection of human rights, upholding constitutional law, as well as freedom of speech and expression.

Soli Sorabjee was educated at Government Law College, Bombay.

Malcolm MacLaren

Malcolm MacLaren is a Habilitand (in comparative constitutional law) and occasional Lecturer (in international law) at the Law Faculty of the University of Zurich. Between 2008 and 2010, he was a Visiting Researcher at the Institute of Federalism of the University of Fribourg. Between 2006 and 2009, he was a Post-Doctoral Fellow in the Swiss National Centre for Competence in Research – "Challenges to Democracy in the 21st Century". Between 2002 and 2007, he was a Research Associate at the Institute for Public International and Comparative Constitutional Law at the University of Zurich.

Dr. MacLaren's research interests are wide-ranging. His Habilitationsschrift is concerned with ethnic conflict, constitution-making, and political participation rights. It is entitled "Constituting the Polity: Can Divided Societies really pull themselves up by their own Bootstraps?" One of the divided societies analyzed is India. His doctoral dissertation was entitled "Rechte, Rechtsmittel und Rechtfertigungen im Völkerrecht – Eine Studie über den Zugang Privater zu internationalen Streitbeilegungsmechanismen" [Rights, Remedies and Rationales in International Law – A Study of Private Access to International Dispute Resolution Mechanisms] and was published in 2008.

Malcolm MacLaren has earned a Dr. iur. from the University of Zurich, a LL.M. from the University of Frankfurt am Main, a LL.B. from the University of Toronto, a M.A. (Modern History) from the University of Oxford, and a B.A. (English and Latin) from the University of Toronto. He is a Member of the Ontario Bar.

Deepa Badrinarayana

Deepa Badrinarayana came to Chapman University School of Law in 2007 from Pace University School of Law, where she completed her doctorate in juridicial studies in environmental law. Between 2005 and 2006, she was a Visiting Scholar at the Center for Global Legal Studies, Columbia Law School, where she also researched for Professor Frank P. Grad on environmental and public health laws.

Professor Badrinarayana has been a Consultant to the United Nations Global Compact on issues of corporate voluntarism and regulations. She is a Member of the World Conservation Union, Committee on Environmental Law.

Before moving to the United States, Professor Badrinarayana was a Research Officer for a Government of India-World Bank Environmental Capacity-Building Project at the National Law School of India University. In addition, she trained government officials and legal professionals in environmental law. Professor Badrinarayana was part of a team that advised the Government of India on its legislation to manage biomedical waste.

Deepa Badrinarayana also holds a LL.M. in Environmental Law from Pace University School of Law and a B.A., LL.B. (Hons.) from the National Law School of India University.

Hiram E. Chodosh

Prior to being appointed Dean of the University of Utah College of Law in 2006, Hiram Chodosh was Professor of Law, Associate Dean (Academic Affairs), and Director of the International Law Center at the Case Western Reserve University School of Law.

Dean Chodosh is an expert in institutional justice reform and author of five books and sixty major articles, book chapters, and special reports. He has served as a Senior Fulbright Scholar in India and as an adviser to the United Nations Development Programme in Asia, the World Bank Justice Reform Group, the International Monetary Fund Legal Department, the State Department, and many supreme courts, ministries, and commissions in the Middle

East and Asia. He directed the Global Justice Project: Iraq, an advisory think tank in Baghdad.

Dean Chodosh is also involved in designing and implementing new educational models to expand leadership experiences for students, interdisciplinary skills training, use of technology, advanced research, and global legal education. He is the Senior Editor of a book series 'Law Across Borders', which seeks to help law professors and law schools transnationalize their curricula.

Hiram Chodosh received his J.D. from Yale University School of Law and his B.A. from Wesleyan University.

Donald R. Davis, Jr.

Professor Davis' research interests range from law and religion in medieval India, the history of religions in South Asia, Malayalam language and literature, Dharmasastra literature, to South Indian history.

His current projects include "Hinduism and Law: An Introduction" (co-edited with Tim Lubin & Jay Krishnan) and a "Cooperative Annotated Bibliography of Hindu Law and Dharmasastra". His recent publications include "The Spirit of Hindu Law" (2010).

Donald Davis, Jr. earned his Ph.D. in Asian Languages & Cultures from the University of Texas at Austin in 2000.

Piyel Haldar

Piyel Haldar is now a Senior Lecturer at the Birkbeck School of Law, having come from Lancaster University in 1994.

Dr. Haldar's research focuses on the historical evolution of legal institutions and legal subjectivity with reference to several separate areas, namely the historical studies of evidential practices, the establishment of common law jurisprudence in British India, and the manner in which law distinguishes legal personality from animality. His work is informed by and engages with critical theory, aesthetics, cultural theory, post-structuralist philosophy, as well as law and literature scholarship.

Dr. Haldar is currently working on a book examining the symbolic importance of animals in iconography, the medieval bestiary, legal trials, and other didactic forms. His last book, "Law, Orientalism and Postcolonialism: The Jurisdiction of the Lotus Eaters", was published in 2007. His doctoral dissertation was entitled "Testimony and the Law of Evidence and the Aesthetics of Courtroom Architecture". He serves as a Managing Editor of 'Law and Critique' and on the Editorial Advisory Board of 'Law and Humanities'.

Piyel Haldar received his doctorate from the University of London and his LL.B. from Middlesex University.

Werner Menski

In addition to being Professor of South Asian Laws, Werner Menski is Chair, Centre for Ethnic Minority Studies; Member, Centre of South Asian Studies; and Member, Centre of Jaina Studies at the University of London.

Professor Menski is specialised in both Muslim and Hindu law, especially concerning issues of personal status, family affairs, and migration. He has also done comparative research on legal systems in Asia and Africa. Professor Menski's interests range from law, socio-legal and cultural studies, to religion and law. His country expertise includes Bangladesh, India, and Pakistan.

The most recent of several books authored or edited by Professor Menski is entitled "Comparative Law in a Global Context: The Legal Systems of Asia and Africa" (2nd ed. 2006).

Werner Menski holds a PhD from the University of London and a MA from Kiel University.

Subrata K. Mitra

Subrata Kumar Mitra is Professor of Political Science of South Asia in Heidelberg, having taught previously at the universities in Hull, Nottingham, and Berkeley. He is a Visiting Fellow at the Centre for the Study of Developing Societies (New Delhi).

Professor Mitra has also held appointments at the Indian Council for Social Science Research (New Delhi) and at the Institut Français d'Opinion Public (Paris).

Professor Mitra's work concerns issues such as democratization in South Asia, the interaction of traditional values and modern institutions, the role of identity and religion in Indian politics, as well as the functioning of political parties and institutions in South Asia.

Recent books include the co-edited "Political Sociology - The State of the Art" (2010) and the co-authored "When Rebels Become Stakeholders: Democracy, Agency and Social Change in India" (2009). Professor Mitra is the Editor or a Member of the Editorial Board of several publications in his field.

Subrata Mitra earned a doctorate in political science at the University of Rochester (NY), a M.Phil in political development at Jawaharlal Nehru University (New Delhi), a M.A. in political science at the University of Delhi, and a Bachelors in political science at Utkal University (Orissa).

Mahendra P. Singh

Mahendra Pal Singh, currently the Vice-chancellor of the West Bengal National University of Juridical Sciences, Kolkata, taught earlier at the universities of Delhi and Meerut. He has also been a Fellow and Visiting Professor at several institutes and universities of international repute, including in Bangalore, Beijing, Berlin, Heidelberg, Hong Kong, New Delhi, Osaka, and Singapore.

Comparative public law including especially constitutional law, administrative law, human rights and legal systems are Professor Singh's major research interests. His many publications include the books "German Administrative Law in Common Law Perspective", "Freedom of Trade and Commerce in India", "Comparative Constitutional Law", "VN Shukla's Constitution of India", "Legal Dimensions of Market Economy" and "Human Rights and Basic Needs - Theory and Practice in India".

Mahendra Singh received a LL.D. and LL.M. from Lucknow, a LL.M. from Columbia, and a B.A., LL.B. from Agra.

Index